Attachment Theory
and Psychoanalysis

Attachment Theory and Psychoanalysis

Peter Fonagy

OTHER

OTHER PRESS
New York

Adapted with permission from Fonagy, Peter (1999) "Psychoanalytic Theory from the Viewpoint of Attachment Theory and Research." In *Handbook of Attachment: Theory, Research, and Clinical Applications* (pp. 595–624). New York: Guilford Press.

ISBN-13: 978-1-892746-70-2

Copyright © 2001 by Peter Fonagy

Production Editor: Robert D. Hack

This book was set in 11pt. Goudy by Alpha Graphics of Pittsfield, NH.

10   9   8   7   6   5

Library of Congress Cataloging-in-Publication Data

Fonagy, Peter, 1952–
    Attachment theory and psychoanalysis / Peter Fonagy.
        p. cm.
    Includes bibliographical references and index.
    ISBN 1-892746-70-0
    1. Attachment behavior.   2. Attachment behavior in children.   3. Object relations (Psychoanalysis).   4. Psychoanalysis.   I. Title.

BF575.A86 F66 2001
150.19'5—dc21   2001032089

Contents

Preamble   1

1. Introduction to Attachment Theory   5

2. Key Findings of Attachment Research   19

3. Freud's Models and Attachment Theory   47

4. Structural Approaches:
   The North American Structural Approach   53

5. Modifications of the Structural Model   65

6. The Klein–Bion Model   81

7. The Independent School of British Psychoanalysis
   and Its Relation to Attachment Theory   93

8. North American Object Relations Theorists
   and Attachment Theory   105

vi / Contents

9. Modern Psychoanalytic Infant Psychiatry:
   The Work of Daniel Stern   117

10. The Interpersonal-Relational Approach:
    From Sullivan to Mitchell   123

11. Psychoanalytic Attachment Theorists   135

12. Summary: What Do Psychoanalytic Theories
    and Attachment Theory Have in Common?   157

13. How Can Attachment Theory Benefit from
    Psychoanalytic Insights?   185

14. Conclusion   191

References   193

Index   247

Preamble

There is bad blood between psychoanalysis and attachment theory. As with many family feuds, it is hard to identify where the problem began.

In the early 1960s, a number of major psychoanalytic figures turned on John Bowlby following the publication of his article in the *Psychoanalytic Study of the Child* (Bowlby 1960). Attachment theory was criticized as mechanistic, nondynamic, and explicated according to thorough misunderstandings of psychoanalytic theory (A. Freud 1960, Schur 1960, Spitz 1960). Opposition to his views provided one small area of common ground for the followers of Anna Freud and Melanie Klein (Grosskruth 1986), and for the next decades Bowlby was a relatively isolated figure in psychoanalysis. These critiques, which were added to at fairly regular intervals by major figures such as Engel (1971), Rochlin (1971), Roiphe (1976), and Hanley (1978), raise a variety of issues but at root they boil down to relatively few simple disagreements. Bowlby is seen as having renounced drives, "the Oedipus," unconscious processes, particularly unconscious fantasy, complex internalized motivational and conflict-resolving systems. He is further seen as having discarded the richness of the array of human emotions, be these affects experienced by the ego and involving socialization or sources of pleasure rooted in the infant's physical body. Attachment theory is seen as ignoring biological vulnerabilities other than those rooted in the caregiver's behavior and as reducing etiological considerations to a single variable: that of physical separation. Bowlby is accused of failing to consider the impact of the developmental state of the ego on the child's ability to make attachments and react to loss. He is also accused of ignoring negative attachment related to the fear of the mother and trauma other than physical separation. Bowlby is seen to be a reductionist in his emphasis on evolutionary considerations at the expense of full recognition of complex symbolic functioning. And that is just the version of the psychoanalytic assessment that is suitable for public consumption. Much worse was said in private. "Bowlby treats humans as though they were animals" (Grosskruth 1987, p. 406). Analysts make dismissive comments about his work yet feel no obligation to read it (Ellingen 1997, cited in Marrone 1998). Although undoubtedly amongst the top ten best known British psychoanalysts, and probably one of the most cited internationally, his work is still not compulsory reading at the British Institute. Nor is the feud showing any real sign of dying down. As recently as 1992, Lilleskov (1992) wrote: "Bowlby's disregard of drive theory may have made observations of behavior easier but has reduced the explanatory power of these observations" (p. 128).

Rather than engaging the historic psychoanalytic figures opposed to Bowlby in debate and taking issue with the crassness of their critiques and the profound misapprehensions of attachment theory they often imply, we should briefly look at Bowlby's presentation of psychoanalysis. This, I am sad to say, is at times unworthy of his genius. In Chapter 22 of his second volume (Bowlby 1973), entitled "Pathways for the Growth of Personality," Bowlby compares two alternative theoretical models to two types of railway systems. The psychoanalytic model of personality development is regarded as a single-track rail along which stops can occur. Adult pathological states are considered as due to fixations at, or regressions to, early phases of normal development. Bowlby's alternative model, derived from the biologist C. H. Waddington (1966), includes a range of alternative developmental pathways, a single main route that then branches out into a range of distinct tracks. While

Bowlby's point is clear, it is also disingenuous. He was very familiar with the work of Anna Freud, Eric Erikson, and others, all of whom posited similar "multi-track" developmental networks. Bowlby seems guilty of combating a psychoanalytic straw man. Similarly, in his 1958 paper Bowlby is at pains to demonstrate that psychoanalysts have been trying in vain to free themselves from what he calls "secondary drive theory." The primary drive, being based on oral and other physical needs, creates a secondary drive for bonding. By contrast, he places social bonds in the position of a primary biological given. Again, Freud and Burlingham in 1944 already recognized the child's instinctual need to be attached to the mother. Even earlier, the Hungarian psychoanalyst Imre Hermann (1923) proposed a primary instinct to "cling" to the caregiver based on primate observations not dissimilar to Bowlby's use of the work of Harlow.

Bowlby (1980c) maintained this blinkered attitude to the end. In his epilogue to the collection of papers edited by Parkes and Stevenson-Hinde, he restated his disappointment with psychoanalysis: "Psycho-analysis gave weight to the internal workings of the human mind and recognized the special status of intimate human relationships, but its metapsychology, already obsolescent, was a handicap, while its fixation on a single, retrospective research method gave no means of resolving differences of opinion" (p. 310). Bowlby here appears to rule out the relevance of psychoanalytic observation on a priori grounds without wishing to explore the ideas in detail. In the same section, he comments that different investigative methods have intrinsic strengths and vul-nerabilities and can be fruitfully used in combination: "the strength of one may make good at least some of the weaknesses of the other" (p. 312). But by this time psychoanalysis has disappeared from his epistemic horizon. In 1988 he characterizes the standard psychoanalytic view as follows: "Anyone who places emphasis on what a child's *real experience* may have been . . . was regarded as pitifully naïve. Almost by definition it was assumed that anyone interested in the external world could not be interested in the internal world, indeed was almost certainly running away from it" (Bowlby 1988, pp. 43–44).

It is interesting to observe, that unlike most of his creative psy-choanalytic contemporaries Bowlby's ideas did not lead to a new psy-choanalytic school. Had they done so there would be no call for this volume. Rather they led to a line of empirical investigation that served to distance attachment theory further and further from psychoanalysis, separated not just by a novel orientation to understanding clinical cases but also by an incompatible epistemology. Bowlby's interest in observation, research, and the representation of the real rather than the reality of the representation ruled him out of bounds for all but the most unorthodox of psychoanalysts for most of the second half of his life. As Jeremy Holmes (1995) so poignantly observed: "Bowlby's theory and its tremendous ramifications for clinical work were for decades virtually airbrushed out of the psychoanalytic record—rather like some dissident in Stalinist times" (p. 20).

Thus, just as psychoanalysts have consistently and somewhat tendentiously misread attachment theory and found it wanting in richness and explanatory power, so Bowlby consistently focused on the weakest facets of the psychoanalytic corpus, almost as if he wished to forestall a mutually corrective interrelationship. Consequently, Bowlby's followers came from the world of empirical science and laboratory observation. There are exceptions to this trend. Bretherton (1987) presented a thoughtful comparative review of attachment theory, separation-individuation theory, and the theory of infant–mother relatedness presented by Stern. There are some other good examples of integrative attempts, including those of Allen (1995, 2000), Eagle (1995, 1997), Holmes (1993b, 1997), and Marrone (1998). We shall review some of these authors briefly after we have considered potential points of contact between attachment theory and the classical psychoanalytic ideas.

This book will undertake a similar integrative attempt with the aim of demonstrating that the relationship between attachment theory and psychoanalysis is more complex than adherents of either community generally recognize. Indeed there are many points of contact, some obvious, others more subtle, yet others perhaps tenuous. There are also points of significant divergence. As psychoanalytic theory is not at this time a coherent set of propositions, there appears to be no shortcut to exploring areas of overlap by looking individually at each major school of psychoanalytic thought in relation to attachment theory. We shall begin with a brief overview of attachment theory and some key findings of attachment research. Our review of psychoanalytic approaches will start with Freud and end with the work of Daniel Stern. Much that is relevant has to be omitted because of constraints of space and the even more significant limitations imposed by this author's ignorance.

1

Introduction to
Attachment Theory

Attachment theory is almost unique among psychoanalytic theories in bridging the gap between general psychology and clinical psychodynamic theory. Many have noted the gulf that exists to this day between theories of the mind that have their roots in empirical social science (largely psychological research), and clinical theories that focus on the significance of individual experience in determining life course, including psychopathology. Paul Whittle (in press) recently described this discontinuity of theories as a fault line that runs across the entire discipline of psychology. Indeed, it is easy to discern the fault line between the tectonic plates of psychoanalysis, where giving meaning to experience is seen as the primary cause of behavior as well as the royal road to its therapeutic change, and the abutting plate of experimental psychology, with its emphasis on parsimony, insistence on reliable observation, and abhorrence of rhetoric and speculative theory-building. Yet attachment theory has a home on both sides of the fault line. How can this be?

John Bowlby's work on attachment theory started when, at the age of 21, he worked in a home for maladjusted boys. Bowlby's clinical experience with two boys, whose relationships with their mothers were massively disrupted, made a profound impact on him. A retrospective study he carried out ten years later, examining the history of 44 juvenile thieves (Bowlby 1944), formalized his view that the disruption of the early mother–child relationship should be seen as a key precursor of mental disorder. The one factor that distinguished the thieves from the clinic children was evidence of prolonged separation from parents, particularly striking among those whom he termed "affectionless." In the late '40s Bowlby extended his interest in mother–infant relations by undertaking a review of research findings on the effects of institutionalization on young children (Bowlby 1951). Children who had been seriously deprived of maternal care tended to develop the same symptoms as he had identified in his "affectionless" young thieves. While giving central place to parenting in general and the infant–mother relationship in particular, the 1951 monograph was silent on the mechanisms by which maternal deprivation might be expected to generate adverse consequences. The maternal deprivation literature was itself wide open to alternative interpretations, particularly ones that de-emphasized the mother-infant bond (e.g., Rutter 1971). At about the same time, James Robertson, with Bowlby's encouragement, spent 4 years documenting on film the impact on 18- to 48-month-olds of separation from the parents during an episode of hospital admission or admission to residential nurseries (Robertson 1962). Later, more systematically collected behavioral observations and descriptions that fully confirmed the Robertson material were collected by Christopher Heinicke (Heinicke and Westheimer 1966).

Bowlby was dissatisfied with prevailing views in the first half of the twentieth century concerning the origin of affectional bonds. Both psychoanalytic and Hullian learning theory stressed that the emotional bond to the primary caregiver was a secondary drive, based on the gratification of oral needs. Yet evidence was already available that, in the animal kingdom at least, the young of the species could become attached to adults who did not feed them (Lorenz 1935). Bowlby (1958) was among the first to recognize that the human infant enters the world predisposed to participate in social interaction. Developmental psychology has made this discovery something of a truism (e.g., Meltzoff 1995,

Watson 1994). Around the midpoint of the last century, however, Bowlby's determination to give central place to the infant's biological proclivity to form attachments to initiate, maintain, and terminate interaction with the caregiver and use this person as a "secure base" for exploration and self enhancement, flew in the face of another kind of (pseudo)biological determinism—one based on the theory of libidinal and aggressive instincts.

Bowlby's critical contribution was his unwavering focus on the infant's need for an unbroken (secure) early attachment to the mother. He thought that the child who does not have such provision was likely to show signs of *partial deprivation*—an excessive need for love or for revenge, gross guilt, and depression—or *complete deprivation*—listlessness, quiet unresponsiveness, and retardation of development, and later in development signs of superficiality, want of real feeling, lack of concentration, deceit, and compulsive thieving (Bowlby 1951). Later (Bowlby 1969, 1973), he placed these interactions into a framework of reactions to separation: protest → despair → detachment. Protest begins with the child perceiving a threat of separation. It is marked by crying, anger, physical attempts at escaping, and searching for the parent. It lasts for as long as a week, and intensifies at night. Despair follows protest. Active physical movement diminishes, crying becomes intermittent, the child appears sad, withdraws from contact, is more likely to be hostile to another child or a favorite object brought from home, and appears to enter a phase of mourning the loss of the attachment figure (Bowlby 1973). The final phase of detachment is marked by a more or less complete return of sociability. Attempts by other adults to offer care are no longer spurned, but the child who reaches this stage will behave in a markedly abnormal way upon reunion with the caregiver. In the Heinicke and Westheimer (1966) study of separations that ranged from 2 to 21 weeks, two of the children appeared not to recognize their mothers upon reunion, and eight turned or walked away. They alternately cried and looked expressionless. The detachment persisted to some degree following the reunion, and alternated with clingy behavior suggesting intense fear of abandonment.

Bowlby's attachment theory, like classical psychoanalysis, has a biological focus (see especially Bowlby 1969). Attachment readily reduces to a "molecular" level of infant behaviors, such as smiling and vocalizing, that alert the caregiver to the child's interest in socializing, and bring him or her into close proximity with the child. Smiling and vocalizing are attachment behaviors, as is crying, which is experienced by most caregivers as aversive, and engage the caregiver in caretaking behaviors in the hope of terminating the noxious stimulus. Bowlby emphasized the survival value of attachment in enhancing safety through proximity to the caregiver in addition to feeding, learning about the environment, and social interaction, as well as protection from predators. It was the latter that Bowlby (1969) considered the biological function of attachment behavior. Attachment behaviors were seen as part of a *behavioral system* (a term Bowlby borrowed from ethology). This is key to understanding the heated nature of the controversy between psychoanalysis and attachment theory. A behavioral system involves inherent motivation. It is not reducible to another drive. It explains why feeding is not causally linked to attachment (Harlow 1958) and that attachment occurs to abusive caretakers (Bowlby 1956).

No specific behaviors can be identified with attachment. After three decades of research there appears to be general agreement concerning the key components of attachment as a psychological mechanism. The behaviors that establish and maintain proximity include: 1) signals that draw the caregivers to their children (e.g., smiling), 2) aversive behaviors (such as crying) that perform the same function, and 3) skeletal muscle activity (primarily locomotion) that bring the child to the caregiver. It is self-evident that the vulnerable infant is better protected in close proximity to a genetically related caregiver, and thus its chances of survival to reproduction are increased. The entire system of behaviors has the common function of optimizing proximity across a range of contexts (crawling, smiling, crying, etc). The system exists to ensure a stable internal organization. The organization has a goal and the individual can respond flexibly to environmental changes in a "goal-corrected" manner. Bowlby's martial analogy was to the heat-seeking missile.

There is a subtle but important difference between Bowlby's formulations and those of object relations theorists (e.g., Fairbairn 1952b) at this molecular behavioral level. The goal of the child is not the object, for example, the mother. The goal that regulates the system is initially a physical state, the maintenance of a desired degree of proximity to her. This physical goal is later supplanted by the more psychological goal of a feeling of closeness to the caregiver. Because the goal is not an object but a state of being or feeling, the context in which the child lives, that is, the response of the caregiver, will strongly influence the attachment system because if the child perceives the attachment goal to have been attained this will affect the system of behaviors.

Attachment theory from the beginning concerned more than attachment. In fact, as a developmental theory it makes sense only in the context of a number of key distinctions about what is *not* as well as what *is* attachment. The *exploratory behavioral system* is subtly interlinked with attachment, with the attachment figure providing the essential secure base from which to explore (Ainsworth 1963). The child's exploratory behavior comes to an abrupt halt when the child finds the caregiver temporarily absent (Rajecki et al. 1978). The absence of the attachment figure inhibits exploration. Thus secure attachment could be expected to be of benefit in terms of a range of cognitive and social capacities. By contrast, the *fear system* activates the attachment systems and the availability of the caregiver reduces the child's reaction to stimuli that would otherwise be perceived as dangerous (Bowlby 1973). When the fear system is aroused by what Bowlby called "natural" cues to danger (e.g., unfamiliarity, sudden noise, isolation), the child immediately seeks a source of protection and safety, the attachment figure. Thus separation involves two stressors: unprotected exposure and the sense of being cut off from the critical source of protection. Bowlby reserves the term *anxiety* for the situation where the fear system is aroused in the experienced absence of the attachment figure. The three behavioral systems—attachment, exploration, and fear—regulate the child's developmental adaptation; in combination they provide a means for the child to learn and develop without straying too far or remaining away too long (Ainsworth and Wittig 1969).

The child's tendency to seek companionship when the fear system is not aroused is accounted for by the activation of a *sociable or affectional behavioral system*. "The child seeks a playmate when he is in good spirits and confident of the whereabouts of his attachment figure" (Bowlby 1969, p. 307). The *caregiving system* is a subset of parental behavior designed to promote proximity and comfort when the parent perceives that the child is in real or potential danger (Cassidy 1999, p. 10). The caregiving system ideally acts reciprocally to the child's attachment system. In reality, there may be instances where the caregiving system is activated when the child's distress is not associated with real or perceived danger. For example, a caregiver responding to the child's distress that arose out of frustration at not being able to explore by further caregiving (e.g., soothing) is going to aggravate rather than ameliorate the situation.

The attachment bond is a subclass of the so-called *affectional bonds or ties*, where one individual has great emotional significance for another and is therefore not interchangeable. Closeness to this individual is desired and distress follows separation. An affectional bond becomes an attachment bond when the individual seeks security or comfort from the relationship (Ainsworth 1989). Thus, whilst affectional bonds may or may not be symmetrical, attachment bonds are appropriately normally profoundly asymmetrical: a parent who attempts to seek security from a child is likely to manifest other signs of psychological disorder and to thus generate disorder in the child (Bowlby 1969, p. 377). Affectional bonds also highlight the relationship between attachment and sexuality. Bowlby recognized that there are unusually close linkages between attachment and sexual behaviors and went on to write: ". . . distinct as the two systems are, there is good evidence that they are apt to impinge on each other and to influence the development of each other" (Bowlby 1969, p. 233). The facts that sex can undoubtedly occur without attachment, and that marriages without sex perhaps represent the majority of such partnerships, prove beyond doubt that these systems are separate and at most loosely coupled.

Children have the propensity to form a number of attachment relationships in early life and there appears to be a hierarchy of major caregivers with a preferred principal attachment figure (Bretherton 1980). Among the factors that determine which caregiver is at the top of the hierarchy are issues such as the amount of time the infant spends in that person's care, the quality of the care, the emotional investment of the adult in the child, and the frequent reappearance of the person (Cassidy 1999, Colin 1996). The multiplicity of attachment relationships is an important point of contact between attachment and psychoanalytic theory.

In the first volume of the *Attachment and Loss* trilogy, Bowlby (1969) was not yet clear about how attachment behavior functioned beyond the termination of the system once physical proximity was ensured. Proximity was the set goal of the attachment system, its measurement was simple and purely behavioral. The absence of the figure generates the biological need; her return and presence turns it off. Little wonder then that the majority of psychoanalysts were horrified by such apparently simplistic approach that bore the hallmarks of the worst excesses of behaviorist reductionism. As it often appears to be the case (and was the case with critical appraisals of psychoanalytic theory itself), critical opinions tend to fix upon early formulations and hold fast and unchangeable, regardless of changes and advances in the object of the critique (often in response to the very same critiques).

In the 1970s the work of Ainsworth (Ainsworth et al. 1978) helped to refine the attachment concept. She recognized that separation (physical absence of the mother) was not the key to understanding the infant's response to the Strange Situation.[1] It was the infant's appraisal or evaluation of the mother's departure in the context of her expected behavior that accounts for the infant's response. At least in older children upset by laboratory separation, it is not the mother's absence but rather her apparently arbitrary behavior that accounts for the child's distress and the relief occasioned by her return. This more elaborate, dynamic-cognitive model could then be extended to the clinical literature on maternal deprivation that had been reviewed by Bowlby. The disruptions occasioned by separation from the primary caregiver are moderated by an increasingly complex set of (unconscious) evaluative processes.

In the second volume of the trilogy, Bowlby established the set goal of the attachment system as maintaining the caregiver's accessibility and responsiveness, which he covered with a single term: *availability* (Bowlby 1973, p. 202). In fact it was not until the third section of the book that he addressed the critical role of appraisal in the operation of the attachment system. Here he asserts that availability means confi-

---

1. This is a 20-minute laboratory test where the child is exposed to two "miniscule separations" of a maximum of 3 minutes each. Mary Ainsworth and her colleagues (Ainsworth et al. 1978) found that the majority of middle-class one-year-old children respond to the mother with proximity seeking and relief at reunion (securely attached—B infants) but about 25 percent respond with subtle signs of indifference (anxious avoidantly attached—A infants) and a further 15 percent respond with proximity seeking but little relief at reunion (anxious resistantly attached—C infants). The results from this assessment will be discussed more fully in the next chapter and throughout the book.

dent expectation, gained from "tolerably accurately" (p. 202) represented experience over a significant time period, that the attachment
figure will be available. The attachment behavioral system thus came
to be underpinned by a set of cognitive mechanisms, discussed by
Bowlby as representational models or following Craik (1943) as *internal working models.* Bowlby's views were actually quite "Piagetian."[2]

The positing of a representational system underpinning attachment permitted a far more sophisticated consideration of individual
differences (Bowlby 1973, 1980a). Given the power of the biological
forces driving the human attachment system, it is assumed that almost
all human beings will become attached. Attachment, as we have seen,
may be secure or insecure. Secure attachment implies representational
systems where the attachment figure is seen as accessible and responsive when needed. Anxious attachment implies a representational system where the responsiveness of the caregiver is not assumed and the
child adopts strategies for circumventing the perceived unresponsiveness of the attachment figure (Ainsworth et al. 1978). Bowlby was pre-
scient in assuming that caregiver responsiveness was critical in determining the security of the attachment system: "the extent to which the
mother has permitted clinging and following, and all the behaviour
associated with them, or has refused them" (Bowlby 1958, p. 370). As
we shall see, considerable empirical support has been gathered for this
assumption (De Wolff and van IJzendoorn 1997, NICHD Early Child
Care Research Network 1997).

Thus the central feature of the internal working model concerns
the expected availability of the attachment figure. A complementary
working model of the self is also envisioned by Bowlby. The key feature of this is how acceptable or unacceptable the child feels in the eye
of the attachment figure. A child whose internal working model of the

---

2. The influence of Piaget on Bowlby is less frequently recognized than that of
ethologists like Konrad Lorenz and Robert Hinde. Yet both Lorenz and Piaget were
attendees of the discussion groups that Bowlby organized at the World Health Organization in Geneva on parental care and personality development. These meetings
were commissioned by Ronald Hargreaves, a friend of Bowlby's and another University College Hospital graduate, who was in charge of the mental health work of WHO
at the time and should be credited with considerable vision in promoting a socially
sophisticated approach to psychiatry.

caregiver is focused on rejection is expected to evolve a complementary working model of the self as unlovable, unworthy, and flawed. Although not explicitly stated by Bowlby, these models of the attachment figure and the self are transactional, interactive models representing self–other relationships. The development of cognitive science and the concurrent increasing prominence of object relations theory in psychoanalysis led to a variety of constructs in developmental, social, cognitive, and clinical psychology, broadly encompassing relational representations or schemas with the primary function of processing social information (Baldwin 1992, Westen 1991). The similarities and differences between the hypothetical structure envisioned by Bowlby, its reformulation by attachment theorists (see below), and current psychoanalytic thought is one of the major topics of this monograph.

Bowlby's original concept has been thoughtfully elaborated by some of the greatest minds in the attachment field (Bretherton 1991, Bretherton and Munholland 1999, Crittenden 1990, 1994, Main 1991, Main et al. 1985b, Sroufe 1990, 1996) and no attempt to review these exhaustively can be undertaken here. However, it might be helpful to summarize the four representational systems, illustrated in Figure 1–1, that are implied in these reformulations: 1) expectations of interactive attributes of early caregivers created in the first year of life and subsequently elaborated; 2) event representations by which general and specific memories of attachment-related experiences are encoded and retrieved; 3) autobiographical memories by which specific events are conceptually connected because of their relation to a continuing personal narrative and developing self-understanding; and 4) understanding of the psychological characteristics of other people (inferring and attributing causal motivational mind states, such as desires and emotions, and epistemic mind states, such as intentions and beliefs) and differentiating these from those of the self.

In the late 1970s the story was elaborated once again by two of the most thoughtful theoreticians in the field, Alan Sroufe and Everet Waters (Sroufe and Waters 1977a). The set goal of the attachment system was "felt security," rather than physical distance regulation. Thus, internal cues such as mood, illness, or even fantasy could be seen as relevant to the child's response to separation, as well as external events and the social environmental context. Felt security as a concept extended the applicability of the concept of attachment from early

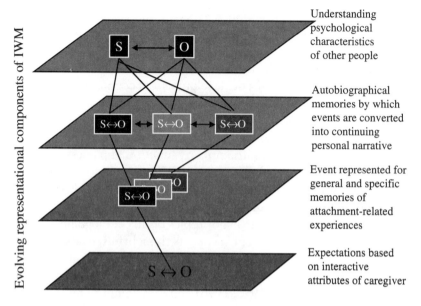

Understanding psychological characteristics of other people

Autobiographical memories by which events are converted into continuing personal narrative

Event represented for general and specific memories of attachment-related experiences

Expectations based on interactive attributes of caregiver

Evolving representational components of IWM

Figure 1–1. The Ontogenesis of the Internal Working Model

childhood to older children and even adults (Cicchetti et al. 1990). Sroufe (1996) was able to reconceptualize attachment theory in terms of affect regulation. Securely attached individuals, who have internalized the capacities for self-regulation, are contrasted with those who precociously either down-regulate (avoidant) or up-regulate (resistant) affect. This is a substantial extension of the Bowlbian notion because the range of experiences that could contribute to felt security is in no way restricted to caregiver behavior. However, as Ainsworth (1990) pointed out, Bowlby's view may be reconciled with the notion of felt security if the latter term is restricted to feelings that accompany appraisals of an attachment figure's current likely availability. Actual closeness of the attachment figure is frequently the means by which the child is able to feel secure (Ainsworth and Bowlby 1991). Thus, the past influences or biases expectations but does not determine these. Both older children and adults continue to monitor the accessibility and responsiveness of the attachment figure. Internalized aspects of the personality may be thought to interact with the quality of the current attachment relationships.

Potential external threats to appraisals of availability take up a considerable portion of the 1973 book. Bowlby is impressed by symbolic communication of abandonment, such as threats of suicide, of leaving, or of sending the child away. While such experiences are posited as "actual," in this domain the reality of a threat and the child's psychic reality clearly overlap. Bowlby, for example, refers to metaphoric communications by the parent (e.g., "you will be the death of me"), interpreted concretely by the child as threatening availability. Domestic violence is a particularly potent source of developmental problems precisely because the fear of harm coming to the parent leads to anticipations of unavailability, confirmed by the inaccessibility of the mother at moments of acute marital conflict (Davies and Cummings 1995, 1998). The consistent observation that open communication can reduce the extent to which disruptive events, such as parental anger, are perceived as threatening (Allen and Hauser 1996, Allen et al. 1996) implies a reduced role for fantasy as a source of bias in the appraisal of availability.

In his later works, Bowlby (1979, 1980a, 1987) was increasingly influenced by cognitive psychology and particularly by the information processing model of neural and cognitive functioning. Just as cognitive psychologists defined representational models in terms of access to particular kinds of information and data, Bowlby suggested that different patterns of attachment reflect differences in the individual's degree of access to certain kinds of thoughts, feelings, and memories. For example, avoidant insecure models of attachment permit only limited access to attachment-related thoughts, feelings, and memories, whereas others provide exaggerated or distorted access to attachment-relevant information. Thus, for Bowlby, cognitive as well as emotional access to attachment-relevant information emerges as a function of the nature of the past relationship between infant and caregiver.

During the late '70s and '80s, attachment research came to be increasingly concerned with child maltreatment, physical and sexual abuse. The disorganized/disoriented classification of strange situation behavior marked by fear, freezing, and disorientation (Main and Solomon 1986) was linked to maltreatment of the child (e.g., Cicchetti and Barnett 1991) and unresolved trauma in the history of the parent (Main and Hesse 1990). The frightened/frightening behavior of the parent is assumed to undermine the child's attachment organization (Main and

Hesse 1992). The attachment figure being at once the signal of safety and of danger can be readily seen to potentially undermine the entire attachment behavioral system. Childhood maltreatment accounts for some but not all attachment disorganization observed in infancy. The potential reasons for the disorganization of the attachment system were therefore extended to include experiences that were more subtle but nevertheless deeply unsettling from an infant's point of view. Moments of dissociation or strange, frightened expressions have been observed in parents of infants whose strange situation behavior was classified as disorganized (Schuengel et al. 1999a; Schuengel et al. 1999b). Infant disorganization has been linked to later psychopathology in a number of longitudinal investigations (Lyons-Ruth 1996b, Shaw et al. 1996), including dissociative symptoms in particular (Carlson 1998). While attachment is still seen as all-pervasive, research and theory on attachment disorganization offers a more satisfactory theoretical link between early attachment experience and personality disturbance than has thus far been available and is therefore the cutting edge of current clinical attachment research (Lyons-Ruth and Jacobovitz 1999, Solomon and George 1999a).

The biological basis of attachment remains rooted in animal studies. Myron Hofer's work with rodent pups identified regulatory interactions within the mother–infant relationship that have clear analogies to what is proposed here (Hofer 1995, Polan and Hofer 1999). Hofer's work over three decades has revealed that the evolutionary survival value of staying close to and interacting with the mother goes way beyond protection and may be expanded to many pathways available for regulation of the infant's physiological and behavioral system. Hofer's view is that the attachment "relationship provides an opportunity for the mother to shape both the developing physiology and the behavior of her offspring through her patterned interactions with her infant" (Polan and Hofer 1999, p. 177). Attachment is not an end in itself—it is a system adapted by evolution to fulfill key ontogenetic physiological and psychological tasks. Hofer's reformulation of attachment in terms of regulatory processes, hidden but observable within the parent–infant interaction, provides a very different way of explaining the range of phenomena usually discussed under the heading of attachment. The traditional attachment model is clearly circular. The response to separation is attributed to the disruption of a social bond, the existence of which is inferred from the presence of the separation response. What is lost in "loss" is not the bond but the opportunity to generate a higher order regulatory mechanism: the mechanism for appraisal and reorganization of mental contents. In this context attachment is conceptualized as a process that brings into being complex mental life into being from a multi-faceted and adaptable behavioral system. Some, but by no means all, of such mental function is unique to humans. The mechanism that generates these (the attachment relationship) has evolutionary continuity across nonhuman species. Just as in rat pups the ontogenetic development of biological regulators crucially depends on the mother–infant unit, so in human development psychological interpretive capacity evolves in the context of the repetitive interactions with the mother.

So how does attachment theory differ from more traditional psychoanalytic ideas? Attachment theory continues to make use of three out of Rapaport and Gill's (1959) five basic psychoanalytic viewpoints. The perspective that Bowlby took forward most forcefully into his new theory was the genetic viewpoint (his developmental view). The structural point of view was also taken forward and elaborated substantially in the context of modern cognitive psychology. The adaptive point of view also has a clear central place in the context of the detailed description of caregiver–child relationship. All three of these principles are evidently at work in Bowlby's original formulations and are still at work in more recent adaptations of the work. However, two points of view were explicitly discarded. These were the economic and the dynamic viewpoints (although in the last volume of his trilogy a whole section is devoted to perceptual defense and other unconscious processes).

To most psychoanalysts of the '50s and '60s the latter points of view were far more critical to the definition of the discipline than the first three. To make matters worse, Bowlby added a number of new perspectives to psychoanalytic thinking that at the time were hard to digest. These were: an ethological (what we now recognize as a sociobiological) perspective on mental function, an object relations perspective, with relationships rather than bodily drives as motivators of behavior, an epistemological perspective that privileged the external environment, and a research perspective that cast aspersions on the value of traditional clinical reports as the sole data source of psychoanalytic inquiry. It is hardly surprising that he was less than popular with his colleagues.

A rapprochement has become possible because of a number of concurrent historical events and changes. These are: 1) A shift within attachment theory from a focus on infant behavior and its determinants in the child's physical environment to a broader concern with internal representations in the infant and the parent; 2) increasing concern within psychoanalysis with systematic observation and empirical research, together with a severe shortage of paradigms that are scientifically acceptable (reliable and valid) and provide information of interest to psychoanalytic clinicians and theoreticians; 3) the breakdown of the theoretical hegemony that governed psychoanalysis in the United States (and to a lesser extent in Europe), which led to more openness to the possibility of plurality in theory, where clinical usefulness and intellectual appeal are the primary criteria for the acceptability of new ideas; and 4) a growing recognition within attachment theory of a certain sense of "paradigm boundedness," recognition of the limitations of a purely cognitive science approach in clinical work and a need for alternative theoretical frames of reference to enrich research and theory building of relevance to clinicians. So on both sides the wish for integration might be developing.

2

Key Findings
of Attachment Research

It is beyond the scope of this brief monograph to offer any kind of comprehensive summary of the findings of three decades of attachment research. Certain empirical observations have already been alluded to above. In this section we shall briefly overview selected findings that have contributed to the development of attachment theory and/or are likely to have a bearing on its evolving relationship to psychoanalysis. There are, fortunately, excellent recent reviews of this work; in particular the edited volume by Cassidy and Shaver (1999) represents a definitive summary, and Allen's (2000) monograph is an accessible yet authoritative integration of clinically relevant findings.

THE MEASUREMENT OF ATTACHMENT
IN CHILDHOOD

Advances in attachment theory have, in part, been driven by discoveries concerning individual differences in attachment behavior in infants and adults. Research on the determinants of attachment security critically depends on reliable and valid measures of attachment class. A range of instruments and coding systems are available to assess attachment classification. As most findings to be considered here depend on these instruments, it is helpful to consider briefly what they are based on and what they offer.

The Strange Situation

The strange situation, devised by Mary Ainsworth and her colleagues (Ainsworth et al. 1978), is a simple laboratory procedure to measure attachment in infants of 1–2 years. It involves two episodes of brief separation between the infant and the caregiver. The infant's behavior during separation, but particularly upon reunion with the caregiver, is classified into one of four categories: securely attached (B), anxiously attached avoidant (A), anxiously attached ambivalent/resistant (C), and disorganized/disoriented (D). The secure pattern of distress at separation and reassurance by the reunion is thought to reflect an internal working model characterized by confidence that the caregiver will be comforting. The anxious avoidant pattern is thought to indicate the infant's lack of confidence in the caregiver's availability, leading to a strategy of trying precociously to control or down-regulate emotional arousal, to show little distress during separation and definite disinterest at reunion, in an immature attempt to cope with separation. Anxious ambivalent/resistant infants, who show distress at separation but are not comforted by the caregiver's return, appear to have adopted the strategy of exaggerating or up-regulating affect in order to secure the caregiver's attention. The disorganized/disoriented infant, in general, seeks proximity to the mother in strange and disoriented ways, for example, approaching the mother backwards, hiding, suddenly freezing in the middle of a movement, or just staring into space (Main and Solomon 1990).

There is current controversy concerning the stability of the classification obtained in the strange situation. The patterns described by Ainsworth are of interest to attachment theorists if they reflect the persistent cognitive emotional structures governing the attachment behavioral system described by Bowlby (1973). While early studies clearly indicated that attachment classification obtained in the strange situation met the criteria of stability, more recent investigations have been quite disappointing. For example, relatively recently, and out of line with previous investigations, Belsky and colleagues reported that less than 50 percent of infants tested were given the same category in the ABC classification upon a retest three months later (Belsky et al. 1996a). The stability of the D classification has been generally high (Lyons-Ruth et al. 1991). On the whole, stability appears to be low in high-risk samples where major changes in family function are common (Solomon and George 1999b).

The Cassidy and Marvin System

The Cassidy and Marvin system is a five-category attachment classification for pre-school and kindergarten children (2 ½ to 4 ½) (Cassidy and Marvin 1992). The reunion of secure children is described as smooth, open, warm, and positive, while those of ambivalent children are described as strong on proximity-seeking but babyish and coy. Avoidant children appear somewhat detached and nonchalant, avoiding physical or psychological intimacy. The disorganized category of infant attachment is sometimes seen at this age as controlling, sometimes as punitive behavior, as well as there being behaviors characteristic of infant disorganization. There is also an insecure other classification for behaviors that cannot be described in terms of the above four categories. There are two alternative systems for this age group: Crittenden's pre-school assessment of attachment (Crittenden 1992) and Main and Cassidy's attachment classification for kindergarten-age children (Main and Cassidy 1988). While the Cassidy and Marvin system is the best investigated of the three, none of these systems has been subjected to the kind of rigorous assessment that the strange situation test underwent, thus attachment data from this age group should be treated with some caution.

Measures Based on Symbolic Representation

There are a range of measures based on the assumption that for children aged 5 and above behavioral measures of attachment will be of limited use and children's symbolic production will provide a more accurate indication of the status of the control system governing attachment behaviors. Coding systems have been developed to assess children's responses to the Separation Anxiety Test (SAT), a range of images depicting attachment related scenes (Slough and Greenberg 1990). In this context secure children would discuss dealing with separation as depicted in the pictures in constructive ways, avoidant children would appear at a loss as to suggesting methods of coping, ambivalent children might combine anger with the parent in the picture with a wish to please the parent, while disorganized children would express fear or disorganized disoriented thought processes (Kaplan 1987). An alternative measure based on symbolic representation is a doll play involving separation and reunion stories (Bretherton et al. 1990). This was developed further by Carol George and colleagues (Solomon et al. 1995) as well as David Oppenheim (Oppenheim et al. 1997). While the SAT is the most commonly used symbolic measure of attachment, there is increasing evidence that the quality of story stem completion narratives might be a highly satisfactory assessment of the IWM in 5–7-year-olds (e.g., Steele 1999).

A similar but more complex and sophisticated approach was recently reported by Green and colleagues (Green 2000). An innovative aspect of the approach is the deliberate arousal of the child's attachment system by the experimenter up to the point when he or she shows concern in relation to the narrative that is being presented in the context of a doll house story completion task. The assessment appears to be acceptable and productive in use with children up to 7 years of age. The classification has good psychometric properties and a strong relationship was found with mother's AAI classification.

The Child Attachment Interview (CAI)

The AAI has been successfully extended to cover lower age groups. The interview has been shown to be valid for adolescents as young as 12–14 (Ammaniti et al. 1990, Ammaniti et al. in press) and was used by Trowell in a study of sexually abused preadolescent girls. The Child Attachment Interview (Target et al. in preparation) is a developmentally appropriate interview and coding system for 8–14 year olds with the potential to be extended for verbal 6–7 year olds. The CAI is a modified version of the AAI with radical changes to interviewer instructions and probes. The interviewer does not expect the child to produce a narrative, and the focus of the interview is not the past but the current relationship with the parent. The coding system offers a secure–insecure classification that has been shown to be reliable and stable as well as strongly associated with parental AAI's.

The Attachment Q-sort

An alternative approach to classifying the child's behavior in the laboratory or mental representations as these emerge in semi-projective or projective tests is the actual observation of the behavior of the child in the home over a relatively prolonged period (2–6 hours over separate visits) (Posada et al. 1995, Waters 1995, Waters and Deane 1985). The measure is both stable and reliable. Recently, some concern has been expressed that the AQS measures a construct somewhat different from the strange situation (van Ijzendoorn et al., in press). The relationship between the strange situation and the AQS is moderate at best and it is possible that the AQS is more sensitive to confounding by temperamental differences than the strange situation. Nonetheless, many results concerned with attachment security do use the AQS as the primary measure of attachment.

The Adult Attachment Interview (AAI)

Foremost amongst the measures of adult attachment that captured the interest of psychoanalysts is the Adult Attachment Interview (George et al. 1996). The interview is a narrative about childhood similar to the sort that might be taken in the course of any psychotherapy assessment. It has the special feature of getting to sensitive childhood issues rapidly and persistently—what Mary Main rather aptly refers to as "surprising the unconscious." Interview protocols are transcribed and classified according to a coding system that privileges narrative form (Main and Goldwyn 1998a,b). At the heart of the system is Grice's (1989) cooperative principle of rational discourse. Interview narratives that score high on coherence come from speakers who give evidence for what they say, are succinct yet complete, relevant to the topic at hand, and clear and orderly. Attachment security in the coding system (the autonomous classification—F) is most closely associated with high coherence. There are three insecure patterns: the dismissing (idealizing or derogatory about attachment—Ds), the preoccupied (angry or passive—E), and the unresolved in relation to loss or abuse (U). The

Ds and E categories map both conceptually and empirically onto the avoidant and ambivalent/resistant infant categories respectively. The U category, while specific to signs of cognitive disorganization in parts of the interview where the subject is questioned about loss or abuse, corresponds to the general disorganization of the attachment system assumed to characterize D infants.

The Adult Attachment Interview was quickly adopted by researchers because of its unique capacity to predict the infant's attachment classification from the caregiver's AAI narrative, even before the birth of the infant. This has now been demonstrated in at least 14 studies (van IJzendoorn 1995). Furthermore, AAI classifications are stable over a two-month period and independent of verbal and performance IQ, autobiographical memory, social desirability, interviewer effects, and general discourse styles (Bakermans-Kranenburg and van IJzendoorn 1993, Crowell et al. 1996, Fonagy et al. 1991b, Sagi et al. 1994). The AAI predicts maternal sensitivity but not sufficiently to explain its association with the strange situation classification (Pederson et al. 1998). A comprehensive review of the impressive body of research findings that have accumulated using the AAI is provided by Hesse (1999).

The Current Relationship Interview

Drawn up to be analogous to the AAI, the Current Relationship Interview assesses the security or insecurity of current attachment relationships (Crowell and Owens 1996). An interview is rated secure if the subject is able convincingly to describe his or her own and the partner's secure base behavior or describe negative partner behavior in a coherent way. Dismissing and preoccupied interviews reflect insecurity by idealization and anxious dissatisfaction respectively. An interview is coded unresolved when a romantic relationship is currently exerting a disruptive influence on cognitive organization. There is a weak but statistically significant relationship between the AAI and the CRI (Gao 1998, cited in Crowell 1999).

Self-Report Measures of Adult Attachment

A wide range of questionnaire measures purporting to measure adult attachment are currently available. Self-report measures of attachment history include: the Attachment History Questionnaire (Pottharst 1990), the Inventory of Parent and Peer Attachment (Armsden and Greenberg 1987b), and the Reciprocal and Avoidant Attachment Questionnaire (West and Seldon-Keller 1994). There are also measures of the security of romantic attachment: the Attachment Style Questionnaire (Hazan and Shaver 1987), and, building on this, the Relationship Questionnaire (Bartholomew and Horowitz 1991). These are simple instruments where brief descriptions are offered of a person's general attitude to relationships and the subject is asked to indicate which description he or she feels greatest affinity with. Descriptions are of a secure, a fearful, a preoccupied, and a dismissing individual. A more traditional questionnaire version of this instrument was provided by Griffin and Bartholomew (1994). Excellent reviews of these and other measures are provided by Stein (1998) and Crowell and colleagues (1999).

DETERMINANTS OF ATTACHMENT SECURITY

Following the Bowlby–Ainsworth model, the determinants of attachment security may be seen as either proximal or distal. Proximal determinants impact on the quality of the parent–infant relationship and principally concern infant temperament and maternal sensitivity. Distal predictors are assumed to act on proximal determinants. But this kind of mediational model is only relatively infrequently explored by researchers and even less often shown to be accurate.

Infant temperament is not generally regarded as a powerful determinant of attachment security. Vaughn and Bost (1999) conclude their exhaustive review thus: "attachment security cannot be considered as redundant with temperament in the explanation of personality and/or in explanation of qualities of interpersonal actions" (p. 218). In general, parent reports of temperamental difficulty, negative reactivity, and emotionality are independent of secure/insecure classification. However, irritability in early infancy does appear to increase the risk of insecurity by potentiating (increasing the impact of) inadequate caregiving practices when social disadvantage places caregivers under specific stress (e.g., Susman-Stillman et al. 1996, van den Boom 1994).

Maternal caregiving makes a clear contribution to attachment security. In particular, maternal sensitivity, responsiveness to distress, moderate appropriate stimulation, interactional synchrony and warmth, involvement, and responsiveness have all been demonstrated to be predictors of attachment security in a large number of studies (see the excellent review by Belsky 1999a). Avoidant attachment is generally predicted by intrusive, excessively stimulating and controlling interactional style with the infant. Ambivalent/resistant infant attachment appears to be related to a generally unresponsive and under-involved approach to caregiving. The strength of these associations, however, is relatively small. A meta-analysis of 66 investigations, which together involved over 4,000 infant–mother dyads, yielded an effect size[1] of .17 (De Wolff and van IJzendoorn 1997)—small by any standards. Restricting the dataset to 30 studies specifically examining the effect of parental sensitivity, the effect size increased to .22. Nevertheless, claims that maternal sensitivity is a primary determinant of attachment security currently appear to lack empirical support.

An alternative line of evidence is far more encouraging for attachment theory. A unique study of experimentally increasing maternal sensitivity for mothers of children with negative temperaments yielded an exceptionally large effect size in terms of increasing attachment security from 28 percent to 68 percent (van den Boom 1994). This suggests that, at least for this socially disadvantaged group, maternal sensitivity was critical to the attainment of attachment security in the infant. The combined effect size of such intervention across more than a dozen studies is .48 (van Ijzendoorn et al. 1995). Paternal sensitivity has a smaller, but still statistically significant, association with security of attachment to father (van IJzendoorn and DeWolff 1997). Similarly, nonparental caregivers are more likely to become secure attachment figures if they show sensitivity in relation to the child (Goosens and van Ijzendoorn 1990).

The most spectacular demonstration of the importance of quality of parenting in determining attachment security does not come from direct observations of mothering. As mentioned above, 14 studies have so far demonstrated that the AAI administered to mother or father will

---

1. Effect size is often used in place of statistical significance as an indicator of the importance or relevance of an association. An effect size of .17, for example, means that having a sensitive caregiver would increase the infant's chance of being securely attached by 6–7 percent.

predict not only the child's security of attachment but, even more remarkably, the precise attachment category that the child manifests in the strange situation (van Ijzendoorn 1995). Thus, dismissing AAI interviews predict avoidant strange situation behavior while preoccupied interviews predict anxious-resistant infant attachment. Lack of resolution of mourning (unresolved interviews) predict disorganization in infant attachment (see below). Temperament (child → parent effects) seems an inadequate account of the phenomena since the AAI of each parent, collected and coded before the birth of the child, predicts the attachment classification of the infant at 12 and 18 months (Fonagy et al. 1991b, Steele et al. 1996a).

Recent evidence by Slade and her colleagues provided an important clue about the puzzle of intergenerational transmission of attachment security. They demonstrated that autonomous (secure) mothers on the AAI represented their relationship with their toddlers in a more coherent way, conveying more joy and pleasure in the relationship, than did dismissing and preoccupied mothers (Slade et al. 1999a). We believe that the parent's capacity to adopt the intentional stance towards a not-yet-intentional infant, to think about the infant in terms of thoughts, feelings, and desires in the infant's mind and in their own mind in relation to the infant and his or her mental state, is the key mediator of the transmission of attachment and accounts for classical observations concerning the influence of caregiver sensitivity (Fonagy et al. 1991a). Those with a strong capacity to reflect on their own and their caregiver's mental states in the context of the AAI were far more likely to have children securely attached to them—a finding that we have linked the parent's capacity to foster the child's self-development (Fonagy et al. 1993b). We have also found that mothers in a relatively high-stress (deprived) group characterized by single-parent families, parental criminality, unemployment, overcrowding, and psychiatric illness would be far more likely to have securely attached infants if their reflective function was high (Fonagy et al. 1994). This is preliminary support for the Freudian notion (1920) that those who do not remember and come to terms with the past are destined (are more likely) to repeat it, at least with their children.

The child's social context is an equally important, even if theoretically distal, determinant of attachment security. On the whole, parents with better functioning personalities are more likely to have securely attached infants (Del Carmen et al. 1993, Maslin and Bates 1983). Children with greater exposure to more severely depressed mothers are more likely to be classified insecure (Lyons-Ruth et al. 1986, Radke-Yarrow et al. 1985, Teti et al. 1995), as are children living with significant marital disharmony (Erel and Burman 1995) and those living with mothers with inadequate social support (Crittenden 1985, Crnic et al. 1986). Many of these effects are small, relatively unreliable, and thus commonly not replicated. Belsky (1999a) suggests that predictors of attachment security should be conceived of as other risk factors in developmental psychopathology and considered to be additive or even interactive with one another. In any case, current evidence suggests that proximal predictors (e.g., mother–infant interaction) of attachment are relatively weak and distal predictors (e.g., parental psychopathology) are weaker still. The weakness of the prediction from either source may suggest powerful genetic effects or the restricted range of measurement in most psychosocial studies, which tend to sample psychosocial environments from within a fairly restricted, homogeneous range (Maccoby 2000).

PREDICTION FROM EARLY ATTACHMENT TO LATER DEVELOPMENT

Bowlby was unequivocal in his conviction that differences in the security of infant–mother attachment would have long-term implications for later intimate relationships, self-understanding, and psychological disturbance. Individual differences in attachment classification have been studied in relation to an exceptionally wide range of later outcomes, spanning cognitive capacities such as verbal IQ, interpersonal capacities, skills, and psychopathology. The findings from these studies only partially support claims for the formative nature of early attachment relationships (Belsky and Cassidy 1994, Thompson 1999). While secure attachment in infancy predicts more positive subsequent parent–offspring interaction in the short term (e.g., Slade 1987), researchers failed to find strong and enduring direct associations between secure attachment in infancy and parent–child interactions at ages 6 and beyond (e.g., Grossmann and Grossmann 1991). Some studies do demonstrate considerable concordance between assessments of attachment classification in parent–child dyads at various ages (Main and Cassidy 1988, Wartner et al. 1994). Substantial continuity of secure versus insecure classifications from the ages of 18 months to 20 years has also been reported using the Adult Attachment Interview (Hamilton in press, Waters et al. in press), 72 percent and 77 percent respectively. Stability has been less remarkable in other samples (Grossman et al. 1999, Weinfield et al. in press). It is highly unlikely that continuity is to be expected in the natural course of development. The likelihood of developmental continuity probably critically depends on important mediating conditions in the ecology of the family life that are not yet known and could not be monitored in these studies.

The Bowlby–Ainsworth model would also lead one to expect accurate prediction from the infant–mother relationship to other close dyadic relationships. There is tentative evidence that a secure infant–mother relationship predicts more harmonious interaction with siblings (e.g., Teti and Ablard 1989, Volling and Belsky 1992), and a substantial body of data suggests that, at pre-school and at age 10, more appropriate relationships evolve between children who were securely attached in infancy and their teachers and counselors (e.g., Weinfield et al. 1999). There are mixed findings concerning the superiority of those with a history of secure attachment in more general social competence. In some studies, such as the Minneapolis Project and the two German samples, secure attachment history predicts greater peer competence even to adolescence. In other studies, long-term follow-ups to pre-school, middle childhood, and beyond reveal small or insignificant effects (Berlin et al. 1995, Howes et al. 1994, Lewis and Feiring 1989, Youngblade and Belsky 1992). Most recently the young adult follow-up of the Bielefeld longitudinal study (Grossman et al., in press), demonstrated substantial continuity on a relatively small sample of 38 young adults in terms of their partnership representations. The young adults' quality of discourse about their partnership was strongly predicted by a composite index of maternal sensitivity and valuing of attachment. Twenty-two-year-olds who had experienced a mother rated as sensitive to a pre-verbal as well as a verbal young child had a coherent discourse about their partnership which gave evidence of self-reflection and respect of the partner's autonomy. Particularly striking in these results was that maternal sensitivity to the infant in the first year appeared to significantly predict by itself the quality of discourse about a partnership at age 22. Thus there are a few reliable, long-term consequences of attachment security in infancy, but do these justify the classic theoretical portrayals of mother–infant attachment as the prototype of all later relationships?

Evidence linking attachment in infancy with personality characteristics is again stronger in some studies than in others. In the Minnesota Study, pre-schoolers with secure attachment histories were consistently rated by teachers as higher in self-esteem, emotional health, agency, compliance, and positive affect, and this persisted to assessment at age 10 (Elicker et al. 1992, Weinfield et al. 1999). The most recent findings from this cohort still show a prediction from infancy to adult measure of psychiatric morbidity with many potential confounding factors controlled for (Carlson 1998, Weinfield et al. 1999). However, not all studies are able to replicate these findings (e.g., Feiring and Lewis 1996). In contrast to Bowlby's prediction, the secure, avoidant, and resistant classifications tend not to be strongly related to later measures of maladaptation; it is the disorganized/disoriented infant category that appears to have the strongest predictive significance for later psychological disturbance (Carlson 1998, Lyons-Ruth 1996a, Lyons-Ruth et al. 1993, Ogawa et al. 1997) and we shall explore this association in detail in the section below. More generally, associations between secure infant attachment and personality characteristics such as ego resilience appear in some samples and not others, and the prediction of behavioral problems from insecurity, when observed, appears to be moderated by intervening experiences such as gender differences, environmental stress, or the child's intellectual capacity (Erickson et al. 1985, Fagot and Kavanagh 1990, Lyons-Ruth et al. 1993). Across a range of studies, it is striking that consistent personality sequelae of secure attachment are difficult to identify. Each of the factors looked at is likely to be influenced by a range of determinants, none of which can be controlled for across these longitudinal investigations. Evidence that suggests that attachment is the foundation for later adaptation is neither reliable nor consistent. It is precisely these kinds of gaps between theory and evidence that, in our view, should call attachment theorists' attention to the need to open dialogue with other theoretical approaches, including numerous psychoanalytic ideas.

To be specific, evidence is accumulating that suggests that, while the residue of early attachment might not be very apparent in overt functioning, it may have discernible effects on the mental processes that underpin personality and psychopathology. This evidence comes from studies that attempt to identify associations between attachment history and representational capacities concerning self, other, and self–other relationships. For example, securely attached children describe themselves in generally more positive terms, but are also capable of admitting that they are not perfect, while insecurely attached children are less willing to admit to flaws, although they are more negative in terms of their self-description (Cassidy 1988). Children with secure attachment histories remember positive events more accurately than negative events (Belsky et al. 1996). In another study, children deemed to be securely attached obtained higher scores on two assessments of emotional understanding, explained by their greater competence in understanding negative emotions (Laible and Thompson 1998). Attachment classification of first-graders predicted the extent to which children attributed benign motives to story characters (Cassidy et al. 1996). Infant attachment has also been shown to predict performance on theory of mind tasks (Fonagy 1997). To anticipate our final argument somewhat, the early relationship environment is crucial not because it shapes the quality of subsequent relationships (for which evidence is lacking, as we have seen) but because it serves to equip the individual with a mental processing system that will subsequently generate mental representations, including relationship representations. The creation of this representational system is arguably the most important evolutionary function of attachment to a caregiver. Adopting this perspective helps redress the prevailing bias against the centrality of the family as the major force in socialization, but it also shifts the emphasis from content of experience to psychological structure or mental mechanism and involves expanding on current ideas of the evolutionary function of attachment.

ATTACHMENT AND PSYCHOPATHOLOGY

Psychopathology in Childhood

Numerous studies of low risk samples failed to identify the simple relationship between insecure attachment in the first two years of life and emotional or behavioral problems in middle childhood (e.g., Feiring and Lewis 1996). In a sample drawn from a high social risk population, children who showed early insecure relations were also consistently observed to be more prone to moodiness, poor peer relations, and symptoms of depression and aggression, right up to pre-adolescence (Weinfield et al. 1999). Two recent follow-ups of this sample showed powerful prediction to psychopathology in adolescence. Anxiety disorder in adolescence was most likely to be associated with ambivalent attachment in infancy (Warren et al. 1997). Overall, avoidant infants showed the highest rate of disorders (70 percent) and resistant infants were no more likely to have diagnosable psychiatric disorder than secure ones. In the same sample, dissociative symptoms at 17 and 19 years were predictable from avoidant classification and disorganized behavior scores (Ogawa et al. 1997).

Lyons-Ruth and her colleagues followed up 64 high-risk infants (Lyons-Ruth 1995, Lyons-Ruth et al. 1989). Seventy-one percent of hostile pre-schoolers had been classified as disorganized at 18 months compared to 12 percent of those originally classified as secure. More than half of children classified as disorganized in infancy and who had a mother with psychosocial problems were seen as hostile in kindergarten, compared with less than 5 percent of those with neither of these risk factors. Similar risk was found in relation to teacher-rated externalizing problems at age 7 in the low IQ subgroup disorganized in infancy. Internalizing symptoms, by contrast, were predicted by avoidant, not disorganized infant classification. Shaw and colleagues (Shaw et al. 1997, Shaw and Vondra 1995), studying a high-risk sample in Pittsburgh, found that attachment insecurity modestly predicted pre-school behavior problems at age 3, and robustly and uniquely predicted problems at age 5. Sixty percent of disorganized children showed clinically elevated aggression compared to around 30 percent of the two other insecure classifications and 17 percent of securely classified children. Children with both disorganized attachment and parental rating of difficult temperament were in the 99th percentile for aggression. Children with just one of these two risk factors were within the normal range. Both these studies suggest that disorganized attachment may be a vulnerability factor for later psychological disturbance in combination with other risk factors. In addition, there is a rich body of literature, reviewed by Greenberg (1999), that shows strong associations between concurrent measurement of attachment and psychopathology. However, cross-sectional investigations always leave open the possibility that nonsecure attachment is but a further indication of the child's psychological disturbance.

Attachment and Adult Psychopathology

There is general agreement that attachment security can serve as a protective factor against psychopathology, and that it is associated with wide range of healthier personality variables such as lower anxiety (Collins and Read 1990), less hostility, and greater ego resilience (Kobak and Sceery 1988), and greater ability to regulate affect through interpersonal relatedness (Simpson et al. 1992, Vaillant 1992). Insecure attachment appears to be a risk factor and is associated with such characteristics as a greater degree of depression (Armsden and Greenberg 1987a), anxiety, hostility and psychosomatic illness (Hazan and Shaver 1990) and less ego resilience (Kobak and Sceery 1988).

Very few studies have linked attachment patterns and adult psychopathology. These have been subjected to detailed scrutiny by Dozier (Dozier et al. 1999). Aggregating across five studies, it seems that psychiatric disorders are nearly always associated with nonautonomous, insecure states of mind and that unresolved status is highly overrepresented in this group. In one longitudinal study (Allen et al. 1996), derogation and lack of resolution of abuse predicted criminal behavior and hard drug use in a high-risk sample. Although it has been suggested that a dismissing state of mind might be associated with antisocial personality disorder, eating disorders, substance abuse, and dependence, and preoccupied states of mind would be linked with disorders that involve absorption in one's own feelings such as depression, anxiety, and borderline personality disorder, the available studies do not support this kind of simplistic model (e.g., Fonagy et al. 1996). Eagle (1999) cites evidence that while preoccupied/enmeshed individuals experience more psychological distress, avoidantly attached individuals show a greater incidence of somatic symptoms and illnesses.

There are several problems with these kinds of studies. First, the co-morbidity of Axis I disorders, particularly in relatively severe clinical groups where co-morbidity is extremely high, preclude any simple links between attachment classification and a unique form of psychiatric morbidity. Second, the coding systems for establishing attachment classes are not truly independent of clinical conditions and some consistent associations might be simple cases of item overlap.[2] Third, the adult attachment coding systems were not developed with clinical groups in mind, and therefore it is not clear if or how the severity of psychiatric morbidity per se might distort the assignment of an attachment classification. Currently we are lacking the validity studies necessary to establish the usefulness of currently available attachment measures for categorization of psychopathology.

More recently a line of work linking attachment classification and treatment outcome has emerged, where attachment classification is used as a predictor within specific diagnostic groups. Dismissing adults appear to be relatively resistant to treatment and within the context of therapy. Arguably, they deny their need for help in order to protect themselves from the possibility that the caregiver will be eventually unavailable. They might be rejecting of treatment, rarely asking for help (Dozier 1990). Preoccupied adults have a more general inability to collaborate with and take in the therapist's words and support, but then become dependent and call therapists between hours (Dozier et al. 1991). A synthetic view of this literature has been suggested by Sidney Blatt and colleagues (Blatt and Blass 1996, Blatt et al. 1995, Blatt et al. 1998). Blatt and his coworkers have proposed a dichotomy that overlaps in a highly informative way with the Bowlby–Ainsworth–Main categorization. They envision a dialectic between two developmental pressures that defines the evolving representations of self–other relationships: the needs for a sense of relatedness and a sense of autonomous identity (Blatt and Blass 1996). These developmental needs are thought to be in synergistic interaction throughout ontogeny and a lack of balance implies psychopathology. *Anaclitic pathology* (an exaggerated need for relatedness—preoccupation/entanglement) is present in dependent, histrionic, or borderline personality disorder. *Introjective pathology* (an exaggerated quest for identity—dismissing or avoidant pathology) is thought to characterize schizoid, schizotypal, narcissistic, antisocial, or avoidant individuals. John Gunderson (1996) writing about BPD from

---

2. For example, if lack of ability to recall early (attachment) experience is a criterion for a dismissing attachment classification (Ds), and memory problems are part of the diagnostic criteria for major depression (MD), any association between Ds and MD could only be taken seriously if the memory deficit in relation to attachment was shown to be something beyond the general memory problems reported by MD patients.

an attachment theory perspective, for example, identifies precisely the anaclitic pathology of these patients when pointing to their total in-capacity to tolerate aloneness.

The person-centered approach of the attachment theory perspective thus has the potential greatly to deepen our understanding of psychiatric disturbance, as categorized by *DSM-IV*, by adding a dynamic developmental standpoint. For example, Blatt and colleagues, using the relatedness–autonomy dialectic, can differentiate two types of depression: a dependent (anaclitic) and a self-critical (introjective) type (Blatt and Bers 1993). Thus, depression in individuals with borderline personality disorder is characterized by emptiness, loneliness, desperation vis-à-vis attachment figures, and labile, diffuse affectivity. For non-borderline individuals with major depression, these aspects correlate negatively with the severity of depression, whereas for borderline individuals, the same symptoms correlate almost perfectly with severity within the limits of the reliability of measurement (Rogers et al. 1995, Westen et al. 1992).

Response to treatment is powerfully predicted by this distinction. For example, in the NIMH trial of psychotherapy for depression (Blatt et al. 1998, Elkin 1994), perfectionist individuals (introjective type) were unlikely to improve after the first few sessions, whereas patients with a high need for approval (anaclitic types) improved significantly in the second half of the treatment (Blatt et al. 1995). In general, it is possible that dismissing patients will tend to do poorly in most short-term treatments (Horowitz et al. 1996). Blatt argues that this may be the consequence of the anticipation of the separation in individuals for whom identity is a clear organizing issue. By contrast, dismissing individuals might do better in long-term psychoanalytic psychotherapy where their self scrutiny is adequately supported, their guilt does not become overwhelming and (unlike the anaclitic, preoccupied types) they do not become so entangled in their therapeutic relationship that they can no longer derive benefit from this (Blatt and Ford 1994, Fonagy et al. 1996). The value of the psychoanalytic approach is highlighted by the fact that the majority of studies of depression neither explores nor differentiates between these groups, although the experience of psychological distress in the two groups is critically different. The person-centered attachment theory approach that takes the representational world as its focus can potentially be very helpful in refining our predictions concerning psychological disturbance.

THE DISORGANIZATION OF ATTACHMENT

The most promising area of attachment research from a psycho-analytic point of view is undoubtedly the study of disorganized/disori-ented attachment behavior. As was described above, disorganized/dis-oriented attachment is marked in the strange situation by displays of contradictory behavior patterns sequentially or simultaneously, undi-rected, incomplete, or interrupted movements, stereotypes, anomalous postures, freezing, apprehension regarding the parent or disoriented wanderings (Main and Solomon 1986, 1990). Main and Hesse's (1990) now classical contribution linked disorganized attachment behavior to frightened or frightening caregiving: infants who could not find a solu-tion to the paradox of fearing the figures who they wished to approach for comfort in times of distress (Main 1995). In the intervening decade, a great deal has been learned about disorganized attachment. A meta-analysis of studies of disorganized attachment (Van Ijzendoorn et al., in press) estimated its prevalence at 14 percent in middle-income samples and 24 percent in low-income groups. The stability of the classification of disorganized attachment is reasonable (r = .36) (Van Ijzendoorn et al., in press), with some indication that lack of stability may be accounted for by increases in the number of disorganized infants between 12 and 18 months (Barnett et al. 1999, Lyons-Ruth 1991, Vondra et al. 1999).

There is no substantial evidence to suggest that temperamental or constitutional variables can account for attachment disorganization (Van Ijzendoorn et al., in press), although an isolated study found that newborn behavioral organization measured by the Brazelton neonatal behavioral assessment scale predicted disorganization at one year. Dis-organization has been shown to be associated with a pattern of mild mental lag, where mental scores lag behind the Bayley Motor scores (Lyons-Ruth et al. 1991).

There is evidence that infants with disorganized attachment be-haviors manifest significantly higher salivary cortisol levels during the strange situation (Hertsgaard et al. 1995, Spangler and Grossman 1993). Cortisol is a stress hormone that in excess is toxic and can cause damage to the hypothalamus. Infants late adopted from East European orphanages (i.e., those who stayed eight months or more in the orphanage) are, not surprisingly, predominantly disorganized in their attachment at age 4 (Chisolm 1998, Marcovitch et al. 1997). Normal diurnal variation of cortisol secretion appears to be altered among Romanian orphans with peak values occurring in late morning or early afternoon rather than on rising as one would normally expect (Carlson et al. 1995). Cortisol elevation appears associated in this group with developmental scores on the Bayley scale (Carlson and Earls 1997). Blunted cortisol responses have been shown in other maltreated samples (e.g., Hart et al. 1995). There is good evidence from animal models that repeated exposure to high levels of circulating steroids such as cortisol results in destruction of actual brain material to which the organism adjusts by becoming hyporesponsive to stress and decreasing cortisol release (Sapolsky 1996, Yehuda et al. 1998). The general pattern of results seems consistent with a model where early overactivity of the ANS leads the organism to respond to subsequent stressors in irregular manner, normal, hypo-, or hyper-reactivity (Figueroe and Silk 1997).

The Causes and Course of Disorganized Attachment

Quite a lot is known about the putative causal associates of disorganized attachment. The prevalence of attachment disorganization is strongly associated with the presence of family risk factors such as maltreatment, major depressive or bipolar disorder, and alcohol or other substance misuse. For example, 82 percent of maltreated infants in a low income sample are classified as disorganized, compared with 18 percent of a matched control group (Carlsson et al. 1989). In a meta-analysis, depressive symptoms in the mother and infant attachment disorganization only showed a marginally significant relationship (Van Ijzendoorn et al., in press). This null finding highlights a weakness of meta-analytic aggregation. The majority of studies exploring the effect of maternal depression fail to examine the critical variable, that is, the extent to which the infant is actually exposed to a severely depressed caregiver over a prolonged period. In individual studies where chronic exposure to severe depression was independently demonstrated, the association with attachment disorganization appears to be strong (Lyons-Ruth et al. 1990, Teti et al. 1995).

Nine studies of 548 infant–mother pairs found an association between disorganization of attachment in the infant and evidence of unresolved attitude to episodes of loss or abuse in the parent's Adult Attachment Interview (van Ijzendoorn 1995). Three studies have helped to

clarify this superficially mysterious association between seemingly easily dismissable slips in the mother's narrative and the infant's bizarre
behavior in the strange situation. Jacobovitz and colleagues reported a
strong association between unresolved status on the AAI before the
child was born and observations of frightened or frightening behavior
towards a firstborn child at 8 months (Jacobovitz et al. 1997). These
behaviors included intrusiveness, baring teeth, entering apparently
trance-like states, and so on. If the loss around which there was lack of
resolution happened before the mother was aged 17, maternal frightened or frightening behavior was more evident. Interestingly, these
unresolved mothers did not differ from the rest of the sample in terms
of other measures of parenting such as sensitivity or warmth.

In a similar study, Schuengel and colleagues found that mothers
classified as unresolved and insecure displayed significantly more frightened or frightening behavior than those classified unresolved secure
(Schuengel et al. 1999a). Surprisingly, however, secure mothers who
were not classified unresolved appeared to display even more frightened
or frightening behavior.[3] Maternal frightened or frightening behavior
predicted infant attachment disorganization, but the strongest predictor was maternal dissociated behavior in interactions with the child.
In an independent investigation Lyons-Ruth and colleagues also found
that frightened and frightening behavior predicted infant disorganization (Lyons-Ruth et al. 1999), particularly when extreme parental mis-
interpretation of the specific content of an infant's attachment related
communication and competing caregiving strategies that both elicited
and rejected infant attachment were also rated. Frightened and frightening and disrupted affective communication behaviors were character-

---

3. Attachment disorganization cannot simply be treated as a fourth attachment
category. The disorganized code in the strange situation may be assigned to infants
who in other ways appear to behave as secure babies and others who are more like
anxious avoidant or anxious resistant ones. Researchers discuss this as "forcing" the
best fitting alternative category on the observation. Similarly, in the coding of the
adult attachment interview, the unresolved category may be assigned to free/autono-
mous or insecure (dismissing or preoccupied) interviews. Once assigned, the disorganization code is mostly treated as an indication of insecurity, so these individuals would
be assigned to insecure groups in most studies contrasting secure with insecure attachment. As we shall see, it appears to matter considerably whether the D code was given
to babies who appear otherwise secure or anxious in their attachment.

istic only of mothers of disorganized insecure infants. Mothers of disorganized secure infants in this study exhibited a fearful inhibited pattern of behavior. There was less hostility in the interaction even when communication was disrupted. In sum, maternal frightened or frightening behaviors appeared to be related to infant disorganized attachment via parental unresolved states of mind. While mothers of disorganized infants appear no less sensitive than do other mothers (Van Ijzendoorn et al., in press), they have been repeatedly identified as deviant in more specific assessments of interactions. For example, disorganized insecure 20-month-olds tended to initiate aggressive conflicts with their mothers, refusing their mother's social initiatives (Hann et al. 1991).

There is general agreement based on both cross-sectional and longitudinal investigations that disorganized infant attachment shifts into controlling attachment behavior in middle childhood. The meta-analysis reports an association of .55 (Van Ijzendoorn et al., in press), although this is based on only two longitudinal studies. George and Solomon described the parenting associated with such controlling behavior on the part of the child as characterized by a sense of helplessness and even fear of the child (George and Solomon 1996). By contrast, the child's model of relationships as derived from doll play appears to be characterized by themes of catastrophes, violent fantasies, helplessness, or total inhibition (Solomon et al. 1995). It is interesting to note that in some studies these children emerge as possessing fewer concrete and formal operational skills (Jacobsen et al. 1994, Jacobsen et al. 1997, Moss et al. 1998, Moss and St. Laurent 1999). In peer relationships, observational studies suggest that disorganized children are less competent in play quality and conflict resolution (Wartner et al. 1994). Jacobovitz and Hazen (1999), observing peer interaction, found that disorganized 4- to 5-year-olds showed quite different models of interaction with two peers. They proposed that this could be explained by the unintegrated internal working models of relationships that such children work with.

Disorganized Attachment and Childhood Aggression

We have considered above the relationship of disorganized attachment history and clinical problems in general. Here we shall restrict our review to three specific clinical problems that have been empirically linked to disorganized attachment: childhood aggression, dissociation, and relationship violence. Both longitudinal (Goldberg et al. 1995, Hubbs-Tait et al. 1994, Lyons-Ruth et al. 1993, Lyons-Ruth et al. 1997, Shaw et al. 1996) and cross-sectional (Greenberg et al. 1991, Moss et al. 1996, Moss et al. 1998, Solomon et al. 1995, Speltz et al. 1990) studies have identified links between disorganized controlling attachment and aggression. While aggressive behavior appears to be a common sequel of disorganized attachment, particularly insecure disorganized attachment, by no means all of those with disorganized attachment histories manifest problems of aggression. Disorganized attachment seems to be a general risk factor for maladaptive behavior (Jacobovitz and Hazen 1999, Lyons-Ruth et al. 1997).

It appears that the sequel to disorganized attachment in early life may be a quite subtle and complex form of relational disturbance that at times includes unpredictable and unwarranted aggression but is perhaps better captured as a general sense of interpersonal incompetence on the part of the child. Since Bowlby's original work on juvenile delinquents (Bowlby 1944), there has been considerable speculation concerning the role of attachment in disturbances of conduct (Atkinson and Zucker 1997, Fonagy et al. 1997, Greenberg 1999, Shaw et al. 1996). The currently popular four- or five-way categorization of attachment patterns is too general to permit the development of a model that may generate specific treatment approaches (Rutter and O'Connor 1999). Insecure attachment may simply indicate inadequacies of parenting of the kind often noted in this group. Alternatively, it may predispose children to transactional experiences that more immediately generate conduct problems (Shaw et al. 1996). Most probably, attachment processes are intimately involved in the development of specific psychological functions or mechanisms that are key in the organization of appropriate behavior. Thus, attachment difficulties may specifically create problems in affect regulation and social cognitive skills, which are known to be dysfunctional in groups with conduct problems.

Importantly, these mental processing deficiencies and biases are present early on and have been shown to predict the course and outcome of preschool disturbance of conduct (e.g., Weiss et al. 1992). Not surprisingly these children have considerable difficulties in the playground and peer rejection can quickly ensue (Kupersmidt et al. 1990). Rejected children tend to forge alliances with other children who are similar to them and with whom they share an interest in deviant activities (Dishion et al. 1995). Behaviors that increase the likelihood of peer rejection (e.g., reactive impulsive behaviors) add significantly to the prediction of later delinquency, beyond the prediction based on aggressive behavior alone (Loeber 1990). Social cognition appears to be strongly associated with family background, independent of the contributions of language and age (Cutting and Dunn 1999). All these facts are at least consistent with the view that disorganized attachment represents the point of origin of one path to conduct disorder.

Not all aggressive children follow the same pathway toward impaired peer relations and social maladaptation. Only half of all children who are physically aggressive in elementary school are rejected by their peers (Bierman et al. 1993, Coie et al. 1996). Those who are aggressive and rejected appear to be at somewhat greater risk (Bierman and Wargo 1995, Coie et al. 1996). Accepted aggressive children use their aggression strategically to attain social goals (Coie and Lenox 1994). Both rejected aggressive and accepted aggressive children show proactive aggressive behavior, but rejected aggressive boys are more likely to show reactive, poorly modulated forms of aggressive behavior (tantrums, outbursts, whining) (Bierman et al. 1993). Pope and Bierman (1999) suggest that rejected aggression may be a marker of social-emotional deficit that affects the process of social adaptation over time. Behaviors manifested by aggressive rejected children (immaturity, angry reactivity, negative affectivity, low frustration tolerance, irritability, social incompetence, frequent expression of personal distress, and inattention) may indicate deficiencies in the capacity to regulate negative affect in the context of interpersonal relations. This is a regulatory capacity that might have been undermined by the early disorganization of attachment (Hofer 1995, Sroufe 1996).

Aggression in these children may be an indication of an incapacity to respond flexibly and strategically in emotionally arousing situations (Fox 1994, Thompson 1994). Emotion dysregulation forces the child to use narrow and rigid response hierarchies (Cole et al. 1994) that lead to impairments in interpersonal relations. Social difficulties that arise directly out of a failure to regulate negative emotion include difficulties in performing regulatory tasks such as shifting attention from disturbing stimuli, suppressing impulsive reactions, engaging in planning and problem-focused coping, engaging comprehensive and unbiased interpretation and evaluation of social information, exploring the environment, and controlling and directing their behavior (Eisenberg and Fabes 1992, Martin et al. 1994). Some children with high levels of aggressive-hyperactive-impulsive-inattentive patterns have been shown to manifest considerable adaptive disability, and it is these children who are most likely to meet diagnostic criteria for ODD and CD (Shelton et al. 1998). The difficulties in interpersonal relations are reflective of the difficulties with the regulation of negative emotion, which may be associated with attachment disorganization (Sroufe 1996). Any deficits in social cognition may be viewed as the key mediators of the impact of disorganized attachment upon the IWM of relationships.

High levels of negative affectivity, emotional outbursts, inattentiveness, and low frustration tolerance predict long-term peer relation problems and negative social outcomes. The regulation of emotions depends on an understanding of internal experience, which is most likely to arise in the context of an early dyadic (caregiving) relationship (Gergely and Watson 1996). Negative affectivity appears to point to the absence of a core capacity to properly regulate negative emotions in interpersonal relations. This may be the sequel of frightened–frightening attachment experiences in early childhood. Because these children cannot inhibit negative arousal or suppress their negative reactivity, they cannot plan effective coping responses or control their attention to reduce exposure to disturbing stimuli. They will inevitably experience considerable difficulty in social relationships, further disrupting their capacity to establish effective attachment relationships and to undo the impact of unfavorable early experiences with more felicitous later ones. For example, a study, which compared 40 preschoolers with conduct problems (assessed by parent report) with a matched control group, reported deficits on a theory of mind task, an emotion-understanding task, and simple executive function tasks (Hughes et al. 1998). Thus, these children may be unable to use their aggression in a strategic, goal-oriented way, and it is probably inappropriate to understand their problems purely in terms of behavioral difficulties (Pope and Bierman 1999). The distinction between effectual and ineffectual aggressors (Perry et al. 1992) may be helpful in drawing attention to the need of these youngsters for the provision of supportive relationships and interpersonal learning experiences that may assist them with developing capacities for regulating emotional processes, which in turn may lead to more competent social behavior.

Disorganized Attachment and Dissociation

Individuals with unresolved trauma or loss experiences as measured by the AAI are demonstrably more prone to dissociative experiences (Hesse and Main 1999). Carlson's (1998) study identified a direct association between dissociative symptoms at 17 and disorganized attachment at 12 and 18 months. An insightful suggestion by Liotti linked dissociative symptoms to parental experience of loss. Basing his prediction on the link between lack of resolution of mourning and disorganized attachment, Liotti (1995) found that individuals with dissociative symptoms were more likely to have parents who suffered a major loss immediately prior to their birth or during the first years of their life. The association was confirmed with a normative sample by Hesse and van Ijzendoorn using a self report scale measuring the propensity for dissociation (Hesse and Main, in press). Not all individuals with attachment histories of disorganization are likely to manifest dissociative symptoms. In the most comprehensive follow-up of the Minnesota sample, scores on the dissociative experiences scale were only shown to be elevated for those individuals with disorganized attachment histories who had suffered major trauma, such as death of an attachment figure or extended separation from the mother before 54 months (Ogawa et al. 1997).

Disorganized Attachment and Relationship Violence

Disorganized attachment in adulthood is generally linked with unresolved states of mind on the AAI (U), preoccupied overwhelmed by trauma (E3) or cannot be classified categories (CC). These categories occur more commonly in groups with severe trauma-related psychopathology (Allen et al. 1996, Fonagy et al. 1996, Patrick et al. 1994, Stalker and Davies 1995) and those with criminal convictions (Levinson and Fonagy, submitted, van Ijzendoorn et al., in press). They are also more common in individuals currently involved in intimate relational violence (Owen and Cox 1997, West and George, in press). Further, mothers who report high levels of partner violence are likely to have infants with disorganized attachment (Holtzworth-Munroe et al. 1997, Lyons-Ruth and Block 1996). In general, evidence strongly links the disorganization of attachment relationships with severe relationship pathologies, normally described as "borderline personality organization" in psychoanalytic writings (e.g., Kernberg 1987).

PATHWAYS FROM INFANCY TO ADULT PATHOLOGY

Attachment theory is of interest to psychoanalysts principally because of the model it provides for the integration of early childhood experience with later development, particularly the emergence of psychopathology. As this brief review has demonstrated, there is considerable, although not overwhelming, evidence for the continuity of interpersonal experience from infancy to later development. There are a number of research-based models to account for observed continuities, which it is interesting to consider side-by-side with the psychoanalytic models (see below). The simplest model, originally posited by Lamb (Lamb 1987, Lamb et al. 1985) and seriously considered by Belsky (1999a) and Thompson (1999), is not in terms of continuity mental structures but merely social environments, more specifically that of the quality of care. The most parsimonious account of the effect of early experience is that correlations between early experience of a pattern of caregiving that is sometimes neglectful, sometimes overtly hostile, and later development are indicative of the continuity of this pattern rather than its particularly strong impact.

There have been numerous attempts at designing studies that might challenge this simplistic account (e.g., Chisolm 1998, Fisher et al. 1997, Hodges and Tizard 1989, Marcovitch et al. 1997). O'Connor and Kreppner (O'Connor et al. 2000) report an adoption study that asked a specific question about the long-term impact of early privation in four contexts: attachment, peer relationships, attention regulation, and cognition. The length of early privation varied between 6, 24, and 42 months but was not correlated with subsequent social experience. Duration of deprivation was strongly linked to attachment disturbance, peer disturbance, inattention and hyperactivity, and cognitive ability. Attachment disturbance showed no signs of improving at age 6 relative to age 4, although peer problems decreased somewhat.

Winnicott (1958a) and Roy (2000) contrasted 19 children from group homes with the same number in foster care (controls). The two groups were unusually well matched. There was a marked difference in observed inattentiveness or hyperactivity between the in-care groups and the controls. Hyperactivity was also far more marked on teacher ratings in children raised in group homes than those raised in foster homes. In general, the results suggest that the different pattern of childrearing in institutional and foster families is the key cause of the elevated levels of hyperactivity and inattention rather than the child's biological background.

Marvin and Britner (1999) looked at attachment classifications in the UK Romanian adoptees at 4 and 6 years. The number of secure children was, overall, less than would be expected by chance. Security of attachment was highest in the group who spent the shortest period in the orphanage, but the percentage of disorganized classifications was particularly striking. It was far above what would be expected in a UK population of comparable IQ and social class. Once again, there was little evidence of recovery with development. These and other similar studies confirm that, at least for relatively extreme levels of deprivation, early experience does not require continuity to have its impact.

A second mechanism that explains continuity involves the representation of relationships. In this framework sensitive, responsive parenting during infancy may be assumed to generate a working model of relationships in which positive expectations regarding intimacy and care from others are indelibly encoded, and this cognitive affective structure goes on to selectively affect perception, cognition, and motivation (Bretherton and Munholland 1999). Because of the reciprocal links between working models of attachment figures and those of the self (see above) it is generally believed that secure attachments will lead to a generalized sense of competence and self-esteem. Expectations of lack of understanding and care might evoke reciprocal parental behavior of increased hostility and negativity though the child's provocativeness or other means (Richters and Walters 1991, Shaw et al. 1997). Thus insecure attachment may come to play a causal role in later maladaptation through the gradual crystallization in transactional parent–child interactions of working models characterized by mistrust, anger, anxiety, and fear (Main 1995). The growing literature of pervasive attributional biases that Dodge and colleagues have repeatedly demonstrated in clinical groups (Coie and Dodge 1998, Crick and Dodge 1994, Matthys et al. 1999) is of course consistent with this view with some direct support (Cassidy et al. 1996).

Attachment may mark changes in neural organizations that are involved in later psychological disturbance. For example, it is possible that emotion regulation established in early childhood may substantially alter fear conditioning processes in the amygdala (LeDoux 1995) or connections between the prefrontal cortex and the limbic system (Schore 1997). There is evidence for elevated cortisol secretion and delayed return to baseline in those with insecure disorganized attachment (Spangler and Schieche 1998). Systematically identifying the potential biological links that underpin attachment will be the task of the current decade.

A further potential pathway for mediation may be rooted in the isomorphism of behavioral disturbance and disturbed attachment behaviors. Greenberg (1999) suggests that behaviors labeled as disruptive may also be viewed as indications of attachment strategies aimed to regulate a relationship with the caregiver. For example, oppositional behavior may serve the function of regulating the caregiver's proximity to and monitoring of the child. Similar links may exist between the controlling behavior of the disorganized attachment pattern (Main and Hesse 1990) and the ambivalent pattern of anxious resistance (Cassidy 1995).

The most likely mediation of insecure or disorganized attachment to later maladaptive or pathological outcome is through a combination of risk factors, none of which singly carry clinical implications but which together may be associated with a substantial elevation of risk. Insecure attachment may combine with family social adversity, ineffective parenting skills, and atypical child characteristics to generate significant risk of behavioral disorder. This is the dominant risk model in modern developmental psychopathology (e.g., Garbarino 1995, Garmezy and Masten 1994, Rutter 1999).

3

Freud's Models and Attachment Theory

It is misleading to attempt to trace commonality and differences between Freud's thinking and current attachment theory. Freud's theory does not represent a homogenous corpus (Sandler et al. 1997). Traditionally, his contribution is divided into four phases. The first is the prepsychoanalytic phase, covering a series of papers, mostly on neurological topics; second is the affect-trauma model, during which Freud put forward the view that the etiology of neurosis rested in the actual events of childhood development (Freud and Breuer 1895); third is the topographical model, which emphasized fantasy driven by biological drive states (Freud 1900, 1905); the fourth phase included the dual instinct theory (Freud 1920) and the structural model of the mind (Freud 1923). Each of these phases has distinct points of correspondence with and divergence from attachment theory, and a skillful Freud scholar could readily construct a picture in which the originator of psychoanalysis is seen as a either a friend or a foe of attachment theory.

POINTS OF CONTACT

Freud, like Bowlby, started his voyage of discovery with concern about the psychological consequences of significant early deprivation (Bowlby 1944, A. Freud 1954). But, whereas Bowlby went on to elaborate the psychological, social, and biological underpinnings of this association, Freud turned away from his "seduction hypothesis" in favor of his second model emphasizing the psychosexual theory of development. Masson (1984) chastised Freud for this "assault on truth," for his defensively abandoning and deliberately withholding evidence supporting the seduction theory of the neuroses. The truth is far more complex than Masson or, from the opposite camp, Crews (1995) allowed. Freud never suppressed the seduction hypothesis. A year after the publication of *The Three Essays* he affirmed that the 18 patients in the *Aetiology of Hysteria* had told him accurate accounts of having been seduced in childhood (Freud 1906). Ten years later he further reinforced his view of the pathogenic significance of actual seduction experiences (Freud 1917). He makes similar points in two further major contributions: *On Female Sexuality* (Freud 1931) and *Moses and Monotheism* (Freud 1939). Uninformed reviewers of Bowlby may take exception to the therapeutic realism of his approach in which cathartic recollections of traumatic events appear, once again, to be occupying pride of place (Bowlby 1977). The critical difference between the naïve realism of Freud's early theories and Bowlby's epistemology lies in Bowlby's attention to the representation of experience (Bowlby 1980a). This refutes any suggestion that Bowlby's theory represents a return to the naïve realist reductionism of the affect-trauma model. Freud's move from the affect-trauma to the topographical model did signal a shift from realist reductionism and extreme environmentalism towards idealism, where phenomena described are chiefly seen as products of the mind bearing no actual relationship to reality. To Bowlby, this shift was unpalatable (Bowlby 1981) and the divergence between the topographical model and attachment theory is far greater than that between Freud's earlier or later ideas.

The social environment again found a pre-eminent place with the fourth phase of Freud's development (Freud 1920, 1923, 1926b). At this stage Freud recognized that anxiety was a biologically determined epiphenomenal experience linked to the perception of both external and internal dangers (Freud 1926b). The prototypical danger situation was one of loss. The loss of the object (the mother) was considered by Freud as a threat of comparable order to the fear of a loss of body part or self-regard. This revision restored adaptation to the external world as an essential component of the psychoanalytic account, as well as recasting the theory in more cognitive terms (Schafer 1983). Already in the early 1930s, Freud's favorite disciple, Ferenczi (1933), was focusing on the reality aspect of children being traumatized by adult misunderstanding of their meaning, anticipating the risks associated with gross insensitivity on the part of the caretaker. His emphasis on interpersonal rather than intrapsychic factors, however, ultimately led to a significant rift with Freud.

Freud's structural model provided a useful background to attachment theory in other ways. Freud (1923, 1933, 1938) hypothesized that conflicts within the human mind were organized around three themes corresponding to three psychic agencies (id, ego, and superego). Attachment theory takes a more complex view of the individual's conflict between wish and moral injunction than did Freud, for whom morality was tantamount to the internalization of the child's perception of the parent's value system. However, Freud's conflict themes concerning wish and reality and internal and external reality remained essential building blocks for Bowlby and other attachment theorists. In particular, the ego's capacity to create defenses that organize characterological and symptomatic constructions as part of the developmental process became a cornerstone of Bowlby's trilogy, particularly the last volume (Bowlby 1980a). Here he considered in detail mechanisms of perceptual and cognitive distortions necessary for the functioning of internal working models.

There are further points of significant contact. Whereas Freud in writing within the affect-trauma model posited little or no mental apparatus beyond the physical conversion of energy (Freud 1954), in later writings he carefully elaborated an internal world of mental processes to establish the developmental determinism that pervades his theory. His genetic developmental propositions, exemplified in his psychosexual theory of development (Freud 1905) consider all behaviors understandable as sequences of actions developing out of earlier or even earliest infantile events. Freud (1917) could be said to have anticipated Main and Hesse's (1990) notion of disorganized attachment in relation to the dependence on an abusive caregiver ("fear without a solution") in his notion of the adhesiveness of the libido, which he describes as the "tenacity with which the libido adheres to particular trends and objects" (p. 348).

Bowlby himself reviewed Freud's contributions (e.g., Bowlby 1958) on the child's attachment to the mother and noted the ways in which his thinking was congruent with that of Freud, as well as points of difference. To summarize briefly: a) he pointed out that Freud's awareness of the importance of the attachment to the mother developed late and was reported only in his 1931 paper on "Female Sexuality" (Freud 1931); b) Bowlby notes Freud's observation (Freud 1920) that abandonment and isolation distressed infants of 18 months; c) anxiety was rooted in fear of the loss of the mother (which Freud saw as a fear of ungratified instincts: see Freud 1926b); d) Freud (1938) acknowledged that the child's relation to the mother was unique and laid down unalterably at an early stage to become the prototype for all later love relations. Here he also acknowledges that there is more to this love relationship than food, and that the experience of being cared for relates directly to self-esteem (narcissistic cathexis); e) Bowlby points out, however, that Freud emphasizes phylogenetic foundations of this relationship in preference to the quality of mothering received by the infant. Thus Freud's theory seems ultimately to hold no place for a primal need to be attached to another person.

POINTS OF DIVERGENCE

Taking Freud's corpus as a whole, it has to be recognized that points of divergence substantially outnumber points of correspondence. The following is an abbreviated list of areas where attachment theory has diverged from Freudian ideas.

- Freud was quite narrow in terms of the cultural and social context he envisioned for development. Although this is not surprising, given the embryonic stage of scientific sociology and anthropology at the early stage of his work, his focus was undoubtedly on cultural absolutes which precluded awareness of the cultural diversity even within his own society.

- Freud's focus on the oedipal period in the third and fourth year of life reduced his interest in early childhood experience. His views of early childhood (1900, 1905, 1920, 1926a) were abstract, fictional, and not based on direct observation. He probably had but the vaguest of impressions of the interaction of infants and caregivers.

- Quite contrary to Freud's (1900) claim that the infant is "forced" to run to objects after primary process "hallucination of the breast" fails to achieve gratification, attachment theory holds that the infant is vitally interested in objects, shows preferences for particular kinds of visual and auditory configurations, and enjoys making things happen in the world. Related to this, and notwithstanding his awareness of the impact of extreme environment, he had relatively little to say concerning the developmental significance of real behavior with real parents. Similarly, the role of instinctual drives was preeminent over other factors such as relationships, phenomenal experience, and environmental determinants.

- Freud was unclear about the synthesizing role of the self. More specifically, in his theory the ego was performing both the function of an organizing agency and of a phenomenal integrative representation, the coherence of which had to be preserved. Freud (1920) accounted for the reemergence in adulthood of childhood patterns of relating in terms of the repetition compulsion, ultimately the death instinct. This is inconsistent with the cognitive formulation of attachment theory, which emphasizes the accumulation of relationship experiences.

- Finally, Freud's view of development was somewhat mechanistic, linear rather than systemic. Although the move from an affect-trauma to a topographical model gave an additional role to the child in shaping his or her destiny, this was restricted to fantasy and conceived of in terms of distortions of reality.

On balance, it would be wrong to consider attachment theory closely related to Freudian theory. There are some points of contact and

Bowlby never denied his intellectual heritage, but his development of Freudian psychoanalysis left far more of the theory behind than it carried forward with it. But Freud does not define psychoanalytic theory. In order to explore points of contact and divergence between psychoanalytic and attachment theories we have to consider major developments of Freud's theory over the past century.

4

Structural Approaches: The North American Structural Approach

Freud's (1923) introduction to the tripartite (or structural) model did not mark the end of the emphasis placed on instincts in his topographical frame of reference. His sequence of stages of libidinal development remained the cornerstone of his theory until the introduction of ego psychology by Heinz Hartmann (1946), first in Vienna and then in New York. A crucial advance proposed by Hartmann was that of *secondary autonomy* (1950). He illustrated how behaviors observed in adulthood could not be traced back to childhood in terms of their function. Thus, proximity seeking may be rooted in the mother–infant relationship, but in adulthood it may be put to quite a different purpose than the one for which it was originally established. To assume such equivalence, a common assumption at the time, Hartmann suggested was a *genetic fallacy* (Hartmann 1955). The autonomous ego was likely to adapt behaviors in the service of optimizing current adjustment.

Hartmann's ideas spread quickly in the post-war psychiatric community of North America. Ego psychology, as it came to be known, detailed the ways in which this structure (the ego), oriented towards internal and external adaptations, came to form a coherently functioning organization that was more complex than the sum of its parts (Hartmann 1952). Within this framework the ego came to be seen to have a developmental line, with fixation points to which, under pressure, an individual might return (Arlow and Brenner 1964). While regressions in the ego are generally considered pathological, Kris (1952) emphasized that they may serve adaptive functions in, for example, artistic or creative sensitivity. Modern structural theorists (see for example Boesky 1989), retain the notion of the tripartite model but dispense with problematic notions such as psychic energy. They retain the central premise of the ubiquitous nature of intrapsychic conflict (see Brenner 1982).

Modern ego psychology is a theory of conflict where all mental contents, thoughts, actions, plans, fantasies, and symptoms are conceived of as compromise formations, as multiply determined by components of conflict. The compromise occurs between four elements of the conflict: 1) intense personal and unique childhood wishes for gratification (drive derivatives); 2) anxiety or depressive affect and their ideational content of object loss, loss of love, or castration (unpleasure); 3) mental operations of varying complexity put in place to minimize unpleasure (defenses); and 4) guilt, self punishment, remorse, and atonement and other manifestations of superego functioning. The representations of self and others are seen as products of conflict between these elements, also as compromise formations. It is accepted, however, that the nature of these compromise formations in their turn affect further compromises between the tendencies above, thus lending the appearance of primary determinants to these products of conflict. The interrelationship of the four tendencies, rather than chronological age or libidinal phase, is the focus of developmental study within modern ego psychology.

Structural theory dominated North American psychoanalysis throughout the development of attachment theory. The fact that no integration was achieved between them, and that attachment theory was treated with considerable hostility by ego psychologists, might suggest that there were few points of contact between the two theories. This, however, was not the case. We shall first turn to issues that would have warranted closer collaboration between ego psychologists and attachment theorists and later explore some possible reasons why such integration proved impossible.

POINTS OF CONTACT

There are several major figures within the ego psychology tradition whose contribution to the attachment field (explicit or implicit) should be given serious consideration.

René Spitz

René Spitz (1959) was one of the first "empiricists" of the psychoanalytic tradition. He had formulated a general understanding of the developmental process in structural terms as early as 1936 in an unpublished paper presented to the Vienna Psychoanalytic Society. He, like Bowlby, drew on scientific fields pertinent to psychoanalysis: Kurt Lewin's (1952) Field Theory and the emerging field of embryology (Spemann 1938). (Bowlby, in contrast, drew on general systems theory and ethology.) Spitz proposed that major shifts in mental organization of the infant are marked by the emergence of new behaviors and new forms of emotional expression, for example, social smiling. These occur when functions are brought into new relations with one another and come to be linked into coherent units. For example, the smiling response at 2 to 3 months marks the initial differentiation of self and object; 8-month anxiety indicates the infant's emerging differentiation between objects, particularly the libidinal object proper (mother). The emergence of the "No" gesture between 10 and 18 months marked for Spitz an advance in self-development manifesting as self-assertion.

Spitz was quite astute in identifying how "psychic organizers," such as smiling, linked to underlying advances in the formation of mental structures. However, it remained for other researchers to demonstrate how these organizers heralded dramatic shifts in the interpersonal interaction of the infants (Emde 1980a,b,c).

Spitz (1945, 1965) ascribed primary importance to the role of the mother and the mother–infant interaction in a theory of developmental stages. His proposal was analogous to that of attachment theorists, in that he saw the child's human partner as "quickening" the development of his innate abilities and mediating all perception, behavior, and knowledge. A number of observational studies demonstrated ways in which constitutional, early environmental, and interactional factors all contributed to the structuring of the self-regulatory process leading to adaptation or maladaptation (Greenacre 1952, Spitz 1959, Weil 1978). All these workers highlighted the role of affect in the development of self-regulation. The mother's emotional expression was seen as at first serving a soothing or containing function that facilitates the restoration of homeostasis and emotional equilibrium. Later, the infant uses the mother's emotional response as a signaling device to indicate safety. Later still, the affective response is internalized and used as part of the child's own emotional reaction, signaling safety or danger (Call 1984, Emde 1980a).

Thus Spitz's views are closely connected to the emphasis placed by modern attachment theorists on emotion regulation as a key developmental function of the attachment system (e.g., Sroufe 1990). Notwithstanding these and other underlying commonalties, Spitz (1960) slated Bowlby's paper on "Grief, mourning in infancy and early childhood," published in the *Psychoanalytic Study of the Child* in 1960 (Bowlby 1960). He claimed the theory to be "oversimplified" and to "make no contribution to the better understanding of observational phenomena" (p. 93).

Edith Jacobson

A second key figure within ego psychology to advance our understanding of constructs closely linked to attachment theory was Edith Jacobson (1954b, 1964). Her contributions were critical, although this is rarely acknowledged, in introducing the conceptualization of "images" or representations of self and other as key determinants of mental functioning. She advanced the idea that the infant acquires self and object representations with good (loving) or bad (aggressive) valences, depending on experiences of gratification or frustration with the caretaker. She introduced the term *representation* to stress that this concept refers to the experiential impact of internal and external worlds and that representations are subject to distortion and modification irrespective of physical reality. Her ideas are clearly closely linked to Bowlby's notion of the internal working model and in some ways are more complex and sophisticated.

Self-representations were seen as complex structures including "the unconscious, pre-conscious, conscious, intrapsychic representation of the bodily and mental self in the system ego" (1964, p. 19). The role she assigned to the bodily self is not comfortably integrated with attachment theory ideas. Further, her suggestion that distributional considerations (good versus bad) shape the future growth of self and other representation, and, particularly, the critical role she assigned to the child's aggression in this process, has not yet been seriously considered by attachment theorists.

A further important contribution made by Jacobson concerns qualitative differences of the impact of the other on the self prior to the formation of self-boundaries. Jacobson (1954a) highlighted that prior to the formation of self–other boundaries, at the level of mental representation, the child's perception of the other directly shaped the structure of the experience of the self. Thus, in the state of primitive fusion, objects became internalized parts of self-images. Her ideas were particularly helpful in elaborating the nature of depression and she was the first to suggest that depression was associated with a gap between self-representation and ego ideal.

In sum, through these and other contributions, Jacobson substantially altered the climate of psychoanalytic thinking. Her contributions ultimately made way for the attachment theory frame of reference, although this took several decades. She anticipated many key constructs, particularly that of the representational world.

Eric Erikson

Eric Erikson (1950, 1959) should be credited for being the first to expand the problematic erotogenic zone model of Freud in his surprisingly subtle concept of *organ modes*. Prior to Erikson, it was commonly appreciated that activity associated with the pleasure inherent in each zone provided the basis for psychological modalities such as dependency and oral aggression, and for specific mechanisms such as incorporation and projection. Erikson's concept of organ modes extended the psychic function aspect of bodily fixation. In 1950 he wrote: "in addition to the overwhelming need for food, a baby is, or soon becomes receptive in many other respects. As he is willing and able to suck on appropriate objects and to swallow whatever appropriate fluids they emit, he is soon also willing and able to 'take in' with his eyes whatever enters his visual field. His tactile senses, too, seem to 'take in' what feels good" (p. 57). In this way he made a critical distinction between drive expression and mode of functioning, which opened up new vistas for the psychoanalytic understanding of human behavior.

The drive expression model binds understanding of social interaction to the gratification of biological needs. The notion of "mode of functioning," on the other hand, frees us to think about *characteristic manners* of obtaining gratification or relating to objects at particular developmental stages. Erikson showed us how a person may find a means of gratification, originally associated with a particular phase or erogenous zone, as a useful way of expressing wishes and conflicts at a subsequent time. This enabled him to introduce a whole series of constructs into the psychoanalytic caucus, including identity, generativity, pseudospeciation, and the one most pertinent to attachment theory: basic trust. He expanded the drive model while remaining in a biological framework. His description of libido theory as one in which the tragedies and comedies take place around the orifices of the body aptly summarizes Erikson's widening perspective enriched by anthropology and developmental study.

For Erikson, *basic trust* was the mode of functioning of the oral stage. The mouth was seen as the focus of a general approach to life—the *incorporative* approach. Erikson stressed that through these processes, interpersonal patterns were established that centered on the social modality of *taking* and *holding onto* objects, physical and psychic. Erikson defines basic trust as a capacity "to receive and accept what is given" (1950, p 58).

In his writings, by emphasizing the interactional psychosocial aspects of development, Erikson, without pomp or circumstance, altered the central position assigned to excitement in Freud's theory of psychosexual development. Although he accepted the libidinal phase model, and its timings, as givens, his formulation was one of the first to shift the emphasis from a mechanistic drive theory view of early development to the inherently interpersonal and transactional nature of the child–caregiver dyad as these are currently understood, related to the child's development of a sense of self.

Erikson became interested in the give and take between infant and caregiver in the sharing and dosing of stimuli at about the same time as John Bowlby. (It so happens that both Erikson and John Bowlby began their work with Anna Freud, the latter in London in her Wartime Nurseries, the former in Vienna.) Like Bowlby, Erikson saw early development as a continuous process, starting within the first few minutes of postnatal experience and extending throughout life, taking different forms at different times. Erikson also shared Bowlby's pioneering lifespan perspective, and his outlook on how "cultures, in various ways, underline and mutualize the child's larger social potentiality" as these gradually become available (Erikson 1950, p. 86).

Erikson's brilliant insight (1950), far ahead of his time, was in identifying that such micro experiences would eventually become aggregated, leading to "the firm establishment of enduring patterns for the balance of basic trust over basic mistrust. . . . [The] amount of trust derived from earliest infantile experience does not seem to depend on absolute quantities of food or demonstrations of love, but rather on the *quality* of the maternal relationship" (1959, p. 63).

Several similarities between current attachment theory and Erikson's views emerge: the notion of the accumulation of lower order episodic experiences in higher order neural structures; broken attachment to the primary caregiver as the opposite pole of whatever was the basis for the continuation of the child's "healthy personality"; the quality of the maternal relationship determines the sense of trust that mothers create in their children, which then persists throughout life; Erikson also anticipated the growing interest amongst attachment theorists in cross-generational cycles of advantage and disadvantage; the notion of coherence of mental representations as the key to how a trustful or secure pattern of relationship may be transferred across generations. He considered basic trust to be transmitted across generations by "the experience of the caretaking person as a *coherent* being, who reciprocates one's physical and emotional needs in expectable ways and therefore deserves to be endowed with trust, and whose face is recognized as it recognizes" (Erikson 1964, p. 117).

Thus, in both spirit and particulars, Erikson's theory is consistent with contemporary research on infant–parent attachment and its roots in interactions with the primary caregiver. His ideas antedated our view of the internal working model (Bretherton 1987, 1990, 1995) and Daniel Stern's (1985, 1994) RIGs and "ways of being with" the caregiver. More importantly, he described the transactional nature of these interactions.

For example, he wrote in 1959: "it is as true to say that babies control and bring up their families as it is to say the converse. A family can bring up a baby only by being brought up by him" (Erikson 1959, p. 55).

Careful reading of Erikson (1959) identifies important insights into the determinants of secure attachment (basic trust). In fact, the classification of attachment security may be helpfully restated in Eriksonian terms. The secure infant trusts the caregiver to return and "he receives and accepts" comfort from her. Insecure attachment patterns are forms that mistrust might take. Resistant infants show an inability to "accept" comfort and reassurance. Avoidant infants cope with a failure of their "mutual regulation" by withdrawing and in the extreme "closing up, refusing food and comfort and becoming oblivious to companionship" (p. 56); they "find their thumb and damn the world" (p. 50). Erikson does not describe the clinically critical disorganized pattern. Otherwise, the correspondence in the respective descriptions suggests that Bowlby and Erikson were describing the same behavioral phenomena from their different theoretical perspectives.

The characteristics of the kind of care that has been shown to predict infant security could have been drawn from *Childhood and Society*. Maternal sensitivity, Ainsworth's key construct, was mentioned above. In a footnote, Erikson describes the importance of moderate stimulation, which he defines as "a certain ratio between the positive and the negative, which if the balance is towards the positive, will help him to meet later crises with a better chance of unimpaired development" (p. 61n). Erikson saw nonintrusiveness of the parent (Malatesta et al. 1986) as the mother not trying to control the interaction too much. Interactional synchrony (Isabella and Belsky 1991) is equivalent to the Eriksonian description of "reciprocity or mutual regulation" (p. 58).

There are two distinct traditions in the literature on the determinants of attachment and both may be found in the work of Erikson. Whereas Erikson invariably stressed the importance of individual or interactional factors such as the ones we have considered above, he was also quick to point out that cultural factors (contextual or ecological factors in attachment terminology) are also critical. Indeed, cultural differences (as well as similarities) in attachment have been clear from the start (see van Ijzendoorn et al. 1992). Erikson also emphasized that the immediate social context of the mother may be critical, and indeed support from the partner (Goldberg and Easterbrooks 1984) and others in the mother's social environment (Crnic 1983) has been shown to be important. In the London Parent–Child Project we found that rather than absolute levels of support, the difference between support anticipated by the mother and actually obtained from the father turned out to be the most potent predictor (Fonagy et al. 1994). This finding again underscores Erikson's point concerning the importance of studying environmental influences in the context of the culturally conditioned expectations of the caregivers.

There is further common ground between Erikson and attachment theory when he explores the long-term effects of trust and mistrust. The most important link made by him was between trust and identity, which, as we have seen, draws on the notion of coherence so central to Mary Main's framework of adult attachment. In his epigenetic sequence of identity formation (Erikson 1956, 1968), he describes a syndrome of identity diffusion that he saw as reflecting deficiencies in a sustained sense of self-sameness, temporal continuity of self experience, and a feeling of affiliation with a social group of reference. Erikson (1950) suggests that mistrust may undermine the outcome of the psychotherapeutic process because such individuals can neither trust the world nor their own mind. He extended this notion, suggesting that the mutuality was central to the achievement of basic truth. Erikson was keen to correct those who mistakenly thought that the achievement of trust was a once-and-for-all event, a misconception reminiscent of arguments concerning the continuity of attachment security. He wrote: "the idea that at any stage a *goodness is achieved* which is impervious to new conflicts within and changes without is a projection on child development of a success ideology" (p. 61n). This statement echoes findings on discontinuities of attachment classifications.

In conclusion, it is clear that there is substantial overlap between the thinking of Erikson and Bowlby. They had in common a deceptive simplicity and appeal to common sense which in their time earned both of them contempt rather than praise from the psychoanalytic community. Like Erikson, Bowlby's breadth of vision was often mistaken for superficiality by lesser minds. They both were misunderstood—their innovativeness and creativity went beyond the reach of almost all their contemporaries within the psychoanalytic movement. Their lack of recognition among psychoanalysts was eloquently underscored by the unusually broad appreciation of their work from the wider academic community. They also had in common a respect for evidence from fields adjacent to psychoanalysis, as well as a commitment to systematization.

POINTS OF DIVERGENCE

How is it that, despite the contribution of Spitz, Jacobson, and Erikson and their followers, attachment theory did not and could never have emerged from the structural frame of reference?

First of all, the pseudo-biological character of the original ego psychology model is fundamentally incompatible with the attachment model, which seeks to identify genuine phenomena in biology in order to achieve concrete reference points for its conceptual framework. Building attachment theory on the structural frame of reference would have required double standards: one taking a metaphorical approach to biological processes, the other treating biological knowledge as providing absolute constraints on theorization. The implausibility of the biological framework for the structural model has been broadly recognized since the 1970s (see, for example, Compton 1981a,b, Klein 1976, Rosenblatt and Thickstun 1977).

The primacy given to sexuality in psychoanalytic explanations of psychopathology is a related incompatibility. Hanley (1978), for example, asserts that it is inconceivable for any behavioral system not to come under the influence of the libidinal instinct. Thus, in the ego psychological perspective, early attachment must, by definition, be formed as part of psychosexual development in the oral phase. Within classical structural theory, although sexuality is the outcome of earlier developmental phases, it is also assumed to undergo qualitative changes during the fourth and fifth years of life with radical implications for later development and neurotic psychopathology. The primacy of sexuality in explanations of psychopathology is regarded as a misconception by many psychoanalysts (e.g., Klein 1980, Peterfreund 1978). There are undoubtedly problems with the ego psychology model besides its incompatibility with attachment theory. Schafer (1974) pointed out that it forced us to consider all forms of sexual pleasure other than genital sexuality as arrested (abnormal or deviant). The observed association of neurotic problems with sexual difficulties and confusions could be reconciled with an attachment theory perspective if we assume that the centrality of conflict related to bodily functions in many forms of psychological disturbance is a consequence of the individual's failure to resolve psychological conflict in the domain of ideas and wishes, hence causing them to be experienced in bodily terms (Fonagy and Target 1995b). Because the body is not an appropriate arena for the resolution of difficulties arising out of relationship problems, the conflict can become intensified instead at the level of drive or instinct.

A further issue concerns the relative emphasis given to the individual ego in contrast to interpersonal relations. Although Erikson stressed the importance of social agents for the facilitation of psychological development and for the ongoing articulation of the individual ego, his emphasis was not on the social relationship but rather on the antecedents and consequences of the attainment of self-identity. Like other psychoanalytic developmental theorists (e.g., Mahler, Spitz, Anna Freud, and others) Erikson placed separation-individuation ahead of social involvement. For example, he wrote, "true engagement with the other is the result and test of firm self delineation" (Erikson 1968, p. 167). The importance of attachment, as we have seen, is not omitted from Erikson's model but is de-emphasized, perhaps as a consequence of his somewhat uni-dimensional schematization of developmental progression, and his emphasis on self-identity as the emergence of the self as separate and autonomous. Thus his emphasis remains psychoanalytic, focusing on the individual rather than on the relationship. Identity consolidation is the central goal, and attachment plays a secondary role. It either facilitates identity development or is its byproduct. Attachment is relegated to the status of an intermediary link in the process of development towards individuation, which, in its turn, is the precondition of a mature relationship. The very concept of identity implies separateness and distinction from others. Franz and White (1985) conclude their comprehensive review of this issue by suggesting that Erikson's theory primarily concerns how identity development produces productive citizens attached to social institutions. His theory, however, diverges from Bowlby's in that he seems less concerned with the movement from a secure, trusting dependency to a mature interdependence with a capacity to tolerate intimacy.

5

Modifications of the Structural Model

There are three major modifications of the structural model, all associated with figures involved in work with children, that have points of contact with attachment theory. These are: a) Freud's daughter, the originator of child psychoanalysis, Anna Freud; b) the American analyst, a pioneer of infant observation, Margaret Mahler; and c) the British colleague of Anna Freud at Hampstead, Joseph Sandler, who contributed enormously to refining the most commonly used concepts of psychoanalysis.

Anna Freud was one of the first psychoanalysts to adopt a coherent developmental perspective on psychopathology. Her model (A. Freud 1965) was both cumulative and epigenetic, each developmental phase constructed on the previous one. She argued that psychological disorder could be most effectively studied in its developmental evolution. Her theory was based on the metaphor of developmental lines (A. Freud 1963). She asserted that it is the profile or patterns among these lines of development that best capture the nature of the risk faced by the individual child. The lines, which are described in terms of their respective beginning and end points, included dependency to self reliance to adult object relations; from irresponsibility to responsibility in body management; from egocentrism to social partnership, and so on. Unevenness of development was considered a risk factor and treatment was seen as incorporating a developmental component (developmental help) to restore the child to the path of normal development (A. Freud, 1970, Kennedy and Moran 1991).

Anna Freud's basic stance, however, remained rooted in the study of conflict and defense (A. Freud 1936). Conflicts were now seen not only as intrapsychic but as also developmental in nature and therefore transitory. The developmental conflicts were associated with libidinal phases but fixation and regression could occur along all developmental lines. Anna Freud's innovation was in encouraging the observation of the child in natural settings and then contrasting these relatively systematic observations with clinical observations from the consulting room (A. Freud 1941–1945).

Mahler offered a developmental model in which object relations and the self were seen as outgrowths of instinctual vicissitudes. Her focus was on tracing the growth of the separate self from the unity of "I" and "not-I." *Separation* refers to the child's emergence from a symbiotic fusion with the mother, whereas *individuation* consists of those achievements marking the child's assumption of his own individual characteristics (Mahler et al. 1975). Mahler's (1968) model assumes that the child develops from "normal autism" through a symbiotic period to the four sequentially unfolding subphases of the separation-individuation process. For the first two months the infant is thought to be surrounded by a "quasi-solid stimulus barrier" (Mahler and Furer 1968, p. 8). From the second month, in the symbiotic subphase, the infant is in a state marked by dim awareness of the object, in a state of "delusional somato-psychic fusion" (Mahler 1975, p. 45). The separation-individuation process is thought to begin at 4 to 5 months. In the *hatching* subphase, the infant begins to differentiate himself from the mother (Mahler et al. 1975). The second subphase from 9 months to 15–18 months is the subphase of *practicing*. The child is practicing locomotion, and reaches the peak of his "magical omnipotence" derived from his sense of sharing his mother's magical powers. The *rapprochement* subphase is dated from 15–18 to 24 months. There is an awareness of separateness, separation anxiety, and an increased need to be with the mother (Mahler et al. 1975). The fourth subphase is the *consolidation* of individuality and the beginning of emotional object constancy (Mahler et al. 1975), which begins in the third year of life.

Mahler's contribution was significant, since it enabled clinicians treating adults to make more accurate reconstructions of the preverbal period, thereby making patients more accessible to psychoanalytic clinical interventions. Mahler's studies were also observational, although the observations were for the most part relatively informal and based on middle-class children who had the benefit of relatively normal parenting. Her ideas, however, have been extensively applied, particularly productively in the understanding of severe personality (borderline) pathology (Masterson 1976, Rinsley 1978).

Sandler's contributions are qualitatively different from the previous two workers. Unlike Anna Freud and Margaret Mahler, his contribution has been conceptual and systemic, rather than content oriented (Fonagy and Cooper 1999). Like Mahler and Anna Freud, Sandler developed a new theory based on the structural model that also encompassed the relational framework of British and modern North American analysts. His major contribution was the restatement of structural theory in representational terms and in the light of observations of child analytic process at the Hampstead Clinic (Sandler 1960c, 1962, 1990, Sandler and Sandler 1978). In essence, Sandler reformulated the structural model of instincts into a model of wishes represented by and acting upon mental representations of role relationships. Sandler has been one of the key figures in the "quiet revolution" that psychoanalysis has undergone over the last 30 years.

The following three sections explore the theories of these three workers in greater depth, examining the specific points of contact and divergence between their ideas and attachment theory.

POINTS OF CONTACT AND DIVERGENCE BETWEEN ANNA FREUD AND ATTACHMENT THEORY

Anna Freud observed and reported on the significance of attachment relationships in her observational work in the Hampstead War Nurseries (A. Freud 1941–1945). At this time, she independently noted the development of attachment in the first six months of life, the early sociability of the infant, the rising ambivalence to the caregiver in some infants at 6 to 12 months, and the parents' use of withdrawal of affection to socialize the child. She and Dorothy Burlingham (1944) also made striking observations on children who survived concentration camp experiences. They described evocatively how children sought safety and security in relationships with each other and continued to seek proximity with each other in preference to adults in moments of stress.

Anna Freud (1965) was probably foremost among psychoanalysts to stress that, for children, the degree of inner equilibrium compatible with normal development could be hard to establish. This is because the forces that influence child development are internal as well as external, and to a marked degree are not under the child's control. The child needs to integrate his constitutional potential, the influences emanating from the parental environment, and the expected vicissitudes associated with the gradual structuralization of personality. When one or other of these aspects of development departs from the expected, disturbances of equilibrium are likely to occur. Although Anna Freud would have resisted this connection, the relationship model she stipulates could readily incorporate attachment as an essential component of the structuralization of personality.

Anna Freud (1963) postulates continuities as the cornerstone of her developmental and epigenetic points of view, in which one layer of psychological attainment leads stepwise to the next. One faulty step leaves a weakness in the structure. This essentially is the same as Bowlby's (1973) conceptualization of the growth of personality. In practice, Anna Freud's notion of developmental assistance leads to a powerful, relationship-oriented therapy (Kennedy and Yorke 1980). Assistance focuses on learning to regulate affect, to tolerate social proximity and to understand the psychological aspects of relating to another (Bleiberg et al. 1997).

Anna Freud's views foreshadowed more recent reconsiderations of the supposedly inevitable pathogenic effects of chaotic environments and early deprivation (A. Freud 1955). In her view the child's developmental course should not be considered to be determined by early experience. Modern attachment theory would endorse such a view

(Emde 1981), although the emphasis in attachment theory has been on continuities rather than discontinuities in development, that is, has focused on those instances when the past predicts the present, rather than those more challenging examples when the direction of the child's development alters course.

Anna Freud's early work on ego defenses (A. Freud 1936) suggests an alternative frame of reference to the association of patterns of attachment and adult outcomes. Attachment patterns could be seen as mechanisms of defense, mustered by the child to cope with the idiosyncratic styles of interaction of his caregivers (Fonagy et al. 1992). Patterns of attachment are habitual ways of relating, developed by the ego to minimize anxiety and maximize adaptation. Avoidant attachment, for example, may be rooted in the infant's behavioral strategy of avoidance, evocatively described by Selma Fraiberg (1982). The anxious-resistant pattern, rooted in the resistant fighting response of the infant aimed at reducing anxiety by replacing a passive strategy with an active one, may further adaptation by maximizing the chances of eliciting the caregiver's attention. The disorganized pattern could be reformulated as an indication of the relative immaturity of the ego and its inability to muster coherent strategies of response.

This reformulation could be of more than semantic significance. In the Anna Freudian framework, for example, there can be no simple relationship between attachment classification and psychological disturbance, the latter only becoming a manifest problem once the mechanisms of defense have proved inadequate to the task of protecting the child from anxiety. Pathology would be the malfunctioning of attachment strategies, rooted in conflict between mutually exclusive strategies, their maladaptive evolution, and their incoherent internal organization. They are neither cause nor consequence, yet they are important as pieces within the complex puzzle of early disruptive behavior. The link between attachment strategies encoded in internal working models of relationships (IWMs), and psychopathology may be found in the inter-relationship of IWMs.

For example, in a longitudinal study of 100 infant–mother and father pairs, we found a tendency for a greater number of early signs of psychological disturbance amongst 5-year-olds who manifested different patterns of attachment with each parent. The security of either parent or child mattered less than the fact that the child's attachment classifications were unmatched, thus calling for different strategies of adaptation (Fonagy et al. 1997). Psychopathology could thus be seen as a consequence of parenting that makes it harder for children to use habitual modes of defense, to adapt and evolve singular internal working models. Such an approach may be more consistent with recent genetic evidence, which highlights the significance of the nonshared environment (Reiss et al. 1995).

Notwithstanding these important points of contact, Anna Freud was deeply unsympathetic to the work of attachment theorists. Despite her own observations to the contrary, in her theoretical writings she based the child's early relationship to the mother on sexual instinctual needs. Although she was well aware of unevenness in ego development she rarely saw this as caused by relationship disturbance. The influence of the external environment was commonly neglected in favor of the vicissitudes of instincts. Even in discussing observations of attachment behavior, she adds the theoretical coda (for which she has no observational evidence) that "by means of the constantly repeated experience of satisfaction of the first body needs, the libidinal interest of the child is lured away from exclusive concentration on the happenings in his own body and directed toward those persons in the outside world (the mother or mother substitute) who are responsible for providing satisfaction" (A. Freud and Burlingham 1944, p. 291).

There is a peculiar disharmony within Anna Freud's work. Her observations were astute, accurate, and innovative. However, her theory was greatly limited by her conservative use of the drives of the structural model. She was unwilling or unable to abandon what she perceived as the most scientific aspects of her father's contributions. Her use of metaphors as part of causal accounts ran the same risk of reification and anthropomorphism as was discussed above in the context of Hartmann's ego psychology. It was rumored at the Hampstead Clinic that when Mary Ainsworth presented her work on the strange situation, Anna Freud sought to reassert the predominance of instinct theory over the attachment perspective. She asked if Dr. Ainsworth knew what these 18-month-olds might do if there was a bucket of coal in the room. Naturally, Dr. Ainsworth had no answer to this question, which must have seemed to her to reflect a lack of comprehension of the underlying issues.

POINTS OF CONTACT AND DIVERGENCE BETWEEN THE WORK OF MARGARET MAHLER AND ATTACHMENT THEORY

Mahler's work is well known to and often cited by attachment theorists. Carlsson and Sroufe (1995), in their comprehensive review of her work, referred to the practicing subphase (9–17 months) of the separation-individuation process and the infant's tendency to return for "emotional refueling" as clearly analogous to Bowlby's "secure base" phenomenon. Similarly, Mahler's proposed link, between histories of well-regulated relationships with the caregiver and the smooth transition towards more autonomous functioning by the age of two, is common ground between the two frames of reference (Burland 1986). The interconnections between the exploratory and attachment behavioral systems were identified independently by attachment theory and Mahler's observations of "emotional refueling" (Mahler et al. 1975). Lyons-Ruth (1991) has also written evocatively and definitively about the relationship of Mahler's observational work and those of attachment theorists.

There are further pertinent aspects of Mahler's model. Mahler and Furer (1968) allude to "mutual cueing," a circular interaction in which the infant adaptively alters its behavior in response to the mother's reactions to the cues presented by the infant in the symbiotic phase. The authors point out that this process creates a unique image of her child for the mother. Elsewhere, Mahler makes clear that it is only with attributes selectively evoked by the mother that the baby establishes a symbiotic dual-unity, which is on the way to self–object differentiation and reciprocal object relations (Mahler 1967, 1975). Lichtenstein's (1961, 1963) elaboration of the identity theme concept and Weil's (1970) introduction to the "basic core concept" offer similar insights as to the way the infant's adaptations to the maternal object gives rise to a rudimentary self-representation that the mother is in a privileged position to respond to. These ideas speak to the recently emerging research on the role of the mother's representations of her infant in mediating the relationship between her general state of mind in relation to attachments and her behavior with the specific infant (Slade et al. 1999a,b).

Mahler and Bowlby make quite different fundamental assumptions concerning the critical issues to be negotiated with the caregiver from

9 to 18 months (Lyons-Ruth 1991). Mahler assumes a positive state of relatedness, symbiosis, between the infant and the caregiver that develops early (2–4 months) and occurs in an intrapsychic context with absence of boundaries between self and other. From 4–10 months the developmental problem is that of beginning to differentiate the representation of the self from that of the other, while from 9–12 months the central developmental issue is one of practicing increased physical separation to continue the differentiation process. By contrast for attachment theorists and other infant observers (e.g., Sander 1962) the period from 9–18 months is the period of focalization on the mother, with emergent physical mobility being marshaled in the service of ensuring access to the mother, both in the context of secure-base phenomena and in the context of social affiliative behavior. The achievement of secure reliance on the caregiver for attachment theorists goes some way beyond Mahler's symbiotic phase.

The normative pattern of infant separation-reunion observed by attachment theorists differs from Mahler's descriptions in a number of ways. Mahler identifies independent or ambivalent behaviors as normative. Independent behavior is seen by Mahler as positive and normative but attachment theorists have identified that it is in fact driven by separation-related anxiety (measurable at the physiological level, Sroufe and Waters 1977b). The later superior functioning of those who do not show autonomy at 18 months and the developmental deficits that emerge in some of these children (Thompson 1999) bear out the attachment theory position. Ambivalent behavior at reunion is, for Ainsworth (Ainsworth et al. 1978), a sign of anxious (resistant) attachment, yet for Mahler it is developmentally to be expected. This is interesting in the light of the relatively recent recognition by attachment theorists that organized if insecure forms of attachment should not be confused with pathological development (e.g., Belsky 1999b). Thus Mahler's intuitions might have been right all along.

Mahler offers a further interesting perspective on the nature of ambivalent or resistant attachment. She describes the behavior of some infants in the second year who shadow their mother at the same time as darting away from her or clinging to her while pushing her away. The term she uses is *ambitendency* (Mahler et al. 1975). She considers such behavior to be both the wish for reunion with the love object and a fear of engulfment by it. Behavioral observations of parenting predictive of such ambivalent behavior in the strange situation, for example, intrusive caretaking, are consistent with the hypothesis that certain types of insecure attachment may be linked to the fear of losing fragile and immature self-representations.

Conflicts of clinging and struggling for separation are also commonly observed amongst infants with disorganized patterns of attachment (Lyons-Ruth 1991). Here the risk of apparently normalizing a disturbed and disturbing pattern of interaction is even clearer. Attachment research alerted us to the developmental risks that such extreme levels of ambivalence might carry. Within the traditional psychoanalytic frame of reference (even with observational data such as those provided by Mahler) there can be a tendency to regard early patterns as "normal sources" of later pathology within the classical regression model. Mahler's focus is on how the mother handles ambivalence, while attachment theory concerns itself with the kind of experiences that might have created these responses. This is an overextension of the developmental metaphor (Mayes and Spence 1994), which is quite inconsistent with the developmental psychopathological approach pursued by attachment theory. Thus while Mahler's focus is on normative development, from which she seeks cues of later pathology, attachment theory focuses on the same developmental phenomena with the aim of identifying truly clinical patterns that might then be prospectively followed to later disturbance.

Followers of Mahler have, however, been helpful in elaborating the specific tasks of parenting in the second year of life that take the field beyond the generic endorsement of sensitivity to be found in the classical attachment literature (Ainsworth et al. 1978). Settlage (1977), for example, identified eight developmental tasks of the rapprochement subphase: 1) mastery of intensified separation anxiety; 2) affirmation of basic trust; 3) gradual deflation of the sense of omnipotence of the symbiotic unity; 4) compensation for the loss of omnipotence through an increased sense of autonomy; 5) firming up of the core sense of self; 6) establishment of affect and drive regulation; 7) healing the tendency to maintain the relationship of the love object by the normal splitting of the object into good and bad parts; and 8) replacing the splitting defense with repression. Thus the mother of the infant in the second year must combine emotional availability with a gentle push towards independence. An excessive push towards independence, or its opposite, undermines the child's potential to invest the environment with sufficient interest and his pleasure and confidence in his own functioning might be impaired. The caregiver's role in gradually dissolving the manifestations of the attachment bond (e.g., the decreasing need for physical proximity, and so on) is not fully considered by attachment theorists.

The rapprochement subphase is seen by Mahlerians as *the critical period* of character formation. Its crucial conflict between separateness and closeness, autonomy and dependency, are repeated throughout development, particularly in periods which accompany loss, illness, drug induced states, and so forth (Kramer and Akhtar 1988). The attachment system seems under particular stress in this subphase, and behaviors associated with anxious attachment are frequently observable in most children. The mother's failure to empathetically support the child during the rapprochement subphase, when the child's ambivalence between autonomy and fusion is at its height, will lead to the collapse of the child's omnipotence. A fixation will occur and the renunciation of omnipotence and the narcissistic enhancement of the self from within (through autonomous activities) will be in jeopardy. Such individuals will therefore have no clear image of themselves or their objects, may wish to avoid or control them, search for symbiosis with a perfect object, and will have difficulty in tolerating criticisms, setbacks, or ambivalence that challenges their view of the other. Although Bowlby (1973) does not explicitly favor the concept of symbiosis, he seems to refer to what Mahlerians call "bad symbiosis" when he discusses the inversion of the normal parent–child relationship in reference to phobias in childhood.

It is this part of her theory that has been put to extensive use by those working with individuals with borderline personality disorder. Mahler and colleagues (1975) observed that some mothers responded to their returning infants in the rapprochement subphase with either aggression or withdrawal, and that the behavior of these infants was similar to that of borderline patients. Residues of rapprochement subphase conflicts are seen in the borderline group in the form of persistent longings for, and dread of, fusion with the mother, and in continued splitting of self- and object representations, which cumulatively prevent the establishment of object constancy and identity (see also Kramer 1979, Mahler 1971, 1972b, Mahler and Kaplan 1977). The search for an "all-good" mother persists throughout life, and coercive clinging and negativistic withdrawal impede the establishment of "optimal distance" (Bouvet 1958).

Masterson (1972, 1976) elaborated Mahler's views of borderline pathology, enriching it with ideas closely tied to Bowlby's (1973) perspective. He suggested that the mother of the borderline individual is likely to have been borderline herself, thus encouraging symbiotic clinging and withdrawing her love when the child strives towards independence. The father did not, or could not, perform his role of focusing the child's awareness towards reality. Masterson believes that the borderline patient experiences a deep conflict between the wish for independence and the threat of loss of love, and thus searches for a clinging attachment bond with a mother substitute. Such a tie will temporarily ensure a feeling of safety, but any wish for self-assertiveness will present him with the terror of abandonment. A lifelong and vicious cycle of brief blissful unions, ruptures, and emptiness and depression will ensue.

Rinsley (1977, 1978, 1982) further elaborated on Masterson's model, based on the internalization of borderline interpersonal relationship patterns (internal working models) from a pathological primary object. Masterson and Rinsley (1975) suggest that dual working models of such objects exist in the borderline individual's mind: a critical withdrawing relationship unit imbued with anger and frustration and containing a self-representation that is helpless and bad; and an alternative relationship representation where the mother is seen as approving, with associated good feelings and an image of the self as compliant and passive. Rinsley (1977) suggests that the persistence of these structures into adulthood, fully compatible with an attachment framework, explains most features of borderline disorder including: splitting into "good" and "bad," part rather than whole object relations, incapacity to mourn, primitive ego and superego, stunted ego growth, hypersensitivity towards abandonment, and the absence of normal phase specificity of development.

There are divergences between Mahler's approach and attachment theory. These are in part epistemological. For example, Mahler was content to define the symbiotic phase largely without reference to behavioral descriptions. For Mahler, this phase is "an inferred intrapsychic state rather than an observable behavioral condition . . . [which refers] to the character of the infant's primitive, cognitive affective life at a time when differentiation between self and mother has barely begun to take place" (Mahler and McDevitt 1980, p. 397). Thus, during the first half of the first year Mahler's infant lives "in a state of primitive hallucinatory disorientation" (Mahler et al. 1975, p. 42). Most attachment theorists would be unhappy with this construct.

The appeal of Mahler's theory for psychoanalysts is that it dovetails with classical oedipal theory, as well as being compatible with the theory of pre-genital drives (see Parens 1980). For attachment theorists this is clearly of little relevance. They are more likely to be put on their guard by the evident empirical difficulties of Mahler's description of the first year of life. As we have seen, according to Mahler, during the first half of the first year, the infant is in a state of primary narcissism; its psychic functioning dominated by the pleasure principle, the structuralization of the mind to id and ego, self and other, inner versus outer, have not yet taken place. Evidence from infant research casts considerable doubt on this formulation. Bahrick and Watson (1985) demonstrated a capacity to differentiate degrees of action-event contingencies and cross-modal stimulus defenses in infants of 3 months of age. There is also innate coordination of perception and action evidenced by imitation of adults' facial gestures based on a short-term memory system at birth (Meltzoff and Moore 1977, 1983, 1989). Similarly, the notion of the lack of object permanence during the first year of life has been seriously questioned (Kellman and Spelke 1983, Spelke 1985, 1990). Recent empirical evidence suggests infants assume physical objects to have cohesion, boundedness, and rigidity.

Gergely (1991) and Stern (1994) both argue that the key feature of these early capacities is the infant's sensitivity to abstract properties, not linked to particular sensory modalities. Infants are able to detect consistencies across modalities (cross-modal invariances), even more than modality-specific, physical features. Thus, the infant seems not to be a concrete experiencer of the physical world as Mahler and classical psychoanalytical theory (see also Klein 1935) assume, but rather biologically prepared for the establishment of early social relationships, as John Bowlby suggested.

As we have seen, Mahler's emphasis is on the process of separation-individuation, the gradual distancing of the child from the mother, the transition from dependency to independent functioning. In fact, Mahler extends this to the entire life cycle, which she regards as constituting a more or less successful process of distancing "from the introjection of the lost symbiotic mother" (Mahler 1972a, p. 130). Followers of Mahler (Blos 1979, Settlage 1980) reaffirm their position that separateness underpins the capacity for self-regulation and object relations. The establishment of relationships is not a developmental goal in its own right. In Mahler's framework it is the disengagement from attachment that would be considered the hallmark of progress and the enrichment of the self. Thus, although Mahler considers emotional availability of the caregiver to be essential, this is viewed as a precursor and precondition of the separation-individuation process. Blatt and Blass (1990) contrast separation and attachment theories and suggest that a full understanding of psychological development requires an integration of theories of attachment and separation. Ultimately, it is an empirical question whether the capacity to maintain a relationship or the capacity to separate from it should be regarded as most formative in the developmental process.

There is a further point of divergence, but here the superiority of attachment theory over the psychoanalytic approach is somewhat more doubtful. Mahler, not surprisingly given her classical psychoanalytic orientation, shows consistent concern with the infant's experience of body boundaries, awareness of body parts, and the development of the body-self (Mahler and McDevitt 1980). The critical aspect of mother–infant relationship in the practicing subphase is the establishment of an experience of contingency in relation to self-initiated physical acts. The mother's support in engendering such an experience of control may be critical in the physical integration of the "I." Mahler thus also sees the development of the representation of the body as a function of the infant–caregiver relationship. Clinical experience with severe personality pathology can strikingly illustrate the ambivalent and chaotic representation some individuals manifest in relation to their own bodies, for example, self-mutilation and self-starvation. In conduct-disordered and delinquent boys, the disruption of attachment (Bowlby 1944, Fonagy et al. 1997c) is often coupled with a limited capacity to experience ownership over one's own bodily actions, which permits interpersonal violence (Bolton and Hill 1996). In general, Mahler's model is far more enlightening as to the nature of aggression than Bowlby's framework. Parens (1979) pointed out that aggression begins to emerge in the second subphase of separation-individuation, in the service of both separation and individuation. This stance marks a clear departure from Freud's nativist views as well as perhaps providing a helpful growth point for attachment theory (Fonagy et al. 1997c).

POINTS OF CONTACT AND DIVERGENCE BETWEEN JOSEPH SANDLER'S WORK AND ATTACHMENT THEORY

Sandler's general approach is fully consistent with the psychological model of attachment theory in that he attempts to describe how complex self- and object representations are shaped by everyday affectively laden experiences, fantasies and memories of the individual alone and in interaction with others. He puts the "shape" metaphor to good use. Identification is the modification of the self-representation to resemble the shape of the object representation. Projection adds unwanted parts of the self-representation to the representation of the other. He attributes a central role to these representations in the causation of behavior (Sandler 1960b, 1974, 1981, 1987b, 1993). Sandler is more concerned about how representations may be distorted by internal states than by external events, but his formulation can deal with both sets of experience equally well.

For example, Sandler (1976a,b, 1987c) elaborated a model of the two-person interaction in which the direct influence of one on the other is accounted for by the evocation of particular roles in the mind of the person who is being influenced. The behavior or role of the influencing person is crucial in eliciting a complementary response from the participant. Sandler suggests that in this way infantile and childhood patterns of relationships may be actualized or enacted in adult relationships, even suggesting that all relationships are guided by individuals' needs to explore the "role-responsiveness" of the other. Thus, there is little substantive difference between Sandler's formulation and the notion of internal working models.

Sandler and Sandler (1978) see mother–infant interactions as the context for the earliest formulations of self- and object representations and as providing the basic unit of self-representation. Emde (1983, 1988a,b), who should perhaps be credited with bringing the notion of mental representation to the forefront of the controversy concerning

developmental continuity, also sees the sense of self and other as arising from the reciprocal exchanges with the mother, exchanges that at
the same time form the basis of a sense of "we" (see also Winnicott
1956, 1965b). Critically, since Sandler's seminal work, most psychoanalytic workers who have adopted the developmental framework
would now assume that the cognitive-affective structures of self- and
other representations regulate children's behavior with the caregiver,
and then behavior in all subsequent significant relationships, including eventually their relationship with their own child. Sandler should
be credited for providing the psychoanalytic theoretical framework for
linking this view with the classical conceptualization, thus providing
a bridge between structural and attachment theory.

Mental representations of the self and other in interaction, as
elaborated by attachment theorists, correspond closely to Sandler's psychoanalytic formulations of self- and object representations and internal object relations (Sandler 1960a, 1962, 1990, Sandler and Sandler
1978). His ego psychological model of the representational world and
the suggestions of developmentalists concerning internal working models of attachment relationships may differ in terms of the respective role
given to fantasy and drives, but even here they agree in many funda-
mentals. The framework proposed by Sandler (1960a, 1985) places an
inborn wish to maintain safety at the center of the infant's motivational
field in a manner analogous to Bowlby's (1958, 1969) emphasis on the
innate propensity for attachment. Sandler's safety concept has reoriented
the psychoanalytic theory of motivation. The unique emphasis on instinctual gratification is replaced by the pursuit of a prototypical sense
of safety as a unifying underlying goal. It is probable that Sandler and
Bowlby were describing analogous ideas. Sandler's description of the
"background of safety" may be the phenomenological counterpart of
Bowlby's secure base concept. The difference between the two approaches
may be attributed to their respective points of origin. Bowlby's concern
is with the external whereas Sandler's is with subjective experience.

The strength of Sandler's formulation rests in the clear framework
it offers to clinicians. It has coherent implications for the transference–
countertransference relationship that most psychoanalytic clinicians
use to guide their work. The motivational system is simplified, as well
as linked to attachment and other theories. Safety is the experience of
the ego not threatened by drive states, moral pressures, the environ-

ment, or its own disintegration. Safety, as a phenomenal experience, arises from the infant–mother relationship (the infant feeling protected, held at the breast) but then acquires autonomy and comes to organize intrapsychic as well as interpersonal life. The abused child seeks contact with the abusing caregiver because, paradoxically, the predictable, familiar, but adverse experience, which includes a clear representation of the child's role, generates a greater sense of safety than an unfamiliar, nonabusive one for which the child has no role-relationship representations. In psychoanalysis, the past is explored because of the light that it sheds on the developmental origin of representations of role relationships. Outdated, maladaptive schemata are worked through and newer, more adaptive relational models are worked towards. Thus, Sandler's model of a structural change is consistent with attachment theory. It is not structures of drives and defenses that are transformed, but rather affectively toned self–other configurations. Sandler's model could be seen as an elaboration of attachment theory from an intrapsychic standpoint.

6

The Klein–Bion Model

The rise of object relations theories in psychoanalysis was associated with a shift of interest towards developmental issues. Regardless of particular theoretical models, psychoanalysis has moved increasingly towards an experientially based perspective. These approaches inevitably emphasize phenomenological constructs, such as the individual's experience of himself or herself, and theory has become increasingly concerned with relationships. Thus, the gap between attachment theory and psychoanalysis has narrowed considerably.

Object relations theories are, however, diverse and do not have a commonly agreed-upon definition (Kramer and Akhtar 1988). In an insightful book, Akhtar (1992) distinguished between a number of object relations theories on the basis of the vision of humankind they offered. The classic view, rooted in a Kantian philosophical tradition, holds that striving towards autonomy and the reign of reason is the essence of being human. By contrast, the romantic view, to be found in Rousseau and Goethe, values authenticity and spontaneity above reason and logic. In the classic view, humans are seen as inherently limited but able to overcome, in part, their tragic flaws, to become "fairly decent" (p. 320). The romantic view sees humans as intrinsically good and capable, but vulnerable to restriction and injury by circumstance. The classic vision approaches psychopathology largely in terms of conflict, while the romantic view frequently sees maladjustment in terms of deficit. Maladaptive, destructive action is viewed as a consequence of deep-rooted pathology in the classic view, while the romantic view understands such acts as manifestations of hope that the environment might reverse the damage done. The romantic view is more optimistic, seeing human beings as full of potential and the infant as ready to actualize the blueprint of his destiny. The classic view is more pessimistic. Conflict is seen as embedded in normal development. There is no escape from human weakness, aggression, and destructiveness, and human life is an unending struggle against the reactivation of the inevitable vicissitudes of infancy. In the romantic view there is primary love; in the classic view it is seen as a developmental achievement.

By these criteria, Bowlby's theory would probably be considered a romantic view, stressing as it does the innate potential of the human infant to relate, but also its vulnerability to insensitive and frightening caregiving. Attachment theorists, however, may differ slightly in terms of the emphasis they give to genetic predisposition. Object relations theories in the romantic tradition include the British Independent School, and Kohut and Modell in the U.S. The classic view is well represented by Melanie Klein and Otto Kernberg. Clearly some differences between attachment theory and object relations models may arise simply as a function of these different views of humans. Even in these instances, however, there are frequent points of contact.

There are several key concepts in the Kleinian model. Klein (1932b) saw mental structures arising out of a variety of internal objects (fantasies about people in the infant's life), which changed in character in unconscious fantasy as the child developed from infancy. The infant's fantasies are modified by his actual experience of interaction with the environment, and the individual is seen as continuing to use his object world in the service of an internal, primarily defensive system of relationships (Klein 1935).

Klein accepts somewhat concretely Freud's philosophical speculations on the death instinct (Freud 1920). Freud's (1920) assumption of an *aggressive drive* is extensively used by Kleinian theorists. In her work with children, Klein (1932a) was impressed that the children she analyzed had extremely ruthless sadistic fantasies about which they characteristically felt very guilty and anxious (Spillius 1994). Klein (1930, 1935) assumes that the infant's self is, from the beginning, constantly threatened by destruction from within by the aggressive drive. She follows Freud (1920) in seeing this as the inevitable result of the organism's wish to dispose of all excitation and reach the ultimate state of nirvana, or total absence of excitation.

Klein assumed that this was a powerful determinant of the stance the infant assumes in relation to the external world. In the Kleinian model, the human psyche has two basic positions: the paranoid-schizoid and the depressive (Klein 1935). In the paranoid-schizoid position, the relationship to the object (the caregiver) is to a part object, split into a persecutory and idealized relationship, and similarly the ego (the self) is split. In the depressive position, the relation is to an integrated parental image, both loved and hated. The individual recognizes his or her destructive wishes toward the object. This brings with it a certain characteristic sadness (hence the term *depressive position*), but correspondingly the ego is more integrated. The paranoid-schizoid superego is split between the excessively idealized ego ideal characterized by the experience of narcissistic omnipotence and the extremely persecutory superego of paranoid states. In the depressive position the superego is a hurt love object with human features. Klein (1957) suggests that early, primitive *envy* represents a particularly malignant form of innate aggression. This is because unlike other forms of destructiveness, which are turned against *bad* objects, already seen as persecutory, envy is hatred directed to the *good* object and arouses a premature expression of depressive anxiety about damage to the good object.

The concept of *projective identification* is central to the Kleinian model of development (Klein 1946). Whereas in classical theory of projection, impulses and wishes are seen as part of the object rather than the self, and identification implies attributing to the self qualities perceived in the object, projective identification involves the externalization of "segments of the ego" and the attempt to gain control over these unwanted possessions via often highly manipulative behavior toward the object. Consequently, projective identification is a more interactive concept then either projection or identification. There is a much closer relation to the object, which now "stands for" the projected aspects of the self (Greenberg 1983, p. 128). The individual is seen as, in part, identifying with an aspect of the unacceptable impulses that were externalized and placed into the representation of the other. This applies equally to internal object relationships; thus, the superego not only contains the projected id impulses, it also contains the projected parts of the ego itself. Bion's (1962b, 1963) work suggests a distinction between normal projective identification, where less pathological aspects of the self are externalized and which may underpin normal empathy and understanding, and pathological projective identification, which is linked to an absence of empathy and understanding.

POINTS OF CONTACT BETWEEN THE KLEINIAN MODEL AND ATTACHMENT THEORY

It is not widely recognized that Bowlby was deeply influenced by Kleinian thought. His training and experience in the British Psychoanalytic Society was predominantly Kleinian. His focus on the first year of life as a crucial determinant of later developmental outcome is, of course, highly compatible with the Kleinian approach. Many of his ideas, or at least the way he expressed them, were however clear reactions against the Kleinian influence prevailing at the time. In a 1981 interview with Ray Holland (1990), Bowlby described Klein as "inspirational, the antithesis of what I try to be." He considered Melanie Klein to be "totally unaware of the scientific method." Nevertheless, despite his apparent rejection of his Kleinian heritage, there is something to be gained from re-examining Kleinian and neo-Kleinian ideas in relation to attachment theory.

Firstly, one may consider whether there might be a significant overlap between the dichotomy of paranoid-schizoid and depressive positions and security and insecurity in infant–mother attachment. Melanie Klein considered that the two positions alternate, but in particular individuals one may predominate over the other.

1) A key marker of the paranoid-schizoid position is "splitting," the attribution of all goodness and love to an idealized object and all pain, distress, and badness to a persecutory one (Klein

1932b). Splitting, brilliantly operationalized as semantic-episodic memory discrepancy, is an important marker of insecurity in Adult Attachment Interviews (AAIs) in the Main and Goldwyn system, particularly in the Ds category (Main and Goldwyn 1995).

2) The paranoid-schizoid position is marked by extreme lability of mental representations. Good is experienced as rapidly turning into bad, the bad gets worse and the good becomes increasingly idealized. This description again resonates with the Adult Attachment coding system, where precisely such contradictions and inconsistencies mark the insecure transcript.

3) By contrast, the depressive position is thought to be marked by the infant's capacity to see the mother as a whole object, the person who accounts for both good and bad experiences (Klein 1935). The operationalization of security in an attachment history narrative seems to manifest as a balance between love and hate, the recognition and acceptance of imperfection in the caregiver.

4) In Klein's view, with the onset of the depressive position the infant becomes aware of his own capacity to love and hate the parent. The child's discovery of this ambivalence and the fear of the threatened loss of the attacked object, opens the child to the experience of guilt over this hostility (Klein 1929). In the AAI, the narrator's recall and recognition of his or her own role in bringing about interpersonal conflict might add to the coherence of the story (coherence being a characteristic of a secure script). Further, the capacity to monitor one's thoughts and feelings as these emerge in the narrative are scored as metacognitive markers of a secure state of mind.

5) Kleinian theory holds that the psychic pain associated with the integration of the split (good and bad) part objects may be so great that the infant may use massive (manic) denial, obsessional reparation, or contempt. Once more, the AAI coding scheme is specifically keyed to identify narratives with derogation (contempt), incapacity to recall (denial), or idealization (manic reparation) as insecure.

6) Segal (1957) linked the capacity for symbolization and sublimation to depressive reparation. AAI coding is strongly oriented

towards the analysis of speech and discourse, with individuals who manifest secure states of mind in relation to attachment showing substantially greater competence in this domain.

7) Spillius (1992) suggested that the depressive position may be initiated by the child's attribution of an "intentional stance" (perception of him/her as thinking and feeling) to the caregiver. Elsewhere, we have suggested that mentalizing[1] or reflective capacity, the ability to describe coherently the actions of one's caregivers and ones own actions in mental state terms, may be crucial in the assessment of attachment security in the AAI (Fonagy et al. 1991a).

As can be seen from this partial list, the Kleinian commentary on infant mental states overlaps with the classification of adult attachment narratives. This may not be surprising, since Klein's description was based on work with children and adults, rather than on the observation of infants. It might be argued that Klein was describing the sequelae of insecure infantile attachment based on the characteristic narratives of her adult patients. Her description of the paranoid-schizoid position may well be considered by attachment theorists as a relatively apt portrayal of an adult's insecure state of mind with respect to attachment. Indeed, it would be a great deal more difficult to attempt to identify paranoid-schizoid features in the behavior of insecure infants in the strange situation. Perhaps, Bowlby's dissatisfaction with the Kleinian perspective was rooted in part in the attempted "adultomorphisation" of the fictional and metaphorical infants of early Kleinian theory.

Modern Kleinian writers (see, for example, Quinodoz 1991, Steiner 1992) see the critical aspect of the depressive position as the child's achievement of separateness and the perception of the object's independence. This brings Kleinian developmental formulations closer to the attachment model of healthy separation. The emphasis on the object's separateness also links the concept of the depressive position to classical ideas about oedipal conflict. Once the object is perceived as a mentally independent entity, it is seen as having desires, wishes, loyalties, and attachments of his or her own, and concerns about the

---

1. Mentalizing is closely related to Bion's notion of "K," as getting to know oneself or the other person, and the evasion of the process, which he calls "minus-K."

feelings of the "third" may arise (Britton 1989, 1992, O'Shaughnessy 1989). These ideas might bring classical notions of the healthy resolution of the Oedipus complex into the purview of attachment theory.

If it is accepted that an overlap exists between the balance of paranoid-schizoid thinking and insecurity in relation to attachment, there are additional implications concerning the categorical nature of the attachment classification. If the AAI may be considered to measure paranoid-schizoid thought, the extent of this tendency may be correlated with the "severity" of insecurity in the individual. Attachment theorists tend to prefer working with the notion of *prototype*, and measuring security on a continuous scale is relatively unusual. Commentary on the psychometric desirability of categorical versus continuous measurement of attachment is, however, well beyond the scope of this chapter. Nevertheless, the Kleinian perspective highlights an approach to attachment security as a mode of mental functioning with cycling, sometimes rapid, between secure and insecure modes. The frequency of such cycles is the stable personal attribute, not the class or category that best fits the individual at any time point.

A second point of contact concerns the notion of projective identification. Melanie Klein (1957) saw projective identification as an unconscious infantile fantasy by which the infant was able to relocate his persecutory experiences by separating (splitting) them from his self-representation and making them part of his image of a particular object. It is assumed that disowned unconscious feelings of rage or shame are firmly believed by the infant to exist within the mother. By acting in subtle but influential ways, he may achieve a confirming reaction of criticism or even persecution. The fantasy of magical control over an object may be achieved in this way. Thus, projective identification is not a truly internal process and involves the object who may experience it as manipulation, seduction, or a myriad of other forms of psychic influence. Spillius (1994) suggested the use of the term *evocatory projective identification* to designate instances where the recipient of projective identification is put under pressure to have the feelings appropriate to the projector's fantasy.

The relationship of projective identification and attachment is undoubtedly complex. Here I would like to draw attention to only one interesting feature. The disorganized attachment pattern in infancy (Main and Solomon 1990) manifests as controlling behavior in the preschool (Cassidy et al. 1989) and early school years (Main and Cassidy 1988). Such children appear to take control of the relationship, sometimes treating the parent in an apparently condescending or humiliating manner. While explanations for such behavioral discontinuity may be offered in terms other than projective identification, the background of such children makes an account in terms of pathological projective identification more likely. Disorganization of attachment has been shown to be associated with parental experience of unresolved trauma (Main and Hesse 1990), infant histories of maltreatment (Carlsson et al. 1989), maternal depression (Radke-Yarrow et al. 1985), and prenatal parental drug and alcohol abuse (O'Connor et al. 1987, Rodning et al. 1991). It is likely that children exposed to such deprivation are repeatedly confronted with intolerable levels of confusing and hostile caregiving, and are forced to internalize aspects of their caregiver that they are incapable of integrating. Their self-structure is thus formed around a fragmented and flawed image that they are forced to externalize in order to retain any measure of coherence. The process of projective identification fits the behavioral description of these children as attempting to experience themselves as coherent selves and force these alien inassimilable parts of themselves into the other. They maintain the illusion that these parts are now outside through subtle manipulative control of the other's behavior (Fonagy and Target 1997).

This suggestion makes use of Bion's elaboration of the concept of projective identification in infancy (Bion 1959, 1962a). Bion assumed that the infant, overwhelmed by impressions of the world, required another human mind (a container) with the capability to accept, absorb, and transform these experiences into meaning. A massive defensive structure is thought to arise if the caregiver fails to contain the overwhelming feelings of the infant by recognizing and reflecting upon the infant's emotional communication. The infant's communications are calculated to arouse feelings the infant wishes to be rid of in the mother (Bion 1962a).

The Kleinian formulation of sensitive caregiving would be of a parent capable of absorbing and retransmitting the infant's psychological experience in a "metabolized" form, responding to the infant emotionally and in terms of physical care, in a manner that modulates unmanageable feelings. Capable (secure) caregivers are likely to experience and transform these feelings into a tolerable form. This involves the combination of mirroring of the intolerable affect with emotional signals that indicate that the affect is "contained," that is, is under control (Bion termed this *alpha function*). The infant can cope with, accept, and re-internalize what was projected, thus creating a representation of these emotional moments of interaction with the caregiver that it can tolerate. In time Bion suggested that the infant internalizes the function of transformation and will have the capacity to contain or regulate his own negative affective states. The mother's capacity for "reverie" ensures the success of containment through alpha function (Bion 1967). The non-verbal nature of this process implies that physical proximity of the caregiver is essential. This is an alternative perspective on the socio-biological root of the infant's need for proximity to the psychological caregiver, the adult mind. It is also the basis of his vulnerability to adults who, incapable of understanding through experience, provide inhumane care. Bion's formulation has much in common with Alan Sroufe's systematization of the attachment relationship as the primary vehicle for the acquisition of emotional regulation (Sroufe 1990, 1996).

A further point of contact concerns the distinction between dismissing and preoccupied patterns of adult attachment and Rosenfeld's Kleinian developmental model of narcissism. Rosenfeld (1964, 1971a,b) described narcissistic states as characterized by omnipotent object relations and defenses that deny the identity and separateness of the object. He distinguished between "thin-skinned" and "thick-skinned" narcissism, and his description closely matches the preoccupied versus dismissing adult attachment categories (Main and Goldwyn 1995). In the case of "thick-skinned" narcissism or a dismissing pattern of attachment, Rosenfeld assumed that, with the assistance of projective identificatory processes, the individual deposits his own perceived inadequacies in others whom he can then dismiss, denigrate, and devalue. In the case of "thin-skinned" narcissism, Rosenfeld assumed that the patient's dependency causes him to feel intolerable vulnerability to the other, which he attempts to ward off through continuous unprovoked angry attacks on those whose dependability appears to mock his own feelings of helplessness and defectiveness. This description fits the angry-resentful subcategory of the preoccupied classification. The former description points to the dismissing attachment pattern where the individual denies the value of the caregiver, or his need of them.

This analogy may be of relevance beyond the level of description. A number of clinicians note the interchangeability of the "thin-skinned" and "thick-skinned" patterns (e.g., Bateman 1996). This should alert attachment theorists to the possibility of a lack of stability in this aspect of the classification in particular individuals who score at extreme levels. Alternatively, Rosenfeld's and other similar psychoanalytic concepts may be helpful in the elaboration of the "cannot classify" category of Adult Attachment Interviews (Main and Goldwyn, in preparation), where the mixture of narrative styles precludes the unambiguous assignment of either a dismissing or a preoccupied classification.

POINTS OF DIVERGENCE

One of Bowlby's central objections to Kleinian psychoanalytic theory was its neglect of actual experience and the assumption that the child's anxieties arose predominantly from constitutional tendencies (Klein 1936, 1959). It is of more than passing interest, as Eagle (1997) noted, that Bowlby's own psychoanalyst, Joan Riviere (1927) wrote: "Psychoanalysis is . . . not concerned with the real world, nor with the child's or the adult's adaptation to the real world, not with sickness or health, nor virtue or vice. It is concerned simply and solely with the imaginings of the childish mind, the fantasied pleasures and the dreaded retributions" (pp. 376–377). One can just imagine the conflict, overt or covert, between this analyst and this patient. Karen (1994) noted Bowlby's marginalia next to the above paragraph: "role of environment = zero."

The criticism is less apt in the case of post-Kleinian psychoanalysts, who have been quite successful at integrating environmental accounts with her ideas (Meltzer 1974, Rosenfeld 1965). The child's capacity to cope with the pain and anxiety of the depressive position, seeing himself as destructive and envious, is also seen as dependent upon external as well as constitutional factors. The strength of the ego is increased with the child's identification with the representation of the internalized good object. The stronger ego can regulate the destructive ideas, reducing the need to project hatred. The weak ego remains at the mercy of paranoid defenses. There is no genuine guilt, nor capacity for reparation. Here again, Kleinian theory leans heavily on attachment-related constructs of emotion regulation and the fragmented, incoherent development of the self consequent on insensitive parenting. The models, however, diverge, in that Kleinian thinking attributes intentionality to the infant, whereas attachment theory ideas avoid anthropomorphizing the infant and describe an equivalent process somewhat more parsimoniously in terms of psychological mechanisms.

Notwithstanding the increased respect for the external environment, at present there is no room in attachment theory for a concept such as the death instinct. Kleinian ideas continue to pivot around the innate destructiveness of the human infant. In truth, the concept may not be as critical to Kleinian theory as often supposed (see Parens 1979). Envy may be triggered by frustration or inconsistent mothering or the child's inadequate capacity to appreciate time and space. However, aggression may not be inevitably linked to deprivation. The child may resent the inevitable limitations of maternal care, find it hard to tolerate the mother's control over it, and might prefer to destroy it rather than experience the frustration (envy). Attachment theory could explore in greater depth the constitutional variability among infants, some of whom may indeed be genetically predisposed to violent responses (e.g., Reiss et al. 1995), which could interfere with the establishment of secure attachment, notwithstanding the sensitivity of the caregiver.

Finally, the concept of "position" to describe a dimension at least analogous to security–insecurity, highlights the nondeterministic nature of the developmental processes that may underlie quality of attachment. Attachment researchers have produced impressive data demonstrating the stability of individual differences predicted by infant–caregiver classification. This can be readily understood in terms of underlying differences in basic mechanisms such as emotion regulation, which are likely to provide continuity for patterns of behavior. An alternative explanation, of course, may be in terms of the continuity of environmental characteristics (Lamb 1987). Kleinian theory highlights yet another possibility. Kleinian psychoanalysts consider the term *position* as implying a particular constellation of object relationships, fantasies, anxieties, and defenses to which an individual is likely to return throughout life. Specific environments may trigger a paranoid-schizoid or a depressive reaction, an insecure or a secure relationship pattern. The infant can develop secure or insecure relationships with different caregivers (Steele et al. 1996b). Consequently, we have to assume the concurrent presence of several, perhaps both secure and insecure, internal working models in the child's mind. Which one becomes dominant for the adult may depend on the importance of the specific caregiver in the child's life. Thus the notion of alterations of working models, in much the same way that Kleinians envisioned the oscillation of positions, is at least a theoretical possibility.

Inspiring though Kleinian ideas might be to some, there is no getting away from the "fuzziness" of Kleinian descriptions. On the one hand, the Kleinian emphasis on fantasy as the building block of mental structure transcends the gap between the experiential and nonexperiential aspects of mental functioning and moves mental structuralization to the experiential realm. This has the advantage of providing experience-nearness and ridding the theory of much reified pseudo-scientific terminology. On the other hand, this creates an unbridgeable gulf between it and the attachment theory approach, which is committed to pursuing questions concerning the nature of the mechanisms underpinning mental functions.

7

The Independent School of British Psychoanalysis and Its Relation to Attachment Theory

Unlike the previous psychoanalytic orientations, the British School should not be considered a unified approach. Fairbairn (1954, 1963) was perhaps the key theoretician. Winnicott (1948, 1958b, 1971a), Balint (1959, 1968), Khan (1974, 1978), and Bollas (1987) may be considered some of the key contributors. These workers do not subscribe to a single coherent framework; hence, their usual collective description as "the Independents" is probably highly appropriate (see Rayner 1991).

The Independents abandoned the libidinally driven structural model and developed a "self-object" theory, in which parts of the self are seen in dynamic interaction with each other and complementary internal and external objects. Self and affect become crucial agents of motivation and for Fairbairn (1954) there is no emotion without the self and no self without emotion. Winnicott (1958b) postulated an inherent desire to develop a sense of self, a desire that could be hidden or falsified.

Fairbairn (1952a) asserted that the basic striving was not for plea-sure but for a relationship. Pleasure and anxiety reduction followed the attainment of a desired relationship between self and other. There was a further important shift away from unconscious contents and repres-sion and towards the notion of incompatible ideas. Fairbairn suggested that the loss of optimal intimacy will give rise to "splitting" in the ego and these conflicting multiple self–object systems are seen as the de-velopmental roots of psychopathology. In contrast to Mahlerian and other ego-psychological rooted theories that emphasize separation, Brit-ish object relations theories focus primarily on attachment and attempt to understand the development of the individual as a unit in interac-tion. The self is seen as being comprised of, and its integrity and con-tinuity being maintained by, the gestalt of past and present interper-sonal relationships. Guntrip (1969) emphasizes the importance of studying relatedness, or what he refers to as "the emotional dynam-ics of the infant's growth in experiencing himself as 'becoming a per-son' in meaningful relationships, first with the mother, then the fam-ily, and finally with the ever enlarging world outside" (p. 243). While Guntrip does not completely neglect the development of the individual as a separate entity, his focus is on attachment and relatedness: "Mean-ingful relationships are those which enable the infant to find himself as a person through experiencing his own significance for other people and their significance for him, thus endowing his existence with those values of human relationship which make life purposeful and worth liv-ing" (p. 243).

Winnicott (1965b) contributed most constructively towards pro-viding a developmental description of the origins of the self in the infant–caregiver relationship. He saw the child as evolving from a unity of mother and infant. Three functions of this unity facilitate healthy development: 1) holding, leading to integration of sensorimotor ele-ments; 2) handling, facilitating personalization (autonomy); and 3) object relating, resulting in the establishment of a human relation-ship (Winnicott 1960b, 1962a,b). The mother's primary maternal pre-occupation of heightened sensitivity to her own self, her body, and the baby offers the infant the illusion that the mother responds accurately to his gesture because she is his own creation, that is, a part of him. Winnicott (1971a) sees object relations as arising from this experience of magical omnipotence. The mother's survival of the infant's "attack" on her facilitates the development of the self. She will be perceived as separate and available for a genuine as opposed to an omnipotent relationship.

By contrast to Winnicott, who assumes no idyllic phase in early childhood, Balint (1952, 1965) proposes that a desire to be loved is a primary form of love. This is conceived of as a lack of differentiatedness felt towards early objects who do not frustrate the infant. A disruption of this state leads to a basic fault, a profound misordering which the individual is conscious of throughout life.

POINTS OF CONTACT

Attachment theory has its psychoanalytic roots in the work of British analysts from the Independent School. What is described as *attachment* in Bowlby's (1969) terms, in Balint's (1952) is *primary love*, in Fairbairn's (1952a) is *object-seeking*, in Winnicott's (1965b) is *ego-relatedness* and in Guntrip's (1961) is *personal relations*. This is explicit in Bowlby's acknowledgments of these analysts, even though he felt he moved beyond them by establishing a firm biological and evolutionary basis for object relations theory. Points of contact between attachment theory and object relations theories of Fairbairn and Winnicott have been extensively and imaginatively reviewed by Sroufe (1986), Holmes (1993b), and Eagle (1995), among others. Here, we shall focus on only certain specific issues less well covered in these reviews.

Bowlby related the attachment concept to the work of the Hungarian school (Hermann 1923). He was influenced by Balint's concept of primary object relations (Balint 1952), but he used it chiefly to add weight to his emphasis on non-oral components of the early need for the object. Balint (1959) identified two characteristic defenses in the child's management of anxiety: one is to love, even to be intensely dependent upon the newly emerging objects (the *ocnophilic attitude*); the other is to dislike attachments to others, but to love the spaces between them (the *philobatic attitude*). Instead of investing in objects, the philobat is thought to invest in his own ego skills. Balint's description is perhaps the clearest statement of the match between analytic accounts of narcissism and a detached-dismissing attachment pattern. The philobatic attitude is a metaphoric statement of an avoidant-dismissing pattern, while the description of its counterpart fits the resistant-preoccupied one.

A first point of contact is between attachment theory and Winnicottian ideas about sensitive caregiving. In Winnicott's view, the true self is rooted in the summation of a kind of sensorimotor aliveness that is assumed to characterize the neonate's mental world (Winnicott 1965a). At this stage the self does not yet exist. Its development is seen as predicated upon the emergence of self-awareness or self-consciousness, the differentiation of me from not-me, and the experience of the infant's own feelings and perceptions as distinct from those of others (Winnicott 1962a). The ego has an inherent potential to experience a sense of continuity. When the child is allowed a basis for being, a basis for a sense of self follows (Winnicott 1971b). Winnicott saw it as developing within the dyadic unit of baby and maternal carer. Attachment theorists now also recognize that an independent, but possibly equally important, primitive dyadic unit can also exist with the father (Steele et al. 1996b). This is of some significance as it implies the presence of multiple internal working models.

Central to Winnicott's ideas is his assertion that this potential for an experience of continuity of being must not be interfered with, giving the infant the opportunity to bring forth what Winnicott calls its "creative gestures" or impulses (Winnicott 1960a, 1965a, 1971b). Also central to his ideas is the radical claim (Winnicott 1962a) that the strength or weakness of the child's ego is a function of the caregiver's capacity to respond appropriately to the infant's absolute dependence at the earliest phases of life. This is the time when the baby's ego is only able to master and integrate the drives insofar as the mother is able to perceive and implement his rudimentary needs and intentions. In this period, prior to the separation of the mother from the self, the stability and power of the infant's ego is thus seen by Winnicott as directly determined by the reflective function of the caregiver. This is Winnicott's justification for the relatively greater importance of maternal sensitivity in the earliest years.

For Winnicott the mother has to be "good-enough," but her failure is expectable and is, in fact, the major motivator of growth. This is consistent with the observation of attachment researchers that moderate degrees of maternal involvement are preferable to highly contingent responses (Malatesta et al. 1989). Moderate levels of acceptance

(Murphy and Moriarty 1976) and maternal involvement (Belsky et al. 1984) are more beneficial to growth than perfect matching. But Winnicott also stresses that the baby must not be challenged too soon, or too intensely, about the mother's "realness" (her independence as a person). This would force the infant to negotiate the "me and not-me" distinction before he acquired sufficient experiences of being omnipotent to form the ego nuclei that will, in time, become integrated in the real experience of the "I" (the true self). Insensitive parenting might have more powerful effects where the child's ego needs are not met. Where the child's knowing, as opposed to willing, is impinged upon or confused this may lead to disintegration, disorientation, withdrawal, and a sense of annihilation—a fragmentation of the line of continuity of being. Measurement of sensitivity could be sharpened if Winnicott's distinction between willing and knowing were to be subjected to separate measurement.

The holding environment provides the setting for the fusion of aggression and love that prepares the way for the toleration of ambivalence and the emergence of concern, both of which contribute to the acceptance of responsibility (Winnicott 1963a). This is Winnicott's version of Melanie Klein's depressive position and an alternative description of the development of a secure pattern of attachment. Winnicott makes a further critical point concerning sensitivity in his often misunderstood and somewhat paradoxical assertion that relatedness is born of the experience of being alone in the presence of somebody else (Winnicott 1958a). The assertion is based on three simple qualities of the holding (sensitive caregiving) environment.

1) A sense of safety must be associated with experiencing the inner world. This statement is related to Winnicott's mirroring (Winnicott 1956) and Bion's containment concept. Distress must be met by a combination of external feedback (e.g., the mother's face and tone), which "explains" to the infant what it is feeling (Gergely and Watson 1996), and a simultaneous communication of having coped with the distress (Fonagy et al. 1995a). The secure caregiver may be thought to soothe by combining a resonant response with an affect display incompatible with that of the child. The finding that the clarity and coherence of the mother's representation of the child mediates be-

tween the AAI and mother's observed behavior towards the child is consistent with this model (Slade et al. 1999b). If secure attachment was the outcome of a sense of safety associated with experiencing the inner world, insecure attachment may be the consequence of the caregiver's manifest defensive behavior in this regard. A dismissing (Ds) caregiver may altogether fail to mirror the child's distress because of the painful experiences this evokes for her, or because she lacks the capacity to create a coherent image of the child's mental state. By contrast, the preoccupied (E) caregiver may represent the infant's internal experience with excessive clarity or in a manner complicated by the parent's ambivalent preoccupation with her own experience at the expense of communicating coping. In either case, the child's opportunity to "experience" its inner world safely is lost.

2) Winnicott makes a second assertion about the holding environment: the infant must only gradually be exposed to external events. Initially, the infant should only be exposed to a reflection of its own internal state and the coping affects of its caregiver associated with this internal state. Because the development of the infant's nuclear self is based on the internalization of the reflection of its own affect in a modulated version, if the infant is instead exposed to the caregiver's defensive reaction, the caregiver's defense being internalized in place of the child's actual experience. This risk is also recognized by attachment researchers: ". . . this dyssynchrony becomes the content of the experience of the self" (Crittenden 1994, p. 89). In other words, avoidant infants can be said to have internalized the excessively muted response of the caregiver, which is why they respond to separation with minimal displays of distress while experiencing considerable physiological arousal (Spangler and Grossman 1993). At an extreme, the internalization of the caregiver's defenses leads to the construction of an experience of self around this false internalization (Winnicott 1965a).

Winnicott (1971a) proposes that the child needs to be able to play alone in the presence of the mother if a stable true sense of self is to emerge. She must be sufficiently unobtrusive for the child to forget her and to focus on self-exploration, which lies at the root of solitary play. A defended or unavailable caregiver will force the child to think about the parent and thus not be able to remember himself. The balance suggested by Winnicott is analogous to the balance between exploration and contact maintenance within the attachment paradigm.

3) Winnicott's third assertion concerns the infant's opportunity to generate spontaneous creative gestures. Winnicott considered sucking one's thumb or smiling after a good feed to be creative gestures, because they were within the infant's control. Sensitive caregiving must therefore actively lend coherence to the physical body of the infant by acknowledging the goal-orientedness of his physical being. Daniel Stern (1985) explored these ideas most fully in his elaboration of the development of self agency in the 4- to 6-month-old, where proprioceptive feedback, as well as the experience of forming plans, were seen as contributing to the continuity of the sense of self. If handled satisfactorily, the infant looks at the mother's face rather than breast. His concerns with mind and meaning can override his preoccupation with his physical needs.

In summary, the crux of Winnicott's discovery is that the true self can only evolve in the presence of an unobtrusive other who will not interrupt the continuity of its experience of itself (Winnicott 1958a). In this regard, Winnicott's view has much in common with Hegel's (1807) assertion that the self both loses itself in the other and also "supercedes" the other "for it does not see the other as an essential being but in the other sees its own self" (Hegel 1807, p. 111). The natural evolution of the self occurs when the person looking after the child does not unnecessarily impinge on the infant by substituting her own impulses while curtailing or redirecting the infant's creative gestures. The caregiver needs to maintain or restore her own sense of well-being before she can act as a tension regulator for the infant. The lack of good-enough mothering causes distortions or deviations in mental functioning and forestalls the establishment of an internal environment that could become the essence of the self.

Attachment theorists are in general agreement that the "harmoniousness of the mother-child relationship contributes to the emergence of symbolic thought" (Bretherton et al. 1979, p. 224). Bowlby (1969) recognized the significance of the developmental step entailed in the emergence of "the child's capacity both to conceive of his mother as having her own goals and interests separate from his own and take them into account" (p. 368). Recently, empirical evidence has accumulated to suggest that attachment security with the mother is a good concurrent predictor of metacognitive capacity in the child (Moss et al. 1995). We have demonstrated a relationship between attachment security to mother and the child's understanding of emotional states in a puppet doll (false-belief test) at 3 ½ to 6 with concurrent assessment of attachment (Fonagy et al. 1997a) and prior assessment at 1 year (Fonagy et al., submitted). In the light of the importance attributed by developmentalists to the child's acquisition of a "theory of mind" around this time (Baron-Cohen 1995, Baron-Cohen et al. 1993), the demonstration of a relationship to attachment security seems quite important. The relationship may be mediated by a number of known associations of attachment security that have been shown to be precursors of "theory of mind" (Dunn 1996).

Here the suggestion is that the capacity to mentalize evolves out of the attachment relationship in the child's exploration of the mind of the caregiver. Secure attachment allows for fuller exploration. Secure children thus learn more about the caregiver's intentional stance and, since the caregiver's mental state frequently reflects their own intentions, they learn more about the way their own thoughts and feelings can affect their behavior (Fonagy et al. 1995b). Severe deprivation undermines the acquisition of mentalization.

A second major facet of Winnicott's theory relevant to attachment theory concerns environmental failure and the infant's reaction to it (Winnicott 1963b,c). On the one hand, internal and external impingements and the lack of a holding environment can lead to aggression and antisocial behavior. This is characterized by the use of physical action as self-expression, a lack of concern for the other, and a definition of the self in opposition to the environment.

On the other hand, external impingement and the substitution of the gestures of the other for the gestures of the self engenders a false self structure (Winnicott 1965a) that appears real, performs and complies, and may be true in highly selected aspects or based on wholesale identification with the object. In either case, notwithstanding the superficially convincing nature of such a presentation, the self put forward by such individuals is fragile, vulnerable, and phenomenologically empty.

Here Winnicott is perhaps describing his assumptions concerning the impact of what may be prototypes of extreme dismissing and preoccupied patterns of parenting. While the former is linked with aggressive and antisocial behavior, the latter is linked with the appearance of a "pretend" personality with pretend relationships. Dismissing caregiving does not threaten the infant's true self as there is no active discouragement of its expression. An antisocial tendency develops because the child cannot cope with the failure or withdrawal of ego support and makes use of antisocial behaviors to protect his sense of self. In the case of preoccupied parenting, we may see the invalidation of the infant's creative gestures. Winnicott conceptualizes the infant's reactions to this as the self acquiescing, hiding its own gestures, undermining its own ability. The false self serves to hide and protect the true self.

From the point of view of attachment theory the two categories of environmental failure may be seen as alternative coping strategies to deal with insensitive caretaking (impingement). Both types of environmental failure would be expected to affect the child's developing capacity to envision mental states in self and other. The developmental failure in each case is, however, different. The aggressive, antisocial pattern could be linked to the defensive inhibition of mentalizing capacity leading to highly abnormal patterns of social interaction (Fonagy 1991). In contrast, a false self structure appears not to be inconsistent with mentalization. We would maintain that this kind of mentalization, as Winnicott suggests, is not genuine. Such individuals have been able to come to an understanding of intentionality in the caregiver, but have achieved this at the expense of self-understanding. They defensively separate mentalization from the actual state of the self. As a consequence, their mentalization may appear "hyperactive"—an intense, but ultimately fruitless pursuit of psychological understanding. Even when accurate, the product of such efforts feel shallow and empty and do not influence behavior.

POINTS OF DIVERGENCE

The attachment theory account of the repetition of early patterns of behavior in later life is primarily cognitive. An account in terms of internal working models risks circularity. What are we trying to explain? An individual's tendency to think and feel in analogous ways to adult attachment figures as they felt and thought about figures of infancy: What is the mechanism of this process? Their internal working models are unchanged: How do we know about their internal working models? We ask them about their thoughts and feelings. The issue that is sidestepped concerns why individuals appear to be unable to relinquish clearly maladaptive models that organize their adult relationships. The object relations account of the persistence of early structures is more dynamic. Fairbairn (1952a) proposed that there was a "devotion" or "obstinate attachment" to certain early perceptions of the object (p. 117). Thus Fairbairn extends the notion of attachment to include attachment to internal organizing principles or specific internal working models, which in his view accounts for the persistence of these patterns notwithstanding their maladaptive features. To adopt new modes of relating might involve a betrayal of the early relationship that is impeded by attendant guilt (Eagle 1997) and the terror of an empty, objectless world where no relationship is available. Thus, in Fairbairn's view, repetition is motivated by the avoidance of guilt and avoidance of the terror of emptiness.

Winnicott's theory is traditionally regarded as highly compatible with attachment theory formulations. The theories evidently agree in placing the self as the focus of the psychology of the mind, seeing self and object representations as intertwined and reciprocally influencing agents, construing relationships as organized to safeguard self structures. Whilst not wishing to dispute this, it may be important to underscore that this view arises out of a somewhat selective reading of Winnicott. For example, in relation to the holding environment, Winnicott assumes that this interpretation of the notion of sensitive caretaking shields the infant from unbearable mental experience, unthinkable, primitive, or archaic anxiety in the vulnerable process of moving from an unintegrated to an integrated state (Winnicott 1962a). It was such extravagant speculations about the internal state of the infant as these that prompted Bowlby to disentangle attachment theory from psychoanalysis on epistemological grounds.

It is important to note that for Winnicott, strongly influenced by Klein and Bion, the infant's predisposition has a highly significant role in determining the nature of the mother–infant relationship. Thus, maternal care is not the only determinant of the holding environment. The stability and balance within the baby itself, the initial balance with which it starts life, contributes to the likely success of maternal care. This is similar to Bionian notions of the infant's envious attack on containment.

There is an important related point of divergence concerning Winnicott's focus on the mother as the root of all the child's potential difficulties. While Winnicott's descriptions of the failed attachment relationships are consistent with attachment theory, many of the "impingements" of the external environment are from sources other than the maternal caregiver. The descriptions of infancy by British Independent analysts all suffer from such "mother-centrism," which can easily give rise to mother blaming.

Winnicott (1965a) was far more deeply rooted in instinct theory than is generally realized. His theory of false self rests on the assumption that internal excitements can be traumatic for the child when the caregiver is not able to contain such demands. In this way instinctual tensions are not experienced as part of the self and are split off or disowned. In a sense, to Winnicott, attachment theory might have appeared as an example of false self development since it placed so little emphasis on sexual drives, physical pleasure, and the individual's struggles with destructive, aggressive aspects of his or her personality.

Similarly, the "good-enough" mother is not simply good-enough in terms of giving meaning to behavior but in terms of permitting the child spontaneous expression of a need or impulse. Mothers who are not good-enough communicate that such impulses are dangerous. Thus Winnicott, unlike Bowlby, does not consider relationships to be independent from instincts and has an integrated formulation where instincts and object relationships are intricately interwoven.

8

North American Object Relations Theorists and Attachment Theory

British object relations theory has influenced North American psychoanalysis over the last thirty years. In some cases (such as the Kleinian influence on Kernberg) this is openly acknowledged. In others (such as Winnicott's influence on Kohut) this is left for the reader to discover. Here we will consider only three of the major North American object relations theorists from the point of view of attachment theory: Arnold Modell, Heinz Kohut, and Otto Kernberg.

ARNOLD MODELL

Modell (1975) attempted to integrate British object relations theory with the structural model by distinguishing two classes of instincts: libidinal and aggressive id instincts, and the newly recognized ego instincts for object relations. Object relations instincts are not strictly speaking biological in nature and are characterized by interaction processes rather than discharge. They are gratified by stimuli in the environment if responses from others are identified that fit with specific needs. Modell sees affects as object-seeking. The main aim of this ego instinct is mastery over the id. This is achieved through identification with good objects. The failure in the taming of the id becomes the major route to psychopathology.

Points of Contact

Modell's object relations theory is reminiscent of Bowlby's early writings, for example Bowlby's report to WHO, where he himself attempted to integrate traditional psychoanalytic ideas with his observations on mothering (Bowlby 1951). In his substantive elaboration of attachment theory, in the 1958, 1959, and 1960 papers to the British Psychoanalytical Society, Bowlby moved away from the instinct metaphor (Bowlby 1958, 1959, 1960). Modell's ideas are important in bridging the gap between classical psychoanalysis and attachment theory.

The key implication of Modell's theory is that the intensification of problems of sexuality and aggression are consequent upon (but do not cause) the incoherent sense of self of the patient. In fact, any anxiety-provoking experience that brings to the foreground the non-cohesive sense of self will be experienced with greater intensity by patients whose object relations needs were not gratified. The prioritizing of attachment over other biological needs is consistent with Bowlby's ideas (Bowlby 1980b). A powerful example of this shift of emphasis is provided by Modell's description of separation guilt (Modell 1984).

Modell's (1975, 1984) description of narcissistic individuals is reminiscent of descriptions of avoidant patterns of attachment. They begin, so Modell claims, to fall back on a compensatory self-structure in order to bypass having to rely on inadequate caregivers. They deny their need for dependency because they experience their caregiver as unable to facilitate their development. Modell points out that their self-sufficiency is illusory and defensive and their autonomy is unreal.

A further point of contact involves Modell's (1963) ideas concerning borderline patients. Modell (1963, 1968) was the first to describe "the transitional relatedness" of borderline patients. This refers to the use the infant makes of inanimate objects to obtain comfort in the mother's absence. Transitional relatedness implies the disorganization of attachment in borderline individuals, a theme to which we shall return later. In his clinical reports Modell highlights how borderline individuals use inanimate objects to relate to in their adult lives, in place of human relationships. Even more striking is their use of other people as if they were inanimate to serve a self-regulating, soothing function, to be used as the toddler uses a teddy bear, in primitive, demanding ways. It is as if their attachment experiences failed to permit the internalization of an emotion regulation strategy (Carlsson and Sroufe 1995). Searles (1986) and Giovacchini (1987) see this as an indication that borderline patients have been treated as transitional objects by their parents.

This formulation adds to Main and Hesse's (1990) observation of frightened and frightening parenting of traumatized individuals. It is conceivable that trauma or loss may prompt the caregiver to use the child to soothe him or herself, as the caregiver's own internalization of affect regulation is inadequate. Modell sees the borderline individual's image of himself as dividing into either the helpless infant or into someone who is omnipotently giving or destructive. The lack of stability of the self and object representation leaves him with what Modell calls a "harrowing dilemma" of extreme dependence and terror of closeness. This pattern of behavior is evocatively described by Mary Main in her observations of disorganized infant behavior (Main and Goldwyn 1998).

Points of Divergence

Unlike British object relations theorists, Modell (1985) only sees object relations theory to be relevant for a restricted group of patients. He also differs from most British theorists in defining object relations (attachment) as a separate instinct of the ego. Many theoreticians feel that the formulation is inconsistent with structural theories of ego psychology (Eagle 1984, Greenberg and Mitchell 1983). Certainly from a structural point of view, it may have seemed more appropriate and more in line with Bowlby's ideas to have considered object relations as an emotional rather than an adaptational need.

HEINZ KOHUT

Whatever one might think of the adequacy of his theories, there can be no doubt that Kohut revolutionized North American psychoanalysis. He broke the iron grip of ego psychology by forcing psychoanalysts to think in less mechanistic terms, in terms of selfhood rather than psychological function, in terms of selfobjects rather than the drive gratification that the object fulfilled.

Kohut (1971, 1977, Kohut and Wolf 1978) made the innovative suggestion that the development of narcissism (originally self-love or self-esteem) has its own developmental path, and that caregiving individuals (objects) serve special functions along this line of development as *selfobjects*. A selfobject functions to evoke the experience of selfhood (Wolf 1988). Empathic responses from the selfobject facilitate the unfolding of the infantile grandiosity, and encourage feelings of omnipotence that enable the building of an idealized image of the parent with whom he wishes to merge. Later the selfobject creates experiences of mild frustration, which permits a gradual modulation of infantile omnipotence through "transmuting internalization of the mirroring function." Transmuting internalization of the mirroring function leads gradually to a consolidation of the nuclear self (Kohut and Wolf 1978). The idealization of the selfobject leads to the development of ideals. At the opposite pole of this "bipolar self" is a representation of natural talents gained through the mirroring function. Selfobjects continue to be needed throughout life, to some degree, to help the maintenance of self cohesion (Kohut 1984). They are experienced as part of oneself, serving to maintain its organization, while objects can become targets of desires once the self-concept is sufficiently demarcated.

Points of Contact

Kohut's self psychology relies on the notion of attachment as a central motivation of the self for the establishment and maintenance of self-cohesiveness (Shane et al. 1997). Consistent with the suggestion of Bowlby, Kohut replaced the dual drives of classical analysis with a relational construct. Some post-Kohutian analysts (e.g., Lichtenberg 1989) integrate attachment constructs fully with their self psychology perspective. Lichtenberg, for example, identifies attachment-affiliation as one of his five motivational systems; although he includes the more traditional systems of libido and aggression, there is a distinct shift in that he considers the latter on a par with attachment motivation. Like Winnicott, Kohut also linked self development to mirroring or maternal sensitivity. Like Modell and attachment theorists, he reversed the relationship of drives and self structure, regarding the self as superordinate and drive conflicts indications of "an enfeebled self" (Kohut 1977). For example, he saw the Oedipus complex as the child's reaction to the parent's failure to enjoy and participate empathically in the child's growth. Unempathic parents are likely to react to their oedipal child with counterhostility or counterseduction. It is such reactions which may stimulate destructive aggression and isolated sexual fixation. Kohut identified castration anxiety and penis envy, as Bowlby might have been inclined to do, as imposed from outside rather than the consequence of a constitutional predisposition to oedipal experiences.

Kohut specified some aspects of the internal working model associated with insensitive caregiving. When parents fail to provide for the child's narcissistic needs, the representation of self as omnipotent and the representation of the caregiver as perfect become "hardened" and will not be integrated into later structures. They continue to exist within the individual's representational world and cause disturbances of interpersonal relationships as well as dysfunctional self representations. For example, the grandiose self may pose a threat to self-organization.

Kohut's view of narcissism (Kohut and Wolf 1978), the most influential of his propositions, is closely linked to attachment constructs. He suggested that primary infantile narcissism is impinged upon by disappointment in the caregivers, which is then fended off by the "normal" grandiose self. The grandiose self would be gradually neutralized by age-specific mirroring responses of the caregivers. If the parent is unempathic or insensitive, the idealized but faulty parental image will be internalized in place of the representation of the child's own capacities. Thus, in attachment theory terms, the internal working model will be a dual one: one component contains a set of omnipotent expectations, based on the child's view of the parent's capacities mixed with infantile omnipotence, and the other component is one of total helplessness and enfeeblement, the expectations of an infant facing an unempathic caregiver.

Kohut provided a particularly valuable description in showing how injured narcissism may call forth rage to protect the self together with fantasies of grandiosity in order to cover a sense of infantile vulnerability (Kohut 1972). Kohut also offers an interesting dual framework for understanding insensitive parenting. The first relates closely to attachment theory operationalizations of parental sensitivity and is framed in terms of the mirroring function. The second is of greater interest because it relates to the evolution of parent–child relations beyond the first two years. In order to facilitate the gradual diminution of infantile narcissism, the parent must be able to help the child appreciate his or her *real* limitations. Parents who, for example, are unable to identify moments when the child himself experiences a sense of achievement but offer uncritical and excessive praise hinder the replacement of omnipotent self representation with a realistic sense of self just as much as do parents who pay little attention to their child. Both leave the child with an unattainable unrealistic or partial system of values and ideas.

Points of Divergence

Unlike Modell and attachment theorists, for Kohut self cohesion is the primary motivation guiding human behavior rather than a biologically predefined relationship pattern. Kohut separated anxiety about object loss from anxiety about self disintegration. At the root of anxiety for Kohut is the self's experience of a defect, a lack of cohesiveness and continuity in the sense of self. This subtle but important shift of emphasis relegates the importance of the attachment figure to second place.

Related to this is Kohut's apparent lack of interest in aspects of functioning other than the individual's relation to his or her own grandiosity and exhibitionism. Incompatible with attachment theory is the lack of consideration for the capacity for intimacy, mutuality, and reciprocity in interpersonal relations.

The concept of self as used by Kohut is in fact somewhat alien to the attachment theory approach. Using the concept as a superordinate structure with a mental apparatus runs into the same problems of mechanistic thinking and reification that, as has been noted, hindered ego psychology (Stolorow et al. 1987). Kohut's motivational metaphor of an attention arc between the idealizing and mirroring functions seems just as abstract and ill-defined in observational terms as was the notion of interagency conflict in the structural model.

The problem of Kohut's approach is that while he presents the self in representational terms he ascribes to it motivational properties and tendencies, such as goals, plans, and self-esteem motivation (Kohut 1971). Thus the self comes to denote almost all of personality and thereby becomes a superfluous term. By contrast, Sandler's (1987b) use of the term, or its use in attachment theory, is logically coherent. It is restricted to a representation that a person forms of themselves (or a mental model) analogous to a mental representation someone else might have formed of him or her.

It is difficult to identify within attachment theory a concept analogous to grandiosity or omnipotence as naturally occurring in infant development. The notion of infantile omnipotence is certainly challenged by findings indicating that on the majority of occasions the infant is not able to elicit synchronous (mirroring) behavior from the mother (Gianino and Tronick 1988). Although infants undoubtedly enjoy experiences of mastery (DeCasper and Carstens 1981), there is no evidence that this leads to a sense of omnipotence. It seems far more likely that we encounter again a central limitation of psychoanalytic thinking—the description of infant behavior in terms of adultomorphic constructs, the very problem that Bowlby's entire theoretical work aimed to address.

OTTO KERNBERG

Kernberg is the most frequently cited living psychoanalyst. His preeminent position is an indication of the remarkable coherence he has achieved in creating a structural object relations theory (Kernberg 1975, 1976a, 1980, 1984, 1987). In Kernberg's theory, affects serve as the primary motivational system (Kernberg 1982). He proposes that psychic structure is made up of combinations of (a) self representation, (b) object representation, and (c) an affect state linking them (which also defines a relationship).

He accepts the existence of drives in the mature child and adult but sees these as the product rather than the motivator of development. He treats them as hypothetical constructs that come to be organized from congruent affect states around the theme of sexuality and aggression if a normal developmental path has been followed. Drives manifest in mental representations as emotional experience. Representations are of the self and object linked by a dominant affect state. The major psychic structures (id, ego, and superego) are also hypothetical constructs that refer to groupings of self–object relationships under the influence of specific emotional states. Self–object relations are internalized relationship experiences colored by the prevailing affective states. For example, the superego may be harsh because the affect state prevailing at the time was one of anger and criticism.

Kernberg's model suggests that the self evolves as part of a relationship (1976a,b) and is a product of internalization. This in its turn is seen as a complex process made up of (a) the wholesale introjection of experience, (b) identification through the distortion of self representation in the direction of the perceived object, and (c) ego identity (which is the overall organization of introjections and identifications under a mature, synthesizing influence). Kernberg differs from most psychoanalytic theorists in that he offers no specific developmental trajectory to explain the current state of the patient's ideation. In contrast to the somewhat caricatured analogy that Bowlby drew of the psychoanalytic theory of pathology as lying along a single track, Kernberg accepts that the complex process of development makes any one-to-one link between the current state and the past implausible.

Points of Contact

There are fewer important points of contact between Kernberg and Bowlby and other attachment theorists than one might expect. This is all the more surprising since Bowlby and Kernberg share a common respect for the empiricist tradition. Kernberg is the only psychoanalyst to have produced a manual of his psychotherapy (Kernberg et al. 1989), who videotapes his sessions, is actively involved in outcome studies, and is publicly committed to empirical research in psychoanalysis (Kernberg 1993).

Kernberg's (1984) model of neurotic pathology fits well with an attachment theory approach. Individuals with high levels of personality organization are considered to be able to integrate positive and negative representations of self and others. They evolved through childhood phases where good and bad representations of self and others were combined across affective valences, and representations containing both loving and hostile elements were formed. Kernberg regards these representations as influential in governing future object relationships. Even relatively well-integrated representations contain units that reflect a defensive or impulsive aspect of conflict.

Anxiety, characteristic of neurotic pathology, is likely to arise when self and object representations are highly charged affectively but are poorly differentiated. For example, the self may be represented as weak and vulnerable and the object as ruthless and domineering. The prevalent affective tone may be violent and hostile. When this configuration is activated in a social situation, the individual may become highly anxious. A defensive aspect may emerge separately, triggered by the activation of the first pattern. In a masochistic character structure, the experience of a good relationship may trigger an unconscious fantasy of sexual intimacy between child and parent. This in its turn propels into consciousness a critical and nagging relationship pattern when the self is experienced as criticized by an unsympathetic and misunderstanding other (Kernberg 1988).

Such a model could be readily restated in terms of internal working models (Bretherton 1995). The main distinction is that Kernberg assumes that the manifest internal working model may be a defense against an underlying or latent but painful internal representation of relationships in which the original source of hostility was the self.

If Kernberg's view of neurotic pathology may be seen in terms of the presence of certain maladaptive internal working models, his view of severe psychopathology (Kernberg 1975, 1977) may be seen as a pervasive dysfunction of the entire system of internal working models. In such cases, Kernberg describes rapid reversals between moments when the patient's self representation is activated while the object representation is externalized, and moments of identification with the other when the self representation is externalized onto the object. Thus, in such cases the activation of the representation of the self as the subject of criticism by an unsympathetic other can quickly shift into an identification with the critic; in this latter case, the object is forced to accept the role of the helpless victim of harsh criticism. Now the critic is experienced as the self who, hurt and mistreated, identifies with the critical stance and ruthlessly chastises the other. The oscillation accounts for many instances of rapid shifts between working models with consequent shifts in impulses into their opposite (active into passive, or good into bad). The "Cannot Classify" classification of the AAI may be describing the same dysfunctional internal representation process.

Even more severe disturbances of internal working model functioning may be found in borderline personality organizations (Kernberg 1984, 1987). Here the self–object–affect triads are thought to dramatically lack integration. The consequences are: profound splitting, impulsivity, lack of empathy, and the unmodulated expression of sexuality and aggression. The underlying cause relates closely to Kleinian formulations of primitive object representations. The units of psychic structure are based, not on genuine internalizations of self–other relationships but rather on so-called "part object" representations originating in states of mind (paranoid-schizoid), in which the representation of the entire person was beyond the capacity of the individual. Instead of the more readily comprehensible, relatively realistic relationship patterns of neurotic personalities, Kernberg identifies highly unrealistic, sharply idealized, or persecutory self and object representations. These part representations could never be traced back into the past as they never actually existed in this form. They represent a specific small fragment of an actual person, experienced at a moment characterized by overwhelming and diffuse affect (positive or negative depending on the affective valance of the part object representation). Of course, insecure attachment, with accompanying inadequate affect regulation, is bound to increase the likelihood of forming such part object representations.

Because object relations are poorly integrated, the reversals and enactments of self–other representations are likely to be extremely frequent and rapid. Relationships with such individuals will be correspondingly confusing and even chaotic. There is evidence from studies of borderline patients using the AAI of exactly such confusing internal representations of attachment (Fonagy et al. 1996, Patrick et al. 1994). Thus, Kernberg's formulation of borderline pathology, translated into attachment theory language might be the activation of poorly structured, highly distorted unstable internal working models with loose assignments of object and subject. Kernberg's criteria for borderline personality disorder include a diffuse sense of identity that may be the consequence of a disintegrated system of models of relationship representations. As Kernberg noted: ". . . [with] extreme and repetitive oscillation between contradictory self concepts . . . the patient, lacking in a stable sense of self or other, continually experiences the self in shifting positions with potentially sharp discontinuities—as victim or victimizer, as dominant or submissive, and so on" (Kernberg et al. 1989, p. 28).

Points of Divergence

Kernberg (unlike attachment theorists and other object relations theorists) does not privilege early experience. In fact, there is little in attachment theory that might preclude giving equal weight to later experience, and the undoubted focus on infancy may be a carry-over from the ethological concept of critical periods or even an historical artifact, due to the relatively slow progress and equivocal measurement properties of pre-school and middle childhood measures (Goldberg 1995).

Kernberg's determination to maintain dialogue with the North American psychoanalytic community obliges him to retain the notions of drives and psychic agencies. These have no place in an attachment theory framework. It should be noted that in contrast to other psychoanalytic writers, for Kernberg these are hypothetical constructs, not biological givens. They are the products of development and integration. It is an open question whether in Kernberg's theory they serve a function other than ensuring communication with the psychoanalytic community at large.

Kernberg (1976a) directly takes Bowlby to task for not taking account of "the internal world" and for neglecting "instinct as intrapsychic developments and internalized object relations as major structural organizers of psychic reality" (p. 121). This is undoubtedly an unwarranted criticism, particularly in the light of Bowlby's emphasis on constructs such as the internal working model (see, for example, Chapter 17 in Bowlby 1969). It would be more accurate to say that Bowlby's conceptualization of the internal world is different from Kernberg's. It is interesting that Kernberg makes no reference to Bowlby's later book (Bowlby 1973). Kernberg is silent on Bowlby's restatement of the psychoanalytic concept of the internal world in terms of "environmental and organismic models" (Bowlby 1969, p. 82).

More substantive discrepancies exist. For example, in Kernberg's model (1967, 1977), the root cause of borderline states is the intensity of destructive and aggressive impulses coupled with a relative weakness of the ego structures available to handle them. He sees this as presenting a constant threat to the good introject, thus forcing the individual to use "primitive" defenses (splitting) in an attempt to separate contradictory images of self and other. Positive images need protection from being overwhelmed by hostile negative ones. The borderline condition is a continuation of an unresolved conflict state. Primitive idealization is a protection from the old bad objects through creating an omnipotent object in fantasy, and so on.

As we have seen, the notion of an aggressive predisposition in the infant is not currently part of attachment theory. A more standard formulation might be one proposed by Shaw (Shaw and Bell 1993, Shaw et al. 1996). Here infant temperament, and negative parental reaction, are seen as leading to avoidant attachment, which in its turn may bring about maternal withdrawal, further aggressive attention seeking, impulsive and unsystematic disciplinary practices, oppositional behavior, and ultimately aggression. The assumption of high levels of innate aggression is clearly reductionist, and it simply short-circuits the more sophisticated transactional developmental model.

THE INTERPERSONAL SCHOOL OF PSYCHOANALYSIS

The interpersonal school of psychoanalysis has tended to distance itself from attachment theory. John Bowlby received merely half a page from Greenberg and Mitchell's classic object relations text (1983). More recently Mitchell (1998) acknowledged his indebtedness to attachment theory ideas. He contrasted Darwin's influence on Freud and Bowlby. For Freud the main message of Darwinism was the ascent of man and thus a justification for the archaic remnants of earlier and more primitive aspects of the psyche underlying our hard-won civilized veneer. Bowlby's Darwin, by contrast, was concerned with adaptation and survival. The main function of attachment was seen as protection from predation and in the environment of evolutionary adaptation there would be strong selective pressure toward attachment behaviors.

9

Modern Psychoanalytic Infant Psychiatry: The Work of Daniel Stern

Daniel Stern occupies a unique place in psychoanalysis (Stern 1985). He has been able to bridge the gulf between developmentalists and psychoanalysts in a highly successful and productive way. Many might not regard his contribution as strictly speaking "psychoanalytic," as his database is infant research rather than clinical observation. In this respect, however, he follows the tradition of René Spitz and Margaret Mahler as psychoanalytic developmentalists.

His primary concern is with the development of self structure. He distinguished four stages of early self formation: 1) the sense of emergent self (0–2 months) involves the process of the self coming into being and forming initial connections; 2) the sense of core self and the domain of core relatedness (2–6 months) are based on the single organizing subjective perspective and a coherent physical self; 3) the sense of subjective self and the domain of intersubjective relatedness (7–15 months) emerge with the discovery of subjective mental states beyond physical events; and 4) the sense of verbal self forms after 15 months.

POINTS OF CONTACT

Daniel Stern (1977, 1983, 1985, 1994) distinguished three types of relationships of self-with-other: self–other complementing, state sharing, and state transforming. While these relationships can be characterized by the degree of attachment or separateness they imply, it is their contribution to the structuralization of the self through the schematization of experience that interests Stern. He takes the concept of relationship beyond the meaning ascribed to it by the separation theories that view self–other relationship as a means toward the development of a sense of self as separate, as well as beyond the meaning ascribed to the relationship by attachment theories that consider the relationship itself a goal. He describes these relationships as the stuff of all human connectedness, intimacy, and trust throughout development, and sees the ability to engage in them as essential to mental health.

Stern's most important point of contact with attachment theory is probably in the elaboration of the internal working model (Stern 1994). In particular he has elaborated the representational world concept. His starting point is the "emergent moment," which is the subjective integration of all aspects of lived experience. The "moment" takes its input from emotions, behaviors, sensations, and all other aspects of the internal and external world. The emergent moment is understood as deriving from schematic representations of various types: event representations or scripts, semantic representations or conceptual schemas, perceptual schemas and sensory-motor representations. He adds to these two further modes of representations: *feeling shapes* and *proto-narrative envelopes*. These schemata form a network, which he terms "the schema of a-way-of-being-with."

The "schema of a-way-of-being-with" is conceptualized by Stern (1998) from the assumed subjective perspective of the infant in interaction with the caregiver. The infant organizes his experience around a motive and a goal. The goals are not only biological, but include object relatedness (see Modell), affect states (see Kernberg), states of self-esteem (see Kohut) and safety (see Sandler), as well as physical need gratification, be it hunger, thirst, sexuality, or aggression (see Freud's structural model). The representation includes a proto-plot with an agent, an action, an instrumentality, and a context, all essential elements in the understanding of human behavior (see Bruner 1990). Stern (1985) and Trevarthen (1984) use similar concepts to describe the intersubjective bond that connects baby and parent. Like Holmes (1997), they both use musical metaphors to describe the interactive patterns suggesting that tone, pitch, timbre, and rhythm all contribute to the eventual security or insecurity of the relationship. Stern (1985) described shared play, in which the parents' tactile interactions with the infant keep rhythm with the infant's vocal utterances. These shared meanings form the nucleus of the capacity for intimacy. Stern's theory elaborates Winnicott's ideas (1971a). Attunement satisfies the infant's need for omnipotence, while the caregiver's capacity to accept protest without retaliation or anxiety satisfies the child's needs to have confidence in the caregiver as resilient to the infant's attacks.

Stern (1994) offers a compelling example of a way-of-being with a depressed mother and describes the infant's reaction to a nonresponsive object by trying repeatedly to recapture and reanimate her. He describes how depressed mothers, monitoring their own failure to stimulate, may make huge efforts to enliven their infant in a forced and unspontaneous way, to which infants respond with what is probably an equally false response of enlivened interaction. This model maps very closely onto Sandler's (1987a) model of projection and projective identification, and the two need to be combined to achieve a fully coherent account. The child identifies with the representation of the mother's distorted representation of him, which is communicated to him by a process of projective identification and eventually evolves into an expectation of "a false way-of-being-with" the other.

The schemata of "ways-of-being-with" come closest to providing a neuropsychologically valid model of the representation of interpersonal experience. Certain features of the model are critical in this regard. First, these schemata are emergent properties of the nervous system and the mind. Second, they make use of multiple simultaneous representations of the lived experience. This is consistent with the clinical observation that, even in pervasive brain injury, aspects of experience are retained. Third, they are based on prototypes, less affected by single experiences and naturally aggregating common patterns of lived experience. Emergent moments are represented in the simultaneous activation of a set of nodes within a network and the strengthening of the connections between these nodes, with each activation automatically constituting a "learning process." By conceptualizing schemata of "ways-of-being-with" as networks, Stern links his model to that of the dominant model of cognitive science, parallel distributed processing (see Rumelhart and McClelland 1986). Fourth, the model allows room for modification from inside as well as outside. In postulating refiguration as a process whereby attention can scan representation, Stern offers a way in which internally generated activation (fantasy) may strengthen or alter and potentially distort objective experience. Fifth, in adopting Edelman's (1987) concept of neural Darwinism, Stern opens an important avenue for further work on the fate of representations that lose out in the process of neural natural selection.

Stern's model is helpful to attachment theory because it casts a new light on the notion of internal working models and brings it into closer contact with mental model theory (Johnson-Laird 1983, 1990). Mental model theory assumes that to understand is to construct mental models from knowledge and from perceptual or verbal evidence. To formulate a conclusion is to describe what is represented in the models. To test validity is to search for alternative models that refute the putative conclusion. Internal working models, like all mental models, such as Stern's schema of a way-of-being-with, may or may not be accessible to consciousness. What matters for Bowlby's, Stern's, and Johnson-Laird's proposed mechanisms are the structures created, which are isomorphic with the structures of the states of affairs to which they pertain, whether perceived or conceived, and which they are thus able to represent.

Johnson-Laird and Byrne (1991, 1993), in their ambitious book on deduction, show that many of the inferences of daily life cannot be accounted for by formal rules that are deductively valid. The process appears to be one in which all thinking may be seen as the manipulation of models, much as Kenneth Craik conceived of as early as 1943. It is a highly attractive aspect of Johnson-Laird's formulation, from both attachment and psychoanalytic standpoints, that irrationality in the sense of invalid deductions is an emergent property of the model. Individuals make inferences that go beyond the semantic information available to them, which inevitably leads them to make some inaccurate inferences. This contrasts with Freud's (1900) and other classical formulations, which distinguish rational and irrational thinking on the basis of discrepant syntactic processes and the extent to which formal rules of inference are used to manipulate representations.

Stern's theory assumes that mental operations are invariant. In the maturation of thought, development is not the evolution of new mental operations, as has been assumed, for example, by Piaget, but the derivation of new concepts and models of the world (see Johnson-Laird 1990). Mental models of the kind envisaged by Stern, and implicitly also by Bowlby, offer a form of data structure that plays a central role in the computational architecture of the mind. Such structures are relevant not only to thinking (deduction) but also perception (see Marr 1982), the comprehension of discourse (see Garnham 1987, Johnson-Laird 1983), and the representation of beliefs and other intentional contents (see McGinn 1989).

POINTS OF DIVERGENCE

Stern's framework has much to offer attachment theory, particularly in terms of the careful integration of infant observation studies with concepts concerning interpersonal development. Nevertheless, it lacks two critical dimensions essential to attachment theory. First, it lacks a genuine longitudinal observational perspective. A great strength of attachment theory is its almost unique empirical handle on longitudinal and cross-generational predictions. Whilst Stern's observations are well operationalized in terms of mother–infant interaction and infant development, they lack operationalization in the context of adult behavior, and therefore longitudinal studies based on Stern's framework have rarely been attempted.

Second, while Stern probably appropriately claims that "schemata of ways-of-being-with" are the building blocks of internal working models (Stern 1998), close links between the two systems have not yet been demonstrated. There is important pioneering work by Beatrice Beebe and her group (Beebe et al. 1997) but the bulk of the empirical work remains to be performed.

10

The Interpersonal-Relational Approach: From Sullivan to Mitchell

The most rapidly evolving theoretical orientation within psychoanalysis of the last decade of the twentieth century (and perhaps the first decade of the twenty-first) is the so-called relational or intersubjective approach. Many major figures are contributing to this orientation. Its identifying tenet is perhaps the assumption that the psychoanalytic encounter is co-constructed between two active participants with the subjectivities of both patient and analyst contributing to generate the shape and substance of the dialogue that emerges. There are a great number of brilliant major contributors more or less committed to relational/intersubjective views, including Ogden (1994), McLaughlin (1991), Hoffman (1994), Renik (1993), and Bromberg (1998), to name just a few in this most fertile of fields (other major contributors working within this framework include Daniel Stern, Jay Greenberg, Lewis Aron, Stuart Pizer, and Stephen Mitchell). Their views are all somewhat different and a definitive intersubjective-relational view has yet to emerge. Having reviewed interpersonal approaches in the early 1980s, Merton Gill was said

to have come to a conclusion analogous to Ghent's witty description
of a psychoanalytic political grouping that agreed to affiliate under a
common designation and then avoided defining the often very different concepts that each had in mind when using a term (Mitchell 1996).
Stephen Mitchell has been singled out for discussion here because the
links between his views and those of attachment theory show the greatest overlap and appear most productive in their convergence.

The key ideas of the interpersonal school form the foundations
of the relational-intersubjective approach. The major classical contributors include Harry Stack Sullivan, Erich Fromm, Frieda Fromm-
Reichmann, and Clara Thompson. Both Sullivan and Thompson
were, in the 1930s, already demonstrating how to treat schizophrenic
young men and schizoid young women patients from the perspective
of interpersonal relations, operationist and humanist, without the libido metaphor. Sullivan never even tried to become a psychoanalyst,
although acknowledged indebtedness to Freud. It was probably Clara
Thompson, originally a training analyst in the New York Psychoanalytic, who blended together Sullivan's interpersonal psychiatry with
Eric Fromm's humanistic psychoanalysis and Ferenczi's clinical and
technical discoveries to generate an interpersonal approach to psycho-
analysis (Thompson 1964). Among contemporary interpersonal writers, perhaps Benjamin Wolstein's (1977, 1994) and Edgar Levenson's
(1983, 1990) work should be mentioned.

One of the key innovations of the interpersonalists' approach is
their replacement of the classic model of the psychoanalyst as observer
without memory or desire (analyst as outside) with a model of the analyst as participant in a shared activity (analyst as inside). They supple-
ment or replace notions of objective truth with subjectivity; the intrapsychic with the intersubjective; fantasy (poetics) with pragmatics
(descriptions of experience or of events); content interpretations
with observation of process; the concepts of truth and distortion with
perspectivism; conceptions of internal sameness within people with
external (and therefore, implicitly, internal) uniqueness; the prevalence
of strong theory with the virtue of trying to denude oneself of theoretical
bias; and countertransference-as-feeling with countertransference-
as-enactment. In the meantime an influential stream of the American
psychoanalytic establishment embraced a complete two-person, mutually participating interpersonal psychology with a very strong empha-

sis on the subjectivity of the here-and-now transference. They are more often exclusively focused on the "playground" than interpersonalists such as Levenson, who always did focus on the here-and-now encounter, but accompanied this with extra-transference patterning. For many decades interpersonal psychoanalysts were considered not to be psychoanalysts at all. Only in the last decade and a half, as the psychoanalytic mainstream appeared to almost have evaporated in the United States, have the contributions of the interpersonalist tradition have come to be acknowledged. The idea of mutual participation in the transference has become part of the general psychoanalytic ethos. The ideal psychoanalyst ceased to be a neutral observer but rather the patient's collaborator engaged in a continuous negotiation about truth and reality—the conversation with the other person being the only way of escaping preconception.

In a number of key books and papers Mitchell established himself as one of the two or three most significant psychoanalysts working in the US today (Greenberg and Mitchell 1983; Mitchell 1988, 1993b; Mitchell and Black 1995). Unlike many contributors to the field, Mitchell is invariably careful to offer his own relational contributions in the context of a detailed explication of other theories. For example he places sexuality (1988) and aggression (1993a) in the relational context, justifying a central place for both in human experience because they are powerful vehicles for establishing and maintaining relational dynamics. Similarly, he offered a relational perspective on therapeutic interaction in the context of a scholarly comparison of interpersonalist and Kleinian approaches (Mitchell 1995). His paper on narcissism builds on the major perspectives current at the time of his paper (Mitchell 1986). Mitchell's contribution is in essence integrative, in that he attempts to show the links between theories and the way they attempt to organize accessible knowledge in unique yet powerfully interconnected ways.

Mitchell's contribution is relational in the sense that his central focus is the interpersonal nature of individual subjectivity. The perspective is clearly elucidated by Stolorow and Atwood (1991): "the concept of an isolated individual mind is a theoretical fiction or myth which reifies the subjective experience of individual distinctness . . ." The experience of distinctness requires a nexus of intersubjective relatedness that encourages and supports the process of self-delineation throughout the life cycle" (p. 193). This perspective is in stark contrast with the traditional Freudian view, which sees individuality as in essence a compromise between the internal, the biological, the primitive on the one hand and the co-operative, the organizational, and the mature, which the social represented. For Mitchell the relational is at the core of psychoanalysis—a core that he shows was present from its very inception. The relational includes individuality, subjectivity, and inter-subjectivity. It is human relating that achieves individuality and renders experience personal, unique, and meaningful. The philosophical bases of this approach are shared by a number of psychoanalytic traditions. Marsha Cavell (1994), drawing on Wittgenstein, Davidson, and others, writes: "subjectivity arises along with inter-subjectivity and is not the prior state" (p. 40). Referring to Descartes's radical skepticism, where the only fundamental is reflective thought, as everything else can be doubted, she adds: "doubting the world and other minds one must be in possession of all one needs to put the doubts at rest" (p. 40). The fact that one has a mind that can raise a question such as "I think therefore I exist," presumes other minds as well as an external world which these minds share.

POINTS OF CONTACT

"All organisms live in continuous, communal existence with their necessary environment" (Sullivan 1953, p. 31). The human environment, Sullivan stresses, includes continual interactions with others and, on a wider level, with the collective achievements of others (culture). It is folly to attempt to grasp the structure of any organism without considering the ecological niche it has adapted to fill. Like the attachment theorists who followed him, Sullivan portrayed the early interactions between the infant and its human environment as shaping an almost infinitely malleable collection of human potentials to fit an interpersonal niche to which that potential becomes finely adapted. Also in agreement with attachment theory, Sullivan stresses that, where there is conflict in the individual, it has been produced by conflictual, contradictory signals and values in the environment. Congruent with this, Bowlby was, without a shadow of a doubt, the quintessential relational theorist. His belief in the power of relationships is a consistent theme throughout his oeuvre, from his earliest work on the effects of institutionalization to the last volume of his trilogy: "intimate attachments to other human beings are the hub around which a person's life revolves, not only when he is an infant or a toddler or a schoolchild but throughout his adolescence and his years of maturity as well, and into old age" (Bowlby 1980a, p. 422).

Further, like Bowlby's, Sullivan's (1964) definition of interpersonal situations privileges the dyadic, albeit in a more subtle way: "Configurations made up of two or more people, all but one of whom may be more or less completely illusory" (p. 33). This might seem confusing since "interpersonal" (e.g., in comparison to "intrapsychic") is ordinarily taken to refer to more than one person. The human environment, with which Sullivan insists the individual is in continual interchange, must involve at least one other in addition to the subject in question. So, just as in attachment theory, the representational system created by the *real* interaction between the attachment figure and the child is then potentially used to distort further interpersonal encounters. Sullivan (1964) suggests that the "correct view of personality [concerns] the doings of people, one with another, and with more or less personified others" (p. 33). The illusory others, by definition, are not derived from or generated in current interaction; the patient brings consolidations and transformations of real others in previous interactions to the current one. Past interactions are recorded, combined, reorganized, and reexperienced in complex relationships with real others in current interactions. Illusory personifications are shaped in early experience. Analysis offers insight into the way these models of relations with past others operate as an organizational grid through which present experience is filtered. Such insights enable the patient to discover potentially new experience in the present (Sullivan 1964). Thus Sullivan's model of parataxic distortions overlaps with and actually antedates Bowlby's description of the IWM, although both were likely influenced by Piaget and other social scientists with structuralist views. Thompson (1964) argued that Sullivan's concept of parataxic distortion encompassed two different dimensions of Freud's clinical theory, both transference and character structure. The same argument can be made for the IWM. The IWM, like parataxic distortions, are means by which residues of the past are displaced into present situations ("transference" for Freud) and that displacement serves to organize the person's current experience and interactions with others ("character" in Freudian ego psychology).

The reformulation of Sullivan's views by Thompson allowed interpersonalist analysts to define themselves in contrast to their classical colleagues as far more focused in the present. Interpersonal authors increasingly emphasized the embeddedness of the patient in the present (e.g., Levenson 1983). In this regard they adopted the same stance as attachment theorists, who came to see the residues of the past as procedures rather than episodic memories (e.g., Crittenden 1994). Attachment theorists have claimed that transference relationships are dominated by procedural memories, separated from past experience that gave rise to them by neuropsychological as well as dynamic barriers (they represent different memory systems) (Amini et al. 1996, Fonagy 1999b, Migone and Liotti 1998). Thus, at quite a profound theoretical level there is agreement between relational and attachment theorists that the past, memory work, and reconstruction are unimportant to clinical work. What is crucial is a clarification of the patient's ways of handling current anxieties and present experience. The problem is not so much residues of the past cluttering and distorting the present, as Sullivan saw it, but irrational attitudes in the present, interfering with more rational, healthier integrations.

The strongest theoretical link between the two theories is an implicit and perhaps rather negative one, concerning the relationship of biological drives and relationships. Mitchell's (1988) work is particularly helpful here. Sexuality is recognized as a powerful biological and physiological force, that emerges inevitably within a relational context, conditioned by an object world. The attachment theory view of sexuality is similarly bodily, but sexuality is seen as conditioned by the specific relationship context of attachment (e.g., Orbach 1978, 1986). The triggering, the experience, and the memory of the sexual response are all shaped by the interpersonal context within which the sexual response arises and takes on psychological meaning. In neither the attachment nor the relational context is sexuality seen as primarily a push from within even if it is experienced so, rather it is a better conceived of as a response, within a relational field, to an external or even internal object. This does not deemphasize the biological, but posits a different understanding of how the sexual behavioral system relates to other systems. Sexuality is conceptualized as a genetically controlled physiological response that emerges within attachment contexts that are mutually regulatory, intersubjective, or relational. These contexts form the medium within which mind develops and operates; sexuality plays a formative role to the extent that it is part of these contexts. More recently a similar powerful relational argument has been constructed for aggression (Mitchell 1993a) that also fits well with attachment theory-influenced formulations (Fonagy 1999a, Fonagy et al. 1993a). Neither sexuality nor aggression are seen by either attachment theory or relational theorists as driving forces of either development or adaptation. Rather, sexual and aggressive responses are seen as understandable in the context of the individual's infantile and early childhood experiences that have "taught him about the specific ways in which each of his object relationships will inevitably become painful, disappointing, suffocating, overly sexualized, and so on. There is no reason for him to believe that the relationship into which he is about to enter will be any different" (Ogden 1989, pp. 181–182).

There is an even more subtle correspondence in Sullivan and Bowlby's attitudes to clinical work. This also follows from their convergence of views about the past distorting interpersonal perception in the present. Both authors suggest a therapist who is to some degree committed to an intellectual effort. In Bowlby's case this is a cognitive effort towards understanding of the unsatisfactory internal working model (Mace and Margison 1997), while Sullivan's concept is one of "participant-observation." This concept was developed to challenge the more traditional assumption that the psychiatrist encounters, gathers, and analyzes data from a more or less detached, objective position. The work of the Sullivanian therapist is investigation: the eliciting of information from the patient and the long and arduous task of sorting out the past from the present, the illusory from the real. For both, the therapist is an expert who is continually checking and verifying the data he is eliciting.

Not only did Bowlby share with interpersonalists an emphasis on relationships, but he shared with Sullivan an interest in observable behavior. Neither could be labeled behaviorist but both have a systematic and consistent interest in what happens between people. For Sullivan, this is "the detailed inquiry" of finding out exactly who said what to whom, while for Bowlby it is principally historical concern about what happened in the past to explain the current state of affairs.

To a large extent attachment theorists share with interpersonalists a reluctance to privilege fantasy over actuality that grew out of their critical attitude to Freud's rejection of his seduction hypothesis. Within Mitchell's relational approach, fantasy and actuality are not necessarily alternatives, they "interpenetrate and potentially enrich each other" (Mitchell 1998, p. 183). Most modern attachment theorists would probably concur (Bretherton and Munholland 1999). Reality is encountered inevitably through imagination and fantasy.

A further point of contact is offered by the interpersonalists' embrace of Fairbairn's notion of attachment to "bad" objects—objects that are unavailable or unsatisfying. In attachment theory, becoming attached to a maltreating or simply insensitive attachment figure may lead to strategies that are somewhat maladaptive or undermine and disorganize the attachment system, as we have seen, but a relationship is established even with a malevolent carer. Similarly, Mitchell extends the notion of a safe base for exploration of the external environment to the exploration of the internal world of preferences, desires, or impulses. Mitchell suggests that the absence of a sensitive attachment figure causes the child to precociously fulfill a missing parental function and thus a worry-free surrender of self to the impulses and desires is lost. This casts an interesting light on the notion of anxious avoidance in infancy or the dismissing quality of adult interviews, where the spontaneous gesture is seen as sacrificed because of adaptational needs that the infant should never have been confronted with. Conversely, the capacity to engage with feelings (negative and positive), which is characteristic of secure attachment, may be seen as an opportunity for a worry-free surrender to the person's own experience with the assurance of a secure base. Thus, secure attachment may be seen as facilitating the development of a personal sense of self. The absence of certain parental functions adaptively forecloses this development.

The interpersonal tradition, for decades alone among analytic approaches in maintaining a two-person point of view, shares with attachment theory-oriented therapeutic approaches an interest in analytic interaction and an attitude of wishing to demystify the therapeutic process. In the great dialectics that characterize the development of psychoanalytic ideas, the field theory emphasis of the interpersonalists and the systems theory emphasis of the attachment theorists have been antidotes to the denial of the analyst's participation that for decades characterized the mainstream Freudian approach. From a clinical standpoint, the strongest link between relationist interpersonalist theory and attachment theory was in providing an understanding of the ways in which the vicissitudes of early attachment experiences play themselves out in current relationships, including one that involves the analyst. The interpersonal emphasis on the analyst's authenticity and Bowlby's somewhat naïve but crystal-clear approach to the clinical process have both provided breaths of fresh "air in the stultifying atmosphere created by the traditional demands to shoehorn the analyst's experience into an overly formal, mechanical, and ultimately deeply disingenuous analytic stance" (Mitchell 1995, p. 86).

POINTS OF DIVERGENCE

Because relational ideas have yet to coalesce into a singular framework of analytic thinking, it is hard to see if there is or is not fundamental agreement between interpersonalist-relational thinkers and attachment theorists. As we have seen above, there are certainly very large and broad areas of agreement concerning the nature and functioning of the adult. The developmental aspect of interpersonalist thought is far more vague, although attachment theory could well be seen as the key developmental dimension to relationist ideas. There are also major differences in world view that might caution against such an integration. Relational theories, in part as a consequence of their historic origins, tend to repudiate the biological in thinking about motivation and human nature. The adult human organism is not thought to be understandable in terms of other sorts of organisms, bestial or infantile, but has its own distinctive nature. It is not "driven" by "special" drives, but is the agent of many kinds of activities, all of which are devoted to the general project of creating, recreating, and expressing itself within its relational context (see Mitchell 1988). Mitchell (1997), in his attempt at reconciliation, offers a distinction "between Freud's and Bowlby's Darwin" (i.e., their different approaches to evolutionary theory) but one is left with the feeling that, while attachment theory stands or falls on its biological foundations and its integration into the natural sciences (Bowlby 1981), the heritage of interpersonal-relational theories are qualitatively different, more at home with post-modern deconstructive ideas than brain-behavior integration and ultimately at odds with the reductionism of the biological context of attachment.

Bowlby's therapist is forever trying to find a way between insight and relationship—between correcting the faulty IWM and a fundamental attempt to offer recapitulation through a positive attachment experience (Mace and Margison 1997). For some, psychotherapy is a new attachment relationship that is able to restructure attachment related implicit procedural memory and modify stored prototypes with new interactions with the affectively engaged therapist that are internalized by the patient (Amini et al. 1996, Migone and Liotti 1998). The Sullivanian therapist is also in a relationship, but this is by no means inevitably one of offering a corrective attachment experience. Sullivan suggests that the psychiatrist *participate* in the events from which he acquires his information: he does not contemplate the therapeutic interaction from an ivory tower (Sullivan 1964). The participant-observer concept was developed to challenge the more traditional assumption that the psychiatrist encounters, gathers, and analyzes data from a more or less detached, objective position. Sullivan repeatedly stresses the therapist's "participation in the data" yet also the therapist's control over the interview, the disastrousness of being surprised, the usefulness of planned work. As Mitchell (1995) puts it: "One way to position Sullivan's epistemology in relation to more recent developments within the interpersonal tradition would be to say that Sullivan was halfway to Heisenberg. Sullivan put great emphasis on the importance of the analyst's participation in and impact upon what he is observing. However, unlike some later theorists, Sullivan believed that through self-awareness, the analyst was able to factor out that participation and apprehend reality in an objective, unmediated fashion" (p. 70).

Interpersonalist analysts have taken this point of view much further, distancing themselves from Bowlby's pre-Heisenbergian epistemology. "The analyst's point of view, even if arrived at through rational, self-reflective observation, cannot be separated from his forms of participation. Observation is never neutral. Observation is always contextual, based on assumptions, values, constructions of experience" (Mitchell 1995, p. 83). This was most eloquently expressed in Levenson's (1972) seminal work, *The Fallacy of Understanding*. "Nothing . . . can be understood out of its time and place, its nexus of relationships.

It is an epistemological fallacy to think that we can stand outside of what we observe, or observe without distortion, what is alien to our experience" (p. 8). By contrast to Sullivan, attachment theory therapy is on the one hand unaware of Heisenberg and on the other more or less condones enactment by the therapist along the lines of a corrective emotional experience. Relational theorists lead the way in highlighting the epistemological problems of assuming the immaculateness of the analyst's perceptions.

There is a range of many different clinical approaches all of which might be considered "interpersonal." Among current authors, Ehrenberg is one of the most radical in her emphasis on countertransference disclosure. The relationship aspect of therapy for interactionist technique is perhaps most clearly formulated in Ehrenberg's concept of a meeting at the "intimate edge" in relatedness (Ehrenberg 1993). This is defined as the locus of the points of maximum closeness between individuals in a relationship over time without violation of the boundaries of either, the interactive boundary between patient and analyst. Trying to achieve such a meeting in the therapeutic context brings into relief and opens for inquiry and exploration in the immediate interaction the obstacles, resistances to, and fears within the patient related to such a meeting. At the same time it facilitates clarification of individual boundaries and allows for contact without violation of these boundaries. In this way the therapeutic relationship becomes a medium for the patient's expanding self-awareness, greater intimate self-knowledge, and increasing self-definition. Ehrenberg places great emphasis on the use of countertransference and particularly on the analyst's disclosure of her own experience as the central vehicle for analytic exploration. Ehrenberg presents her approach as an antidote to fallacious claims to analytic objectivity. The patient is repeatedly confronted with what she did interpersonally, which places the focus on the "intimate edge." Ehrenberg makes "the immediate interactive experience the crucible of the work and the arena for working through" (p. 6). At that edge, the analyst can be most authentically engaged and here has the greatest opportunities for understanding and growth. While there might be superficial ways in which this is seen as related to the emotional engagement by the therapist conceived by attachment theory oriented clinicians (Amini et al. 1996, Mace and Margison 1997, Migone and

Liotti 1998), careful study of the respective clinical material cited makes it clear that the interpersonalist therapist does not have the provision of a corrective attachment experience as an aim. Rather, the emotional heat at the "edge" is evidently felt to strengthen the impact of statements that are (in attachment theory terms) aimed to be corrective in the IWM.

11

Psychoanalytic Attachment Theorists

A number of major authors in attachment theory have been significantly influenced by psychoanalytic ideas. In fact, in the case of these authors the two theories overlap so much that it is difficult to assign primogeniture. The views of these authors are intellectually very close to the present writer's ideas, and the task of a comprehensive review of their work belongs to a more impartial critic. Here I would simply like to acknowledge that the bringing together of psychoanalysis and attachment theory is a major thread in the writing of several significant intellects and contributors to the field by highlighting some of their key ideas. The reader interested in the possibilities of integration of these two fields should closely examine the work of these authors.

KARLEN LYONS-RUTH

The work of Karlen Lyons-Ruth has been covered at several points in this volume: her groundbreaking research into the nature, causes, and consequences of disorganized attachment in infancy (Lyons-Ruth et al. 1999a), her views on the relationship of separation-individuation and attachment (Lyons-Ruth 1991), her contribution to the work of the Boston Change Process Study Group (Lyons-Ruth 1999), and elsewhere. The extensive coverage of her work is entirely appropriate since she has worked hard on both sides of the chasm, both on the tectonic plate of psychoanalysis and that of attachment theory. In brief, she is one of the few in the current generation of psychoanalysts who is simultaneously making a contribution to the advancement of empirical science and psychoanalytic theory.[1] In this context I would like to briefly review her psychoanalytic model of disorganized attachment— the relational diasthesis model (Lyons-Ruth et al. 1999a).

As we have seen, disorganized attachment is principally a set of rather contradictory and certainly unintegrated behavioral strategies. In this group's development contradictions emerge between behaviors and mental contents and also between mental contents. The phenomena covered by this term are diverse (punitive behavior towards the caregiver alternating with unsolicited caregiving; frightened or frightening behavior, etc.). The causes are equally multifarious: unresolved state of mind with regard to loss or trauma, disorganization of attachment in infancy, frightened and frightening caregiving behavior (Lyons-Ruth and Jacobovitz 1999). The relational diasthesis model is the only psychoanalytically inspired explanation currently available to account for most of the complexities inherent to these data (Lyons-Ruth et al. 1999a).

The model places fear and its modulation into a relational context. It argues that attachment disorganization is probably a function of both the intensity of the fear-producing experience and of the background level of safety that the infant can experience, given the past history of attachment relationships. Thus two parameters need to be considered: the severity of trauma and quality of the attachment relationship. A dichotomy is proposed where at one end extremely severe

---

1. Some of the other members of this small but elite group to be saluted, in my view, include Ricardo Bernardi, Carlos Edson Duarte, Robert Emde, Stuart Hauser, Enrico Jones, Horst Kächele, Ranier Krause, Guillermo Lancelle, David Lopez Garza, Joy Osofsky, Roger Perron, Steven Roose, Mark Solms, Per Vaglum, Sverre Varvin, and Daniel Widlöcher.

trauma is required to disorganize the attachment strategy of the child or adult whose attachment relationships are adequate, and at the other end experiences that are hardly out of the normal range can disorganize attachment responses given that the primary caregiver is not providing optimal attachment experiences. In these latter cases caregiving is thought to be frightened or frightening because of experiences of unresolved fear that the caregiver experiences in response to the infant's attachment behaviors. If early attachment relationships continue to remain disorganized/controlling through to middle childhood, then further trauma may not be required and the intergenerational transmission of disorganization will still occur. Within this model, insecure but organized attachment relationships are seen as providing adequate protection, as long as the traumatic experiences are not of overwhelming intensity. However, extraordinary severity of trauma or loss will even in these cases lead to the kind of mental lapses that are thought to index attachment disorganization.

Importantly, if the level of protection, communication, and mental organization that the caregiver is able to offer the child falls below the quality that organized secure or insecure caregivers provide, in these cases disorganization may occur in the absence of specific traumatic experiences. Lyons-Ruth brings pertinent evidence from animal models of attachment (Suomi 1999). Maternally deprived peer-nurtured monkeys will show atypical social behaviors only when stressed. Thus Lyons-Ruth's model is one of vulnerability created by a flawed early relationship. She links this to Bowlby's discussion of mourning (Bowlby 1980a) and Freud's mourning and melancholia (Freud 1915). Bowlby's model identifies patterns of affectional bonds (e.g., characterized by ambivalence, compulsive caregiving, and a claim for self-sufficiency) that in his view place an individual at higher risk of pathological mourning following a loss. The more insecure the underlying attachment, the harder the mental resolution of loss will become. At present, we cannot be certain if lack of resolution in the AAI leading to infant disorganization is the long-term consequence of attachment disorganization in the caregiver's infancy or disorganization caused by later trauma or some combination. But the prediction of the relational diathesis model is that trauma will occur more frequently and will be harder to resolve in an already disorganized caregiving-attachment system. Thus Lyons-Ruth updates Bowlby by including both direct and later indirect disorganization as potential determinants of later outcome. As we have seen from the long term follow-up of the Minnesota sample (Ogawa et al. 1997) there is preliminary data that is consistent with the Lyons-Ruth model.

The psychoanalytically most pertinent aspect of the relational diasthesis model is the account it provides of the sometimes dramatically contrasting behavioral styles that constitute the disorganized attachment category. If a caregiver's experience does not include comfort and soothing in relation to fear evoking episodes, the caregiving relationship will quite likely evoke unresolved fearful affects when the caregiver is confronted with pain and fear in the infant. This disruption in the continuity of experience may include memories of a sense of helplessness or merely the affect state itself. To protect herself from reexperiencing the trauma, the caregiver restricts her attentional field and will be unable to respond in a fluid way to the infant's attachment-related cues. This is also the essence of the model originally proposed from a psychoanalytic perspective by Selma Fraiberg (1975). The pervasiveness of the attentional restrictions on the caregiver is expected to be commensurate with the extent to which the caregiver's states of mind take precedence over the infant's attachment related cues. This will lead to an imbalanced exchange and the infant–caregiver dyad will lack mutual regulation.

The construct of unbalanced relational processes is a further development of the internal working model. As the model depicts the relationship between self and other, when the actual relationship is unbalanced by the caregiver's preoccupation with her internal state, the infant's internalization of this relationship will be necessarily discontinuous and potentially self-contradictory. The relational polarities will be skewed and contradictory procedures such as, "I should accept external control and take no initiative" and "I need to control the other and override their initiative" will exist side by side. The lack of integration of such contradictory procedures is considered to be at the root of the phenomena of disorganization. Control will be a critical feature in all such relationship representations. There is an asymmetry of power in which attachment-related goals of one participant are elaborated at the expense of the other's goals. The child's controlling behavior in the strange situation is one pole of this relational model. Helplessness is the other. Since such internal models encompass both relationship roles (control and helplessness), in any one interpersonal situation the response may be of either type. However, Lyons-Ruth argues that the predominance of overwhelmed by trauma (E3) and cannot classify (CC) sub-groups of the AAI correspond to an unbalanced/helpless versus a hostile/controlling internal working model (Lyons-Ruth et al. 1999a). The behavioral manifestations may be either helpless or hostile interpersonal stances or indeed the two in alternation.

The model has many aspects that link a formulation oriented to research findings with psychoanalytic clinical considerations. The great strength of the model is in addressing the real-life situation where all loss and other trauma occurs in the context of a relationship, even if that relationship is highly unsatisfactory. The psychological mechanisms that underpin the relational diathesis model are not yet clear. However, Lyons-Ruth's contribution to the work of a group of eminent researcher psychoanalysts working in Boston, who are currently involved in attempting to understand the change process in psychoanalysis, promises to deliver an integrated psychological model of the encoding of relationship experience, as well as the mechanisms whereby these might be therapeutically altered (Lyons-Ruth 1999). While the relational diathesis model is not yet fully integrated with psychoanalytic ideas, it is undoubtedly the most sophisticated attachment theory model to be advanced from a psychoanalytic point of view by a psychoanalytic researcher since John Bowlby.

MORRIS EAGLE

Eagle has been a major theoretician of psychoanalysis, long before his interest focused on attachment theory (e.g., Eagle 1984). His angle on the integration of the two fields is of particular interest because he approaches the task from the very broad standpoint of the problems posed for psychoanalytic theory by taking on board the relational (object-relationship) perspective. From Eagle's standpoint (1997, 1998, 1999) the most important contribution of attachment theory overlaps with that of object relations theory in highlighting the importance of the subjective experience of infancy, "felt security," in the child's development and throughout the lifespan. Eagle considers attachment theory to have been a "reaction against and corrective to" (Eagle 1997, p. 217) certain aspects of classical analytic theory, in particular Freudian and Kleinian theory. He emphasizes the radical difference between traditional psychoanalysis and attachment theory in relation to the role of external versus internal factors in development. He also vigorously challenges attachment theory from a psychoanalytic viewpoint.

In several writings, Eagle takes issue with Bowlby's assertion that IWM's are veridical reflections of actual behaviors or actual interactions with the caregiver because 1) the child's immature cognitive capacities, conflicts, wishes, and fantasies could generate distortions in his or her perceptions and understanding of the caregiver's behaviors, and 2) given individual differences between infants in constitution and temperament, it seems inevitable that different infants will experience the caregiver's behavior in idiosyncratic ways (Eagle 1995, 1997, 1999). Here Eagle is not making the common point that different infants could elicit different reactions from caregivers depending on their temperament (the so-called child → parent effect), but rather that the identical caregiver behavior might be experienced differently by different infants depending on their constitution. Thus, IWM's could never actually be veridical and must include constitutionally determined experiential components. Unfortunately, while Eagle's logic is sound, modern genetics takes it to an infinite regress since constitution itself appears to be dependent on experience (Kandel 1998, 1999). Constitution is not an absolute, the genotype is far from the phenotype (Elman et al. 1996), and it may indeed be Bowlby's IWMs that best predict if a particular gene, a particular part of the infant's constitution, is likely to express itself or not. However, this is a subtle point; Eagle's critique of attachment theory's exaggerated claim to objectivity is well taken.

Eagle points to the relatively sparse treatment of sexuality and pleasure in attachment theory (Eagle 1995). He makes the challenging suggestion (1997) that the adult consequences of unresolved or poorly resolved oedipal conflicts might be accurately conceptualized as forms of insecure adult attachment. For example, the inability to integrate sexual feelings and attachment feelings tends to manifest as some kind of avoidance or ambivalence, closely mimicking adult attachment styles. The exciting integrative suggestion here is that the failure to resolve oedipal issues in these cases forces the insecure infantile attachment problems to the fore. If the oedipal conflicts had been developmentally appropriately addressed, we might see no signs of these infantile patterns of relating. Eagle (1999) also draws a parallel between avoidant defensive exploratory activities (marked in the strange situation by the continued exploration of the avoidant infant in the mother's absence, which is known to be associated with heightened autonomic arousal [Spangler and Grossman 1993]) and work as a pseudo-sublimatory activity that Winnicott drew attention to with the phrase "marking time."

The broadest integrative suggestion offered by Eagle (1997) links the notions of the repetition compulsion (Freud 1920) with the IWM. Citing evidence indicating that insecure IWMs could predispose an individual to elicit behavior from others that maintains and perpetuates early attachment patterns (e.g., Sroufe 1990), he links this phenomenon to that of the transference, as well as the need that the neurotic individual feels to repeat his self-destructive mode of action. Eagle here aims to replace extravagant Freudian notions such as the "adhesiveness of infantile pleasures," or the need for unconscious punishment to expiate unconscious guilt, or the death instinct with the far more parsimonious idea of the IWM (Eagle 1998). He points to the pervasive property of the mind to represent repeated episodes and events in terms of generalized and invariant features. These features include rules and expectations regarding one's own behavior, the behavior of the other, and the nature of the interaction (Eagle 1998). The interactional representational structures constructed to mediate these, once formed, are resistant to change. They influence perceptions and expectations about new relationships so that relationships are formed and transformed so that they conform to earlier schemes. The IWM embodies persistence.

In advancing these views, Eagle is not far from Sandler's concept of role responsiveness (Sandler 1976a,b, 1981; Sandler and Sandler 1998) or Joseph's (1989) concept of the total transference. Eagle (1999) also cites Merton Gill (1982) in suggesting that the therapist also emits clues that influence the patient's transference reactions. However, Eagle (1998) also notes that the "representational unconscious" structures like the IWM and such as those proposed by Stern (1985), Weiss and Sampson (1986), and others, are almost polar opposites of Freud's irrational, primary process constituted by wishful impulses and characterized by exemption from mutual contradiction and timelessness. Eagle (1988) squares the circle by returning to the ultimately subjective nature of the infant's perception of the caregiving he has received. The interactions aggregated into the representational unconscious are not veridical, rather they have been distorted by wishes and fantasies. He points out that the attachment theory assumption of multiple internal working models and the defensive structures identified within the AAI leaves plenty of room for a more dynamic unconscious, more in his view than is posited by the views of Stern or self psychology (Eagle 1995, 1996).

Eagle (1997) goes beyond the authors who propose a representational unconscious. He links the persistence of past patterns of relating to the unconscious loyalty individuals show to early objects (Fairbairn 1952b). "To relate and live differently not only involves betrayal of one's early figures and its attendant guilt . . . but is experienced as equivalent to living in a psychological world that has been emptied of those self, object and interactional representations that normally make up one's inner world and that defines oneself" (Eagle 1997, p. 222). Eagle (1999), to support the notion of the intense attachment to pathological modes of relating, cites evidence for the intensification of attachment behavior in maltreated individuals to the person of the abuser. The need for holding on to past ways of relating with the tenacity observed in our patients is, however, not regarded by Eagle as adequately captured by attachment theory ideas. Fairbairn (1952b) observed that the truly bad object is both rejecting and abusive and alluring (Eagle 1999). He proposes an integration of Fairbairnian and Bowlbian notions in explaining the need to remain tied to early objects, not just for the assurance of security but also because the ties constitute a person's very sense of self and the raw material of his or her inner world.

Clinically, Eagle (1997) stresses that attachment theory speaks to the importance of classical notions of insight, awareness, remembering, and self-reflection at a time when these ideas are frequently regarded as outmoded by the new wave of psychoanalytic theoreticians. However, he takes a strong position against those who link autobiographical competence (coherence) to progress in psychoanalytic therapy. He questions the assumption that those who tell competent, plausible narratives are indeed genuinely securely attached. They are merely defined as such by attachment theory for heuristic purposes. Eagle's point is that those individuals who are able to be coherent about their attachment experiences (i.e., are appropriately reflective) will develop secure attachments with their children regardless of the security of their own attachment systems. This conservative formulation by Eagle seems particularly appropriate in the light of more recent longitudinal studies that find only weak relationships between AAI narratives and childhood attachment classifications (Grossman et al. 1999, Weinfield et al., in press). The more general point here is that improvements in the coherence of narratives might be a byproduct of successful psychoanalytic therapy, but these should not be confused with its substantive goals. The key to improvement is the strengthening of the observing ego functions (as conceived by classical psychoanalytic theory) and this improvement might be captured in greater coherence in self narratives as a byproduct of improved mentalizing capacities gained through the therapeutic interaction.

Finally, Eagle (1999) offers a useful distinction between therapeutic tasks entailed in the psychotherapeutic treatment of individuals with avoidant and entangled attachment styles, which are quite similar to suggestions of Blatt (1996). Avoidant/dismissive individuals need to get in touch with the cut-off feelings of loss, sadness, and anger in response to severe disappointments in their past relationship with primary attachment figures, thus overcoming the defensive exclusion mentioned by Bowlby. The enmeshed/preoccupied are also immensely preoccupied with attachment concerns and the central therapeutic task is to help them to relinquish the fantasy of recovering a lost relationship that never existed but is itself a fantasy. In these treatments it is primarily the patients' negative transference reactions that need to be addressed in the context of the background safety provided by the positive transference aspects of the therapeutic situation (see also Kernberg 1984).

In sum, while Eagle is critical of attachment theory he is also appreciative of its strong points, particularly its empirical foundations. Unlike Lyons-Ruth his research is somewhat independent of the mainline of work in attachment and this gives him an opportunity to consider a number of key concepts (such as the link between security of attachment and narrative coherence) in a far more critical light than those whose proximity to the trees might at times risk an obscuring of the forest of larger issues and fundamental assumptions. While Eagle is by no means a relationist theorist (and has been quite critical of that tradition in the past), it is interesting to note that his particular brand of integrating psychoanalytic and attachment theories comes quite close to those of relational theorists such as Mitchell (see above).

JEREMY HOLMES

The oeuvre of Jeremy Holmes embodies a theoretical and clinical integration of psychoanalytic and attachment theory ideas and probably represents the fullest exposition to date of an "attachment theory psychotherapy." Holmes (in press) finds the basis of a rapprochement between psychoanalysis and attachment theory in epistemological and theoretical changes in the former. He points to the strengthening of empirical research in psychoanalysis, the increasing recognition of the relevance of sexual and physical abuse, the flourishing interpersonal school, and the proximity of attachment theory and object relations approaches. He suggests that urgent tasks face psychoanalysis if it is to retain its place in the scientific and medical domains and argues that attachment theory might be a useful ally in this work.

Holmes (1996a) makes many fascinating links between attachment theory and psychoanalysis—a number corresponding closely to those advanced in previous chapters of this volume. For example, he also suggests connections between Kleinian and attachment theories. He points to the similarity between the description of the secure individual and the person who has reached the depressive position as both being able to view the object in a coherent and consistent way and to attach and detach from it with appropriate freedom and fluidity. Bringing good and bad object together is a mark of coherence, and the ability to tolerate loss suggests a secure sense of self. Further, in both avoidant and ambivalent attachment there is an underlying fear of intimacy and the splitting of the self, typical of the paranoid-schizoid position. In avoidant attachment the patient may be seen as clinging to himself and cannot tolerate the other's point of view. To do so would mean rendering the self vulnerable to attack or abandonment. In ambivalent attachment there is also a fear of intimacy: the clinging self is a false self, in that aggression and autonomy are denied for fear that they might be unacceptable and drive away a secure base.

Holmes (in press) points to the disagreement between attachment theorists and psychoanalysts regarding the mother–infant relationship in the first few months of life. Attachment theorists stress the ways in which the mother and the infant seek each other out to relate to one another from the moment of birth. Mahler's (1975) classical account, by contrast, holds that there is an undifferentiated symbiosis that covers the first few months. In Holmes's view, Myron Hofer's research argues for a physiological symbiosis arising out of the relationship: the mother's actions change the infant's physiology (Hofer 1990, 1995, 1996). Holmes (2000) suggests that affects are part of a human psychological immune system, which serves to alert the individual as to the safety or danger of self and other. The secure relationship with the other can offer the emotional equivalent of the physical protection that the immune system offers. Trauma overwhelms and disrupts the psychological immune system. Holmes links this to affect dysregulation in borderline personality disorder and suggests that a part of the difficulty of individuals with BPD arises as a consequence of disturbance of the early mother–infant psychophysiological regulatory system as a consequence of early trauma, maternal depression, or some similar catastrophic experience.

The idea that early disturbance of mother–infant relationship might lastingly disrupt physiological response systems is supported by recent work on bonnet macaque monkeys (Rosenblum and Coplan 1994). In these studies, mother monkeys are experimentally manipulated so that they need to spend more time foraging and can be less attentive to their infants. These infant monkeys, as adults, have hyperreactivity to a noradrenergic agent and hyporesponsivity to a serotonergic agent. Holmes (in press) interprets this finding as indicating that an attachment bond is a complex psychophysiological state. Further evidence for this proposition is garnered from studies of mother–infant interaction in relation to the development of the visual system (Schore 1997), the release of peptides during mating associated with the cementing of pair bonds in voles (Insel 1997), and the SPECT analysis of serotonergic changes in the psychodynamic therapy of BPD (Vinamäki et al. 1998). Whatever the strength of arguments that can be mustered from these individual studies, Holmes makes it clear that by accompanying the return of attachment theory to its biological foundations, psychoanalytic ideas might also find unexpected verification or at least limited support.

Like other psychoanalytic attachment theorists (e.g., Eagle 1997), Holmes (1997, in press) compares the Freudian unconscious with the unconscious in attachment theory. The Freudian unconscious is readily seen as a seething cauldron of unbridled sexuality, self-centeredness, and aggression that needs to be actively held at bay by defense mechanisms such as repression and splitting. By contrast, the unconscious of attachment theory sees no war intrinsic to the functioning of the mind. Both theories agree that our actions are shaped by forces over which we have little actual control. Holmes suggests that underlying this dichotomy is a possible hierarchy of unconsciouses. At the bottom is a physiological unconscious. Above this might be a layer of the behavioral unconscious implicit in attachment theory. Going through this we arrive at Freud's preconscious, which is akin to cognitive behavior therapy's unconscious that generates the automatic thoughts and feelings lying at the root of depression, anxiety, and other personality problems as conceived by cognitive psychologists (Beck 1987, Beck and Freeman 1990, Young 1990). Finally we arrive at the classical Freudian unconscious, in which disturbing thoughts are actively kept out of awareness by mechanisms such as repression and splitting. Thus Holmes's integration admits of a number of processes outside of awareness, all of which influence conscious experience and behavior. Yet these influences might at times be confused by theoreticians. It is simply not yet clear which mechanism is required to account for which type of clinical experience.

Holmes (in press) finds a common evolutionary basis for the attachment theory unconscious and the psychoanalytic unconscious. The attachment behavioral unconscious is rooted in the selective advantage to the vulnerable infant of protection through social relationship. Similarly, the Freudian or psychoanalytic unconscious is rooted in vulnerability, though born of the selective advantage of self-deception rather than protection. Citing Nesse (Nesse 1990, Nesse and Lloyd 1992), Holmes argues that self deceit might be adaptive for a hurt child with a stressed rebuffing mother who might gain some minimum comfort if he can persuade her that his demands are not limitless. The child is more likely to achieve this if he deceives himself first, by repressing the full extent of his felt neediness and rage. This is likely to be the case particularly while the child is small and vulnerable and from the point when the biological need of the mother becomes incompatible with that of the child's. (After a certain point the mother's best chance of reproducing her genes rests with further mating and childbirth rather than taking care of her toddler [Trivers 1974].) Oedipal feelings (the wish to have total possession of the mother) are thus best repressed, at least over the first decade of life. Later on, when the individual is stronger, selective advantage might accompany an integrated self with full awareness of its internal states.

Similar arguments might be mounted for the attachment theory behavioral unconscious from an evolutionary perspective. Holmes suggests that the avoidant child might keep near enough to a rejecting parent to remain in touch and therefore achieve some measure of protection but not so close as to get hit and suffer injury. The ambivalent clinging child again senses the inability of the parent to provide secure consistent long-term support, so clings on in the hope of extracting as much nurture as he can in as short a time as possible. Attachment theorists have made similar arguments for the adaptive nature of insecure attachment (Belsky 1999b, Belsky et al. 1991). In addition, Holmes suggests that, as with the offspring of variable foraging condition monkey mothers (Rosenblum and Coplan 1994), insecurely attached children will be handicapped when it comes to handling their emotions as adults.

Holmes places attachment theory at the heart of psychotherapy (Holmes 1993a,b). He profoundly disagrees with Bowlby's off-the-cuff comment that psychotherapy is merely about providing a secure base. He concurs with Bowlby that attachment is a lifelong set of needs, albeit modified according to developmental need. He makes the assumption that coherence, plausibility, and other characteristics of autobiographical competence indicate secure attachment, while autobiographical incompetence indicates insecure attachment (Holmes 1993b). Psychotherapy fits into the developmental context of this behavioral system (Holmes 1997). Attachment figures provide secure-base experiences throughout the life span, but the self is a critical one of these. The work of therapy according to Holmes (1998b) involves both story making and story breaking. The therapist helps the patient at once to tell a story coherently and also to allow for the story to be told in a different and perhaps more healing light. The aim of psychotherapy, dynamic or cognitive, is to enhance consciousness of our own mental life; "narrative competence" is seen by Holmes (2000) as a psychological equivalence of immunological competence. His view is that psychological help (closely linked to secure attachment) depends on a dialectic between story making and story breaking, between the capacity to form narrative and to disperse it in the light of new experience. For example, therapeutic interventions with avoidant patients involve "breaking open" the self-contained narratives with which they protect themselves from feelings of insecure attachment (Holmes 1998a). The patient needs to be able to stand outside his or her own story and see his or her attachment at the level of representation. The therapist needs to have a mind of his own.

Holmes (1998b) defines three prototypical pathologies of narrative capacity: 1) clinging to rigid stories (dismissing), 2) being overwhelmed by unstoried experience (preoccupied), or 3) being unable to find narrative strong enough to contain traumatic pain (unresolved). These pathologies of narrative capacity have profound and distinct effects on the clinical process. The first category has nodal memories, rigid inflexible versions of the patient's story that block the way, that need to be reworked, unpacked, and reassembled. By contrast, work with preoccupied adults involves the therapist finding a way of capturing the confusion and vagaries of overwhelming feelings. Holmes (in press) argues that the sense of self, which evolves coherently if supported within a stable attachment relationship during the first years of life, is made more robust, ready to offer the experience of safety, by psychotherapy. Psychotherapy provides a limited analogue to the mirroring experiences that traditionally psychoanalysts (Kohut 1977, Winnicott 1956) and more recently attachment theorists (Gergely and Watson 1996) have seen as the primary mode of creating a coherent representation of internal states. This outcome is achieved through increased competence in autobiographical memory (Holmes 1996b). The sense of self is the place where the intersubjective phenomena of attachment theory genuinely come into a common frame of reference with the intrapsychic concern of psychoanalysis with a fragile sense of self. The avoidant individual has a split-off self while the ambivalent individual has a deficient sense of self and has to cling to another person in order to know who she or he is. Role reversal or compulsive caring associated with disorganized attachment might have its origins in the extraordinary sensitivity to the mother's moods that occurs when the mirroring relationship is distorted or reversed.

Holmes proposes a specific therapeutic approach, BABI (brief attachment based intervention), which is a relatively well-structured intervention for moderately severe psychological disorders. It is a time-limited approach with a strong emphasis on formulation, uses handouts, suggests homework between sessions, and is integrative in using Rogerian, dynamic, and cognitive behavioral techniques. Its unique features include a focus on attachment considerations (e.g., exploration, loss, assertiveness, and appropriate anger, the internal working model), the modification of attachment styles, and the enhancement of reflexive function. It is a promising integrative therapy that is as yet untested.

Holmes's contribution to an integration of psychoanalysis and attachment theory has been multifaceted. His central contribution is linking a model of psychological change in all forms of the "talking cure" to attachment theory ideas via the notion of coherence and biography. The model also generated a particular therapeutic approach with techniques focused on autobiographical competence, which Holmes and colleagues are in the process of manualizing. A second thread in Holmes's project is the strengthening of both the attachment and the psychoanalytic approach by creating links to advances in biological psychiatry. The third aspect of his work concerns an evolving developmental model that draws on both psychoanalytic and attachment theory ideas. In all these respects, Holmes's contribution stands alone as a thoroughly coherent attempt to build a new school of psychoanalytic psychotherapy based on attachment theory.

ARIETTA SLADE

Arietta Slade has been one of the major figures in North America linking clinical practice of psychoanalytic therapy and attachment research (see Slade 1999a for an outstanding review of the work of clinical application of attachment theory). She points out that, to Bowlby's great surprise and disappointment, clinicians were slow to take an interest in attachment theory as a tool for facilitating or supporting clinical work (Bowlby 1988). Slade's own view is not that attachment theory dictates or gives rise to a particular psychotherapeutic approach but rather that an understanding of the nature and dynamics of attachment informs rather than defines intervention and clinical thinking (Slade 1996). Attachment theory offers a broad and far-reaching view of human functioning that has the potential to change the way a clinician thinks about and responds to patients, the way he or she understands the therapeutic relationship and interventions.

Slade drew attention to the clinical implication of attachment theory's focus on narrative (Slade 1996, 1999b, in press). She demonstrates that listening for features such as changes in voice, lapses, irrelevances, breakdowns in meaning, and for more subtle ongoing disruptions and fluctuations of the structure and the organization of patient discourse in the attachment and clinical contexts are broadly the same. The therapist, by focusing on the failures of the narrative, is alert to issues and topics where the patient is unable to mentalize an experience and thus where therapeutic intervention may be helpful and even welcome. In fact this stance is the one the therapist normally uses to identify the ways the patient chooses to defend himself or herself against the intrusion of unacceptable feelings or thoughts. Slade (in press) claims that such gaps in the narrative also offer hints about the nature of the experience of the patient as a child, which might have been causal in generating the deficits and maladaptations with which the patient presents. Thus, Slade sees an interaction between attachment theory and clinical practice at the most fundamental levels of technique. The therapist follows the material with an image of an infant and caregiver, not at the level of memories or fantasies but rather at the level of the insights offered by considering the gaps in the patient's narration. These gaps are evocative of the mechanisms the patient uses to regulate affect and to bring together a comprehensive narrative concerning the experience of the self.

Slade's approach to memories in therapy follows the suggestions of Mary Main quite closely. The capacity to provide appropriate memories to support the generalizations included in the narrative might be critical in substantiating the generalizations, regardless of the accuracy of the memory recalled at that moment. Listening to autobiographical narratives, the therapist must become attuned to the interfacing of general claims (the semantic system) and actual episodes that fit more or less well with these generalizations—when these different levels or layers of the internal working model are poorly integrated the therapist is alerted to the presence of defenses and distortions in the representational system, ostensibly created by unfavorable experiences with the caregiver. Slade (in press) points to the distortions of language that reflect the child's efforts to maintain his connection to the caregiver, even if this requires fragmenting his feelings and knowledge. This way of hearing language has important implications: 1) it implies that experiences of seeking comfort and care constitute nodal, organizing events in early development. The consideration of these events as conveyed in language in the analytic context may be a critical part of the analytic work for some patients; 2) listening at the level of the structure of discourse influences the way the analyst imagines the patient's earliest experience and thinks about how the experience has impacted on the patient; and 3) it might also enhance the analyst's quality of empathy by enabling them to imagine the patient's experience in suboptimal caregiving situations more concretely.

Slade (1999a) recommends using the Main and Goldwyn classification system alongside other types of diagnostic approaches to help the therapist come to an understanding of the patient's experience. For example, for avoidant-dismissing individuals the free expression of (particularly negative) affect is minimal and the structures for regulating, containing, and suppressing affect are highly organized and rigid. Similarly, affects, memories, and cognitions that play a part in the attachment behavior system are probably overregulated. Comparable diagnostic information would be available from identifying resistant-preoccupation in the patient. Slade has more difficulty in painting a coherent clinical picture of the patient whose attachment is unresolved-disorganized. She suggests that this picture resembles most closely the resistant-preoccupied pattern, typified by unusually high levels of incoherence and disorganization. But the lack of consistency within this heterogeneous category is troubling for attachment theory.

Slade (1999a) is astute in identifying the superficial incompatibility in frames of reference between the psychoanalytic interest in developmental process on the one hand and the attachment theorist's concern with mutually exclusive categorization on the other. In Slade's view this is perhaps the key reason for the psychoanalytic clinician's lack of interest in attachment theory-based clinical approaches—clinicians simply cannot see patients staying stable in categories across sessions. She points out the shortsightedness of this stance: attachment categories tell a story about the individual, about how experiences have shaped the pattern of affect regulation of the individual, about what experiences are in general allowed into consciousness, and to what degree that individual has been able to make meaning of his or her primary relationship.

Using Holmes's characterization of narrative pathologies (see above), Slade considers technical implications of each of the primary insecure patterns. Dismissing patients constrict their emotional experience. Ways need to be found in therapy for allowing affects into experience and into consciousness (i.e., story breaking). The therapist must pay attention to finding ways into the patient's affective experience and memory. Preoccupied patients' treatment revolves around the slow creation of structures for the modulation of affect. They are so driven by feelings that focus and inner purpose are hard to identify, and the characteristic pattern is one often regarded in the past as dominated by primary processes. Slade is most helpful in describing the challenges of and suggesting techniques for dealing with unresolved, disorganized individuals. Much of the affect underlying the lack of resolution of trauma or loss has been dissociated with these patients and profoundly, therefore substantially, distorted. There is often a slow and painstaking recreation of what might have happened that might involve further terror and dissociation. Countertransference becomes a major issue, as the therapist's mind is taken over by the patient's disorganized self-structure. Here the secure attachment of the therapist, the availability of a relatively robust sense of self, might be particularly important. The investigation by Dozier and colleagues (1994), which demonstrates that secure therapists were more able than insecure therapists to hear and respond to the dependency needs of their dismissing patients and were thus less vulnerable to intense countertransference, is consistent with this view. Insecure therapists might become entangled with such patients, responding to their obvious needs rather than their underlying needs.

Finally, Slade (1999b, in press) considers the relevance of attachment theory and research for clinical work with children. Two issues are highlighted. First, for the child, attachment is not the past but the current and the real context of treatment, defined by his or her own past experience and shaped by the parents' history of attachment experiences. It is important to note that especially with children, but perhaps with adults too, we work with the past but also with what the child carries forward from the present into the future. Clearly, this touches on the longstanding controversy concerning the relative importance of the therapist as a real or alternative object for the child, with all the complexities of the controversial corrective emotional experience (Alexander and French 1946). Second, Slade highlights her own work concerning the parent's mental representation of the child, the extent to which this is determined by her own attachment experiences, and the extent to which these are modifiable in the course of therapeutic work with the family. The conception of a link between the mother's capacity to represent and recognize her child and the child's recognition of himself as a thinking and feeling person is at the heart of the clinical work she elaborates.

In summary, Arietta Slade's contribution has been to bring attachment theory to the practicing clinician as a coherent set of helpful propositions to improve the day-to-day work of diagnosis and clinical practice. Unlike Holmes, Slade does not introduce a new integrated theoretical model. Rather her approach is that of the practitioner, identifying and elaborating those aspects of attachment theory that are most likely to be helpful for the psychoanalytic psychotherapist.

ALICIA LIEBERMAN

Infant–parent psychotherapy evolved in an effort to treat disturbances in infant–parent relationships in the first three years of life. Fraiberg (1980) established this approach with a simple and coherent rationale: disturbances between the infant and the parent in the first three years of life are manifestations in the present of unresolved conflicts that one or more of the babies' parents have with important figures in their own childhood. The paradigmatic writing is Selma Fraiberg's paper, "Ghost in the Nursery," where she writes: "In treatment, we examine with the parents the past and the present in order to free them and their baby from old 'ghosts' that have invaded the nursery, and then we must make meaningful links between the past and the present through interpretations that will lead to insight. . . . We move back and forth, between present and past, parent and baby, but we always return to the baby" (Fraiberg et al. 1975, p. 61). The link between attachment theory and the work of psychoanalytic infant–

parent psychotherapy has been only recently but powerfully forged by Alicia Lieberman (Lieberman 1991).

The central ingredient of this approach to psychotherapy is the presence of the baby in the sessions. The recognition that parental reporting is no substitute for direct observation of interaction was Fraiberg's essential innovation, but also an epistemic bridge to the direct observational methodology of attachment theory. The present is a bridge to the past—Fraiberg's simple aphorism is loaded with implications, particularly the reminder of the crippling hold that a sad, frightening and deprived childhood might have on adult experience. While Fraiberg's suggestion has the virtue of simplicity, it was Alicia Lieberman who fully recognized the resistances infant–parent therapists are likely to encounter in a simple direct approach to trying to discover obstacles to good-enough care in the mother's past (Lieberman and Pawl 1993, Pawl and Lieberman 1997). Her clinical approach is to focus on the feeling states involving salient current relationships and exploring how these feeling states may also be present in relation to the baby (a vivid clinical example is provided in Silverman et al. 1997).

In addition to insight-oriented interventions, Selma Fraiberg (1980) described three other therapeutic modalities in infant–mother psychotherapy. These were: brief crisis intervention, developmental guidance, and supportive treatment. Additionally, across therapeutic modalities concrete assistance with problems of living (e.g., a ride to a doctor, advocating for improved housing) can strengthen the therapeutic alliance. The combination and integration of these elements actually fits far better within an attachment theory framework than the psychoanalytic framework from which the components originate (Lieberman and Zeanah 1999). An example of this is the role of the infant as a transferential object. Fraiberg originally suggested that the baby was the appropriate focus of the transference. In the context of attachment theory this would be seen as the best opportunity for the observation of the mother's IWM of attachment relationship. The mother most commonly identifies with the baby and plays out residues of her own experience with her mother in the role of caregiver. The immediacy of the experience arises through the simultaneous activation of the attachment and caregiving systems prompted by the birth of her child.

The mutative factors of mother–infant psychotherapy are also better explained in the context of attachment theory than that of classical psychoanalysis. The internal working model for caregiving is altered in many of these cases by the therapist's positive regard, attentiveness to the parents' need, and empathic responsiveness. The patients learn ways of relating characterized by mutuality and caring rather than the more readily available models based on anger and fear (Lieberman and Pawl 1993). Negative expectations about how to be with an other are corrected or at least expectations are expanded to include nonhostile interchanges, presumably biologically primed in any case in the mother's mind by the arrival of the child and the activation of the caregiving system (Lieberman 1991). Thus the concept of an internal working model permeates clinical practice. Within the classical formulation intergenerational transmission is accounted for as the enactment of unresolved conflict with the parent—the unconscious impulses are displaced or projected from their original object to the current transference object represented by the infant (Fraiberg et al. 1975). Lieberman's position would be that internalized early experiences provide a structural framework that serves to sort out, select, and encode the experience of caring for an infant (Lieberman and Zeanah 1999).

As well as providing assistance in understanding the parents' experience, the IWM concept is also used in the understanding of the infant's putative internal experience. Lieberman and her colleagues (Lieberman and Pawl 1993, Lieberman and Zeanah 1999) conceive of the infant's behavior in terms of defensive operations along the lines outlined by Ainsworth and colleagues (1978). Interestingly, the attachment classification of defensive behaviors are almost identical to the dramatic mechanisms of self-protection in the infants that Fraiberg observed in a clinic setting (Fraiberg 1982). In fact, with the benefit of hindsight, one would guess that Fraiberg's observations of infantile defenses might have been far less organized and coherent pieces of behavior than they appear from her narrative descriptions. Current experience with clinic samples is that disorganized patterns of defensive behavior would be expected to predominate in these infants (Lyons-Ruth et al. 1991, 1999). Although Fraiberg mentions Ainsworth in her paper, it seems she does this more to distance or to distinguish her ideas from those of the attachment theorist than to suggest an integration. Yet the psychoanalytic theory she is committed to (modern ego psychology) has no model for the psychic structure of infancy that could readily accommodate infantile defenses. Only object relations theories, particularly Kleinian developmental theory, equip the infant with sufficient mental structures to consider these as mechanisms of defense.

Alicia Lieberman has been a charismatic leader of the infant–mother psychotherapy movement. Attachment theory enabled her and her colleagues to integrate a range of interventions into their therapeutic model. Her work is in no sense limited to psychoanalytic interventions. Indeed it could be argued that the most potent parts of her treatment approach have more to do with social work than with psychotherapy. Yet within the framework of attachment theory these "nonanalytic" interventions sit quite comfortably alongside the interpretive work, focusing on here-and-now concerns with the infant and emotional reactions triggered by other life circumstances.

12

Summary: What Do Psychoanalytic Theories and Attachment Theory Have in Common?

As psychoanalytic theory cannot, at its current stage of evolution, be reduced to a singular coherent set of propositions, in this volume we have been forced to consider points of contact between attachment theory and particular traditions of psychoanalytic thought. Here we summarize the points of contact between the two approaches in more general terms, offering illustrative arguments to put to rest the prevailing view of incompatibility between these two frames of reference.

PERSONALITY DEVELOPMENT IS BEST STUDIED IN RELATION TO THE CHILD'S SOCIAL ENVIRONMENT

As we have seen, Freud and Bowlby both began their theoretical contributions with concern about the psychological consequences of early deprivation (Bowlby 1944, Freud 1954). Freud's celebrated turning away from the seduction hypothesis (Masson 1984) did not compromise his position on the pathogenesis of childhood trauma (Freud 1917, 1931, 1939). Conversely, modern psychoanalytic readers might criticize Bowlby for the therapeutic realism of his approach, and his emphasis on the therapeutic qualities of cathartic recollections of traumatic events (Bowlby 1977). However, Bowlby's attention to the representation of experience (Bowlby 1980a) was not a return to the naïve realism of Freud's early theories. It represents an elaboration of the fourth phase of Freud's theory, the structural model (Freud 1923). Freud, like Bowlby, recognized that anxiety was a biologically determined epiphenomenal experience linked to the perception of both external and internal dangers (Freud 1926b), the psychological template for which was loss of the object. The move toward recognizing that adaptation to the external world had to be an essential component of the psychoanalytic account, and that such an account necessitated a reorganization of the theory in terms of a quasi-cognitive structure (Schafer 1983) is the essential common background for both ego psychological and attachment theory elaborations of the classical psychoanalytical model.

Bowlby was not the first psychoanalyst to focus on interpersonal rather than intrapsychic factors in pathogenesis. The Hungarian psychoanalyst Ferenczi (1933) pointed to the potentially traumatic nature of the adult's failure to understand meanings in the child's psychological world, thus anticipating risks associated with lack of sensitivity on the part of the child's primary objects. We have seen that emphasis on the quality of caregiving has featured in most of the dominant psychoanalytic traditions since Ferenczi, playing a particularly dominant role in the work of Spitz (1945, 1965), Erickson (1950, 1959), Winnicott (1962a), and Anna Freud (1941–1945, 1955). The common perception that there is an underlying epistemic difference in the ways that psychoanalysts and attachment theorists conceptualize the influence of the social environment glosses over the fact that these views have much in common. There are four key points of epistemological overlap.

Actual versus Psychic Reality

It is a fundamental tenet of both theories that social perception and social experience are distorted by expectations, both conscious and unconscious. In the structural model Freud (1923) described the ego's capacity to create defenses that organize characterological and symptomatic constructions as part of the developmental process. This idea became a cornerstone of Bowlby's trilogy, particularly the last volume (Bowlby 1980a). Anna Freud's (1936) description of common mechanisms of defense can be readily restated in terms of mental representation, or rather its typical distortions (Sandler 1987a, Sandler and Rosenblatt 1962). Crittenden's (1990) work has made it possible to understand behaviors typical of avoidant and resistant attachment patterns in terms of the language of the defensive behaviors of infancy (Fraiberg 1982). More recently, we have attempted to demonstrate that transgenerational consistencies in attachment classification may be understood as internalization of the caregiver's defenses mobilized by the infant's distress (Fonagy et al. 1995a). Both modern attachment theory and modern psychoanalysis have as their fundamental epistemic aim the description of the internal mechanisms responsible for the discrepancy between actual and psychic reality.

Emphasis on Early Life

It is easy to show that both psychoanalysts and attachment theorists privilege the first years of life in their consideration of the relationship between social environment and personality development. Within psychoanalysis, this bias took some years to fully emerge and did so more or less contemporaneously with the development of Bowlby's ideas. For some time Melanie Klein's attempts to consider the first year of life as setting a template for subsequent phases of personality development (Klein 1935) were treated with skepticism by psychoanalytic developmentalists, particularly because of the level of cognitive sophistication she appeared to be willing to attribute to the infant in the first year of life (Yorke 1971). However, more sophisticated methods of observations of infant behavior revealed that the human infant possesses relatively complex mental capacities, even at birth, in some cases exceeding what was presupposed by Kleinian theory (Gergely 1991). Margaret Mahler is commonly credited with bringing observational methods to bear on the earliest phases of development. Her systematic observational studies, however, were based on children in the second half of the first year of life (Gergely 2000). In fact much of the later criticism of Mahler's theories (e.g., Klein 1981, Stern 1985) focuses upon the fact that her characterizations of the earliest phases of the psychological birth of the infant are still to some extent based on retrospective pathomorphic explanations, even though intensive and careful observation of infants in the first three years of life was a powerful source of inspiration for these. The emergence of self psychology as an alternative psychoanalytic framework (Kohut 1971) has contributed further to placing the earliest phases of development in the center of psychoanalytic theoretical interest. As concern with the real as opposed to the reconstructed infant grew within psychoanalysis, so psychoanalytic interest in attachment theory increased (e.g., Lichtenberg 1995).

Maternal Sensitivity and Mirroring

Beyond this converging interest in the early stages of development, there is a more specific common focus on maternal sensitivity as a causal factor in determining the quality of object relationships and, therefore, psychic development. However, attachment theory and psychoanalytic theories of development conceptualize the construct of maternal sensitivity in significantly different ways. Attachment theory describes sensitivity in a variety of ways that all involve behavior or personality characteristics of the caregiver (e.g., global ratings of responsiveness, accuracy of individual responses, personality traits of the caregiver, the quality of mental representation of the infant in the caregiver's mind [De Wolff and van Ijzendoorn 1997]). In psychoanalytic formulations sensitivity tends to be considered in terms of its consequences, its organizing impact on the child's self-development. There is also considerable heterogeneity amongst these conceptualizations. The Kleinian formulation of sensitive caregiving would be of a parent capable of absorbing and retransmitting the infant's psychological experience in a "metabolised" form (Bion 1967). The infant can accept and reinternalize what had been projected and transformed, thus creating a representation of these internal moments of interaction with the caretaker that it can tolerate. In time, Bion suggested, infants internalize the function of transformation and will acquire the capacity to regulate their own negative affective states. The nonverbal nature of this process implies that physical proximity of the caregiver is essential. Thus Bion's ideas may provide us with an alternative perspective of the sociobiological root of the infant's need for proximity to the psychological caregiver, the adult mind.

In a slightly different vein, Winnicott (1956) proposed that when the baby looks at the mother who is reflecting the baby's state, what he apprehends in the mother's expression is his own self-state. Thus, the mother's mirroring function is seen as essential for the establishment of the baby's self-representation. In Kohut's work (1971, 1977), probably as a consequence of his clinical interest in narcissism, the empathy concept was closely tied to considerations of self-evaluation (self-esteem). The psychoanalyst whose formulation most closely matches attachment theory concerns with caregiver behavior was Eric Erikson (1950). Erikson (1964), for example, conceived of basic trust as arising out of "the experience of the caretaking person as a *coherent* being, who reciprocates one's physical and emotional needs and therefore deserves to be endowed with trust, and whose face is recognised as it recognises" (p. 117).

There is a further indication that psychoanalytic concepts of sensitivity and those of attachment theorists pertain to related phenomena. Both attachment theorists and psychoanalysts have come to the conclusion that the ideal level of caregiver sensitivity from the point of view of infant development is moderate rather than perfect, both in terms of intensity and responsibility for the infant's state. Certainly, this idea is at the heart of Winnicott's notion of "good enough" parenting (Winnicott 1962a), Kohut's model of transmuting internalization (Kohut and Wolf 1978), and, most explicitly, in Erikson's writings. In *Childhood and Society* he suggests: "A certain ratio between the positive and the negative, which if the balance is towards the positive, will help him to meet later crises with a better chance of unimpaired development" (Erikson 1950, p. 61n). Erikson saw nonintrusiveness of the parent (Malatesta et al. 1986) as the mother not trying to control the interaction too much. Interactional synchrony (Isabella and Belsky 1991) is probably equivalent to Erikson's description of "reciprocity or mutual regulation." There is a shared common assumption that a well-regulated relationship with the caregiver leads to an autonomous, robust sense of self. Thus, while attachment theory and psychoanalytic formulations certainly differ in terms of their respective emphasis on caregiver behavior versus infant experience, in neither domain has a definitive formulation as yet emerged. We will suggest later that this critical facet of social development for both theories may provide an important area of cross-fertilization.

The Motivation for Forming Relationships

Contrary to Bowlby's prejudiced claims, modern psychoanalysis shares the fundamental assumption of attachment theory that the infant–caregiver relationship is not based on physical need but rather on some kind of independent autonomous need for a relationship. Bowlby's motivation to assert divergence from psychoanalysis on this point (Bowlby 1958) may have in part been rhetorical. As with any new theory, new ideas are brought into sharpest relief by asserting a dichotomy, even if this represents an oversimplification. More importantly, a lack of clarity arises out of overwhelming heterogeneity in psychoanalytic formulations on this point. Arnold Modell (1975), for example, suggested the existence of object relations instincts characterized by interaction processes rather than discharge. In the work of the British object relations school, the need for relationships is considered as a constitutional predisposition, which is described variously as "primary love" (Balint 1952), "object seeking" (Fairbairn 1952a), "ego relatedness" (Winnicott 1965b), or just "personal relations" (Guntrip 1961). In certain places Bowlby was explicit in his acknowledgment of these analysts, but felt he went beyond them by establishing a firm biological and evolutionary basis for their constructs.

Even within the British school, however, there is ambiguity in the treatment of the relationship construct. While for Balint and Winnicott the construct is unequivocally primary, for Fairbairn and Guntrip it is described as a need secondary to a primal need for psychic organization. This latter view is also implicit in Kernberg's model, which suggests that the self evolves as part of a relationship (Kernberg 1976a,b), as a product of internalization (introjection, identification, and ego identity). Yet other psychoanalytic writers appear to assume that the need for relationships arises as a defense against the vicissitudes of the child's internal world. We have already seen how the concept of proximity seeking may be derived from Bion's notion of containment (Bion 1967). Eric Erikson's closeness to the drive theory tradition may have also led him to infer that attachment played a secondary role, either facilitating identity development or being its by-product; it has the status of an intermediary link in the process of development towards individuation (Erikson 1968). In summary, modern psychoanalysis does not differ from attachment theory in the sense that it overlooks the child's need for a relationship. There are, however, too many competing formulations as to the nature and origin of this need. Thus, the relevance of a singular and coherent account drawn from attachment theory should be evident. This kind of argument is beyond the scope of this work.

THE COGNITIVE UNDERPINNINGS OF EMOTIONAL DEVELOPMENT

A major strength of attachment theory is the relative clarity with which Bowlby describes the representational system that mediates and ensures the continuity of interpersonal behavior (Bowlby 1969). Bowlby's model has been elaborated and developed by two pioneers in the field: Inge Bretherton (Bretherton 1987) and Mary Main (Main et al. 1985a). Notwithstanding these advances, there are many critics of the internal working models concept, particularly from amongst developmental psychologists (e.g., Dunn 1996). At the heart of such critiques is the lack of specificity of Bowlby's model. How do expectations concerning the likely response of a caregiver to the infant's distress develop into generalized templates for social interaction? Mary Main's work on adults' discourse concerning early relationships demonstrated suggestive links between infant behavior in the strange situation and adult conversational styles, manner of speech rather than narrative content (Main and Goldwyn, in preparation). Thus attachment theory and research have increasingly focused on procedural as opposed to episodic or semantic memory systems (Schachter 1992) in understanding the continuity of social behavior from infancy to adulthood. A case could be made that a similar family of ideas is emerging in the field of psychoanalysis. There are several issues of relevance.

The Representation of Relationships

Originating in the work of Edith Jacobson (1954b), it is now generally accepted that mental representations of relationships of self and object are key determinants of interpersonal behavior. She introduced the concept of *representation* to stress that these referred to the experiential impact of internal and external worlds and were subject to distortion and modification irrespective of physical reality. A number of theorists have elaborated these notions in postulating that roles are encoded for both subject and objects. For example, Sandler (1976a, 1987c) elaborated a model of the two-person interaction when the direct influence of one on the other is accounted for by the evocation of particular roles in the mind of the person who is being influenced. The behavior of the influencing person is seen as critical in eliciting a complementary response from the participant. Sandler suggests that in this way infantile patterns of relationships may be actualized or enacted in adult relationships. Daniel Stern (1994) and his co-workers in the Boston Psychoanalytic Institute (e.g., Morgan 1998, Sander, in press, Stern 1998, Tronick 1998) have gone a step further in developing the idea that therapeutic change occurs not as a consequence of insight or reflection on episodic memory but as a consequence of experiences that change procedural (implicit) memory. Stern discusses the schemata of ways-of-being-with as an emergent property of the nervous system that naturally aggregate the invariant aspects of interpersonal experience. He suggests (Stern 1998) that these are the building blocks of internal working models and, while this remains to be demonstrated, his work suggests a route whereby the micro-experiences of infant–mother interaction could become aggregated into enduring structures and subserve stable patterns of behavior.

The Relationship Context of Cognitive Development

Both attachment theory and psychoanalytic theory assume that early relationships provide the context within which certain critical psychological functions are acquired and developed. Alan Sroufe (1990) offered an imaginative framework whereby early interaction patterns between infant and caregiver were thought to translate into individual styles for the regulation of affect, which in their turn determined patterns of interaction. Affect regulation is seen as internalized in the course of infant–caregiver interaction. Bretherton (1979) and Main (1991) both claim that the development of symbolic function is crucially dependent on the harmony of mother–infant interaction. These workers suggest that secure attachment frees attentional resources necessary for the full development of symbolic cognitive capacities.

The notion that psychic functions may be internalized from primary object relationships is present in the writings of a number of psychoanalytic authors. Rene Spitz (1945), in particular, saw the child's human partner as quickening the development of his innate abilities and mediating all perception, behavior, and knowledge. Spitz made specific reference to the role of mother–infant interaction in the development of self-regulation (see also Greenacre 1952, Spitz 1959). Bion's (1959, 1962a) model of containment also assumes that the infant internalizes the function of transformation exercised by the caregiver, and through this acquires the capacity to contain or regulate his own negative affective states. Winnicott (1953) makes a strong claim concerning the evolution of symbolic function in the "transitional space" between infant and caregiver. Winnicott bases this assertion on an assumption that three conditions pertain: 1) a sense of safety associated with experiencing the inner world; 2) an opportunity for the infant deliberately to limit concern with external events; and 3) an opportunity to generate spontaneous creative gestures. These parameters may be considered analogous to Bowlby's (1969) secure base notion. Both see the evolution of cognitive structure as a function of infant–mother interaction.

Mentalization in Attachment Theory and Psychoanalysis

Mentalization is a specific symbolic function that is central to both psychoanalytic and attachment theory and that emerged concurrently in psychoanalytic and attachment theory thinking. Developmentalists over the past ten years have drawn our attention to the universal and remarkable capacity of young children to interpret the behavior of themselves, as well as others, in terms of putative mental states (e.g., Morton and Frith 1995). Reflective function enables children to conceive of others' beliefs, feelings, attitudes, desires, hopes, knowledge, imagination, pretense, plans, and so on. At the same time as making others' behavior meaningful and predictable, they are also able flexibly to activate from multiple sets of self–other representations the one most appropriate in a particular interpersonal context. Exploring the meaning of actions of others is crucially linked to the child's ability to label and find meaningful his or her own experience. This ability may make a critical contribution to affect regulation, impulse control, self-monitoring, and the experience of self-agency (Fonagy and Target 1997).

Reflective function is closely linked to attachment. The frequency of both prospective mothers' and fathers' references to mental states in their accounts of their own childhood attachment experiences powerfully predict the likelihood of their children being securely attached to them (Fonagy et al. 1991a). If secure attachment is conceived of as the acquisition of procedures (implicit memories) for the regulation of aversive states of arousal (Carlsson and Sroufe 1995, Cassidy 1994, Sroufe 1996), it may be argued that such information is most likely to be consistently acquired and coherently represented when the child's acute affective state is accurately, but not overwhelmingly, reflected back to the child. Secure attachment may thus have a great deal in common with successful containment (Bion 1962a). What is critical is the mother's capacity mentally to contain the baby and respond, in terms of physical care, in a manner that shows awareness of the child's mental state yet reflect coping (mirroring distress while communicating an incompatible affect [Fonagy et al. 1995b]). If secure attachment is the product of successful containment, insecure attachment may be seen as the infant's identification with the caregiver's defensive behavior. A dismissing caregiver may fail to mirror the child's distress, while a preoccupied caregiver may represent the infant's state with excessive clarity. In either case, the opportunity for the child to internalize a representation of his mental state is lost. Proximity to the caregiver is in this case maintained at the cost of a compromise to reflective function. Bowlby (1969) recognized the significance of the developmental step entailed in the emergence of "the child's capacity both to conceive of his mother as having her own goals and interests separate from his own and to take them into account" (p. 368). A number of empirical findings support the relationship of attachment security and reflective function. Attachment security is a good predictor of metacognitive capacity in the domains of memory, comprehension, and communication (Moss et al. 1995). Attachment security with mother has been found to be a good predictor of belief-desire reasoning in 3½- to 6-year-old children in both cross-sectional (Fonagy et al. 1997a) and longitudinal studies (Fonagy 1997, Meins et al. 1998). On the basis of such findings, we have argued that the child's acquisition of reflective function, the tendency to incorporate mental state attributions into internal working models of self–other relationships, depends on the opportunities that he had in early life to observe and explore the mind of his primary caregiver. The parent of the secure child engages in behaviors such as pretend play, which almost obliges the child to contemplate the existence of mental states.

The caregiver's understanding of the child's mind encourages secure attachment; the caregiver's accurate reading of the child's mental state, moderated by indications that the adult has coped with the child's distress, underpins the symbolization of the internal state, which in turn leads to superior affect regulation (Gergely and Watson 1996). Secure attachment provides a relatively firm base for the acquisition of a full understanding of minds. The secure infant feels safe in thinking about the mental state of the caregiver. By contrast, the avoidant child shuns the mental state of the other, while the resistant child focuses on its own state of distress to the exclusion of intersubjective exchanges. Disorganized infants may represent a separate category; hypervigilant to the caregiver's behavior, they may appear to be acutely sensitive to the caregiver's mental state yet fail to generalize this to their own mental state (self-organization), which remains disregulated and incoherent.

Is this model, derived from attachment theory, any different from traditional psychoanalytic accounts? We would argue "no" on a number of grounds: 1) the notion of reflective function or mentalization is already present in Freud's (1911) notion of *Bindung*, or linking. *Bindung* refers to the qualitative change from the physical (immediate) to the psychological (associative) quality of linking; 2) Melanie Klein (1945), in describing the depressive position, stressed that it necessarily entailed the recognition of hurt and suffering in the other, that is, the awareness of mental states. Although her emphasis is upon individual recognition of destructive wish, clearly this cannot arise without awareness of intentionality in both self and other; 3) we have already touched on Bion's (1962a, 1962b) description of containment. He delineates the transformation ("alpha function") of internal events experienced as concrete ("beta elements") into tolerable, thinkable experiences; 4) Winnicott (1962a) was perhaps closest to these ideas from attachment theory in recognizing the importance of the caregiver's *psychological* understanding of the infant in the emergence of the true self, and in acknowledging the dialectical aspect of this relationship. The psychological self develops through perception of oneself in another person's mind as thinking and feeling. Parents who cannot reflect with understanding on their child's inner experience and respond accordingly deprive the child of a core psychological structure that he or she needs to build a viable sense of self; 5) independently, French psycho-analysts developed a notion of mentalization, largely rooted in the eco-nomic point of view. Marty (1968) considered mentalization to be a protective buffer in the system preconscious, with a capacity to prevent progressive disorganization. He saw mentalization as the function that linked drive excitations and internal representations and thereby cre-ated flexibility (both "fluidity" and "constancy") (Marty 1990, 1991). Thus, according to Marty, mentalization ensures freedom in the use of associations as well as permanence and stability, a description strikingly similar to Bowlby's account of the capacities of the securely attached child; 6) another French psychoanalyst, Pierre Luquet (1981, 1988), discussed the development of different forms of thinking and the reor-ganization of inner experience alongside this development. In his chap-ter on the theory of language (Luquet 1987) he distinguished primary mentalization (which is really the absence of mentalization or reflective capacity) from secondary (symbolic) mentalization. While this form of mentalization was still seen as closely connected to sensory data and pri-mary unconscious fantasy, it was also seen as representative of these pro-cesses and observable in dreams, art, and play (see also Bucci 1997). His third level was verbal thought, which he considered the most dis-tant from bodily processes. Similar distinctions have been proposed by Green (1975), Segal (1957), McDougall (1978), and more recently in the United States by Frosch (1995), Busch (1995), and Auerbach (1993, Auerbach and Blatt 1996).

Thus the notion of an intersubjectively acquired abstract reflex-ive implicit awareness of mental states, to be distinguished from intro-spection (Bolton and Hill 1996), has always been at the core of many psychoanalytic formulations of self development. The fruitful integra-tion of this classical idea with the relationship constructs of attachment theory serves to illustrate the potential of bringing psychoanalytic ideas to bear on attachment theory and, perhaps, vice versa.

Mentalization and the Complex Relations between Actual and Psychic Reality

We have in past papers attempted to draw together clinical and research evidence to show that a normal awareness of the relationship between internal and external reality is not universal, but rather a developmental achievement (Fonagy and Target 1996, Target and Fonagy 1996). It is the consequence of the successful integration of two distinct modes of differentiating internal from external in the young child intricately tied to the earliest relationships. We see development as normally moving from an experience of psychic reality in which mental states are not related to as representations, to an increasingly complex view of the internal world, which has as its hallmark the capacity to mentalize: to assume thoughts and feelings in others and in oneself, and to recognize these connected to outer reality (but only loosely). Initially, the child's experience of the mind is as if it were a recording device, with exact correspondence between internal state and external reality. We use the term *psychic equivalence* to denote this mode of functioning, to emphasize that, for the young child, mental events are equivalent in terms of power, causality, and implications, to events in the physical world.[1] Equating internal and external is inevitably a two-way process. Not only will the small child feel compelled to equate appearance with reality (how it seems is how it is), but also thoughts and feelings, distorted by fantasy, will be projected onto external reality in a manner unmodulated by awareness that the experience of the external world might be distorted in this way.

---

1. The term *psychic equivalence* may, with hindsight, be unfortunate in the light of Segal's concept of the "symbolic equation," which may appear to overlap with the formulation proposed here and in the previous papers. Our understanding of Segal's important concept entails the relationship of signified and signifier, rather than internal and external. Segal discusses confusions often observed in psychotic states, where the symbolic character of a representation is lost and there is an equation between the symbol and the thing it represents. Thus, playing the violin no longer carries a symbolic meaning of masturbation, it becomes that activity. Our concept of psychic equivalence is more restricted. We are concerned with the quality of states of mind, and here the term *equivalence* does not denote an equation of the symbolic vehicle with the idea represented, but rather the assumption that what is thought about has to be actual. This is not unidirectional, as the child also assumes, in an omnipotent way, that everything that is actual is known to him. There is, however, an area of overlap between Segal's and our descriptions that might be helpfully clarified. Take, for example, a 3-year-old who cannot go to sleep because a man's dressing gown hanging behind his bedroom door terrifies him. He says that he knows it is only a dressing gown, but when he starts going to sleep it turns into a bad man who is going to steal him from his bed in the night. Evidently, the dressing gown may be considered as symbolically equated with the frightening man, and the child reacts as though they were the same.

Perhaps because it can be terrifying for thoughts and feelings to be experienced as concretely real, the small child develops an alternative way of construing mental states. In *pretend mode*, the child experiences feelings and ideas as totally representational, or symbolic, as having no implication for the world outside. Even though the 2-year-old knows that when he pretends to be a policeman he does not become one, this is not because he understands that he is being a pretend policeman, but rather because the form of psychic reality that allows him to pretend requires strict separation from external reality (Gopnik and Slaughter 1991). His play can then form no bridge between inner and outer reality. Only gradually, and through safe closeness to another person who can simultaneously hold together the child's pretend and serious perspectives, does the integration of these two modes give rise to a psychic reality in which feelings and ideas are known as internal, yet related to what is outside (Dunn 1996).

The Background of Security and a Theory of Self-Development

We have suggested that the emergence of mentalizing is deeply embedded in the child's primary object relationships, first in the mirroring relationship with the caregiver. This is conceived somewhat differently from the traditional psychoanalytic concepts of mirroring proposed by Kohut (1977), Bion (1962a), and Winnicott (1956). It is much more akin to the model recently described by Gergely and Watson (1996). We suggest that the infant only gradually realizes that he has feelings and thoughts, and slowly becomes able to distinguish these. This happens mainly through learning that his internal experiences are meaningfully related to by the parent, through her expressions and other responses. These habitual reactions to his emotional expressions focus the infant's attention on his internal experiences, giving them a shape so that they become meaningful and increasingly manageable. Primary representations of experience are organized into secondary representations of these states of mind and body (Fonagy and Target 1997). The experience of affect is the bud from which eventually mentalization can grow, but only in the context of at least one continuing, safe attachment relationship. The parent who cannot think about the child's mental experience deprives him of the basis for a viable sense of himself (Fonagy and Target 1995a). This is a familiar idea in psychoanalysis. Bion (1962a) described how, for the infant, repeated internalization of the mother's processed image of his thoughts and feelings provides containment; Joyce McDougall (1989) has said "a nursling, through its cries, bodily gestures and somato-psychic reactions to stress, gives nonverbal communications that only a mother is able to interpret. She functions, in this respect, as her baby's thinking system" (p. 169). This "adequate" response not only involves interpreting the baby's physical expressions, but also giving him back a manageable version of what he is communicating (Winnicott 1956). The absence or distortion of this mirroring function may generate a psychological world in which inner experiences are poorly represented, and therefore a desperate need is created for alternative ways of containing psychological experience and the mental world. These ways may, for example, come to involve various forms of self-harm or aggression towards others (Fonagy et al. 1993a, Fonagy and Target 1995a).

Within a secure or containing relationship, the baby's affective signals are interpreted by the parent, who is able to reflect on the mental states underlying the baby's distress. For this reflection to help the baby, it needs to consist of a subtle combination of mirroring and the communication of a contrasting affect. The nature of the object's mirroring may be most easily understood in the context of our description of the parent's pretend play with the child: thus, to contain the child's anxiety, the mother's mirroring expression will display a complex affect, which combines fear with an emotion incompatible with it, such as irony. At one level, this communicates that there is nothing truly to worry about, but more importantly the parent's reaction, which is the same yet not the same as the baby's experience, creates the possibility of generating a second order (symbolic) representation of the anxiety. This is the beginning of symbolization. We have also discussed how language is well adapted to this task (Fonagy and Fonagy 1995), for example, speakers frequently, quite unconsciously, combine two patterns of intonation, each characteristic of a different emotion. The listener is affected by both, even when only one of the affects expressed is consciously perceived. We believe that the infant is soothed (or contained) through much the same process. If the parent is unable to respond in this way, the infant's distress is either avoided or mirrored without first being "metabolized" and the child tends to internalize her defenses. In extreme cases, the process of self-development may be compromised, and a vulnerability is created to a highly maladaptive defense, that of inhibiting mentalization. Even in less extreme cases, parent–child relationships in which mirroring has been inadequate may lay the groundwork for subsequent distortions of personality development in one of two ways. These correspond to the two early modes of experiencing psychic reality. The mother may echo the child's state without modulation, as in the mode of psychic equivalence, concretizing or panicking at the child's distress. Alternatively she may avoid reflection on the child's affect through a process akin to dissociation, which effectively places the mother in a pretend mode, unrelated to external reality, including the child's genuine feelings or intentions. The mother may then ignore the child's distress, or translate it into illness, tiredness, and so on. Both ways of sidestepping the child's communication strip it of the potential for a meaning that he can recognize and use. It may also lead to a currency between parent and child of interpretation of feelings in physical terms, so that the physical state is the "real" thing. Lynne Murray (Murray and Cooper 1997), in her work with mothers suffering from puerperal depression, has provided some vivid illustrations of such mothers offering an alternative reality, marked by the exaggeration associated with pretense, and not related to the infant's expressions. The infant has not been able to find a recognizable version of his mental states in another person's mind, and the opportunity to acquire a symbolic representation of those states has been lost. Normally the child achieves control over affect partly through this kind of symbolization. The representation of his feelings is increasingly associated with the modulation included in her reflection of them. The reflection is clearly related to the original feelings, but is not the same. The infant will map the mother's modulated reaction on to his own feelings, and slowly learns that symbolic "play" with affect can bind his emotional and physiological reactions. Clinically this would mean that the child who has not received recognizable but modified images of his affective states may later have trouble in differentiating reality from fantasy, and physical from psychic reality. This may restrict him to an instrumental (manipulative), rather than signal (communicative) use of affect. This instrumental use of affect is a key aspect of the tendency of borderline patients to express and cope with thoughts and feelings through physical action, against their own bodies or in relation to other people. Central to understanding this, we suggest, is the fact that delayed or absent secondary representation of affect constrains the development of the child's psychic reality. The integration of the two primitive modes of experiencing mind (equivalence and pretence) normally begins in the second year of life and is partially completed by the fifth or sixth years (Target and Fonagy 1996). We see this integration as the achievement of mentalization, which has been described in the psychoanalytic literature under various headings (see the excellent review by Lecours and Bouchard 1997).

Awareness of the physical separateness of bodies, and even of mental states, does not immediately bring with it the capacity to identify or attribute a plausible mental state to another person. Common observations of the young child, toddlers, and even 3- and 4-year-olds readily confirm that, as far as the boundaries of the psychological self are concerned, a young child readily assumes that his object's desires are the same as his own. A boy of 4, in a considerable temper, warned his mother that he no longer wanted to sleep in her bed, or have a birthday party, or even have a Megazord (a prized model from the Power Rangers). He assumed that his mother's desires were identical to his and her sense of loss at these deprivations would be as great as his. A borderline child treated by George Moran offered food to the analyst when George asked whether he was hungry. The mental boundaries of the self probably remain permeable throughout development and perhaps even in adulthood. Sandler (1992) stressed the importance of primary identification as underpinning empathic gestures (for example, correcting one's stance when seeing somebody else slip). Normally these experiences are circumscribed, preconscious, and limited to the earlier stages of perception. Nevertheless their very existence underscores the importance of intersubjective states that lay the ground for self-knowledge. *At the core of the mature child's self is the other at the moment of reflection.* The mental representations of mental representations are object-images congruent with internal states, yet not identical with them. They share elements of the child's self sufficiently coherent and stable for the formation of a symbolic link and for the child to construct further self-representations in the physical absence of the object.

The Role of Trauma in Preventing the Integration of the Two Modes of Psychic Reality

We know that trauma plays a significant role in the psychogenesis of borderline states (Johnson et al. 1999). When perpetrated by an attachment figure, we suggest that trauma interferes with the developmental process described above. Evidence of this can be seen in severely abused children in one or more of the following ways: a) the persistence of a psychic equivalence mode of experiencing internal reality; b) the propensity to continue to shift into a pretend mode (dissociation); and c) a partial inability to reflect on one's own mental states and those of one's objects. We are suggesting that these ways of thinking persist into adulthood, and play an important role in the symptoms of borderline personality disorder.

The maltreated child cannot afford the luxury of seeing the parent's expression as indicating only a psychic reality, as nonconsequential, since the parent's feelings can carry terrifying repercussions. Normally, the child between the ages of 2 and 4 will increasingly notice discrepancies between his or her internal states and the world outside, or other people's states of mind. However, the child who is surrounded by threat or actual trauma will have little opportunity to develop an awareness of any distinction between inner and outer. His or her focus needs to be maintained so closely on the outside world and its physical and emotional dangers that there is little room for attention to the internal world. In normal circumstances, a parent will be able to protect the child from some of the frightening force of reality, not so much by concealing some events and feelings but by conveying to the child that there is more than one way of seeing things. Perhaps the child has seen the parent being angry, even frightening; if the parent is able to recognize the child's experience, but also to communicate that that fear is unjustified, the child is safe. However, in cases of maltreatment, the child is not safe. Any reassuring communication of containment will be false, further undermining the child's capacity to trust inner reality. Thus, abuse inevitably reinforces a psychic equivalence mode of functioning. It forces the child to attend primarily to the physical world, to mistrust any opportunities for playfulness, and to be suspicious of the internal world in general, because the object's internal world is incomprehensible, terrifying, or painful.

However, parents who cannot enter a "pretend" mode with their child are by no means always overtly abusive, neglecting, or mentally ill. We speculate that the capacity on the parent's part to adopt a "pretend" stance may be essential for the child to experience his projections as contained. This may be one of the reasons why many characteristics of children who have experienced maltreatment may also be found in those whose childhoods have apparently been relatively benign. The parent may have been emotionally inaccessible to the child. This would prevent the child from forming the image of his internal world in the parent's mind that he needs to internalize in order to form the core sense of himself. Some parents may, in addition, unconsciously reveal states of mind (hatred, sadism, disgust) that, if pervasive, constitute a psychological form of abuse, because the child has to recoil from the image of himself that is contained in the parent's attitude. These, as well as the overtly maltreated children, experience inescapable victimization. The most perturbing aspect for the child might be to contemplate the frankly malevolent intent of the caregiver towards the child. He can have no protection from this, other than barring all ideas about feelings and thoughts in others and in himself from his consciousness. The maltreated child can thus grow up to fear minds, and to repudiate knowledge of mental states with the persistence of psychic equivalence as the inevitable by-product of this process.

Furthermore, as Main and Hesse (1992) have pointed out, it is almost as disruptive to the child for the parent to be experienced as frightened as for her to be seen as frightening. There may be at least two processes in operation here. First, as at this early stage the infant perceives the object as part of the self, the child will tend to assume that his own mental state is dangerous or even catastrophic, because it is associated with frightening behavior from the parent. For instance, a baby might bite the mother's breast in excited pleasure, and produce a reaction of anger or disgust. If such experiences were frequent, then they could be expected to have a disorganizing effect on the baby's understanding of his own states of mind; excited pleasure becomes equated with anger and rejection. Second, the child may perceive the caregiver's image of him as a frightening, unmanageable person, for instance, a reminder of an abusive figure from the mother's own history (the excited, biting baby might cause the mother to react with fear or shock), and this may be internalized as an unacceptable and confusing part of the child's self-image. We have previously discussed the role that this process may have played in the case of Rebecca (Fonagy and Target 1996).

Trauma may also disrupt functions involving the representation of feelings, thoughts, beliefs, and desires by creating a propensity for shifting into the mode of pretend. Some traumatized children grow up with an apparent hypersensitivity to mental states, needing to guess immediately what those around them feel and think in order to pre-empt further trauma. As part of this, a pseudo-knowledge of minds will develop, which is superficial and may be very selective, scanning for particular danger signals, and avoiding reflection on deep meanings. Commonly, the "expertise" in the psychological world of the other develops at the expense of knowledge of his own internal states. In such cases the analyst may anticipate a great deal of psychological manipulativeness from the patient, which might lead him or her to expect a comparable sophistication of understanding, reflectiveness, and insight into the self. Such "hyperactive mentalizing," however occurs in the pretend mode, without firm ties to internal and external experience that is felt to be real. In some instances, particularly when such individuals have received psychotherapeutic treatment, an overly analytical form of mentalization develops that is ultimately inaccurate and ineffective, in that it cuts the individual off from deep genuine contact with other people. An awareness of this possibility, and of the function of this pseudo-reflectiveness, is critical in working with such individuals.

Most commonly, however, mindless treatment, or neglect, of the child leads to the disavowal of reflection and rejection of mentalization (Fonagy et al. 1997b). This should be understood not simply as a deficit but as an *adaptation* that has helped the child to attain some distance from a traumatizing situation. Although restriction of mentalization was originally adaptive, there is a clear and powerful link between this restricted capacity and vulnerability to later trauma. The inability to reflect upon the mental state of the perpetrator, as well as the reaction of the self, may prevent the child from resolving the original traumatic experience or coping with subsequent assault. Conversely, mentalizing is an important component of the self-righting capacity of individuals who are able to withstand early adversity (Fonagy et al. 1994). Thus, there is a bi-directional developmental relationship between trauma and mentalizing; trauma may undermine the child's willingness to play with feelings and ideas (felt as too real) in relation to external events. At the same time, the lack of a full mentalizing mode of internal organization will create a propensity for the continuous repetition of the trauma, in the absence of the modulation that a representational view of psychic reality brings.

The Rigidity of Relationship Patterns and the Petrification of Systems of Representation

We have described in an earlier paper (Target and Fonagy 1996) the ways in which the development of reflective capacity benefits people in terms of making both internal and external worlds more meaningful. We suggest here that some aspects of borderline pathology arise from the inadequate integration of early forms of the representation of internal experience, which would normally form the basis of a mentalizing mode of experiencing psychic reality. Perhaps the single most important indicator of this is the quality of rigidity that imbues the internal representational world, the experience of the self, and relationships with others. In borderline patients particular ways of relating, idiosyncratic ways of understanding the world, are held to with a tenacity far beyond what would be associated with habitual patterns of defense, and place a major obstacle in the path of therapeutic change. These individuals, like other patients, organize the analytic relationship to conform to their unconscious expectations, but for borderline patients these expectations are experienced with the full force of reality, and there is no sense of alternative perspectives. At those moments when the external reality does not fit with the tenaciously held active schema, there is only a sense of emptiness.

Just as behavior and interpersonal relations are rigidly restricted, so is internal experience; of the total spectrum of experiences only some are registered and felt, frequently leading to a discontinuity in self-experience. As a consequence of the lack of flexibility of the representational system for mental states, the individual does not have the capacity to evoke psychic experiences in any way other than by enactment and provocation. Even relatively simple and common subjective states, such as worry or concern, cannot be experienced except through creating them in another person. Many have noted the manipulative aspects of eating disorders and other forms of self-harm (e.g., Bruch 1982, Main 1957), but mostly in the context of the projection or projective identification of intolerable parts of the self, or as part of interpersonal communication. Here our emphasis is somewhat different. It is the creation of an internal experience akin to reflection, normally intrapsychic, which is established through interpersonal interaction. *Not being able to feel themselves from within, they are forced to experience the self from without.*

An important aspect of such rigidity is the persistence of psychic equivalence as a predominant mode of experiencing psychic reality. Much of the apparent inflexibility of such patients may be understood in terms of the increased weight they give to psychic reality. When mental experience cannot be conceived of in a symbolic way, thoughts and feelings have a direct and sometimes devastating impact that can only be avoided through drastic and primitive defensive moves.

> A borderline young man, described more fully in an earlier paper (Fonagy 1991), was prone to long periods of silence during an early phase of his analysis. The silences were impenetrable, and for some time unexplained. On one occasion, the trigger was a two-minute delay in the analyst's arrival for the session, which led to over a week of silence. Interpreting the silence as punishing the analyst, replicating a sense of exclusion, communicating frustration with the process or a sense of not being understood, failed to break the deadlock. Eventually it transpired that on this and many other occasions, the analyst's lateness created an image in the patient's mind of being with someone uncaring, unreliable, or even mad. "You are just an unprofessional, uncaring bastard, and you know it." At that moment, the analyst was experienced as someone totally unsafe to be with.

While there is little that is exceptional about this image, it was the tenacity with which the patient retained this idea, and its imperviousness to any consideration of other times that had been experienced equally definitively as showing an opposite reality. What was noticeable was the extent to which each view replaced the other completely, and each was seen as so clear that it was not even worth discussing. This is based in a lack of ability to "play with reality." The patient is mesmerized by an idea and unable to experience it as psychic rather than concrete reality. The only way to deal with this technically is to accept it. At this stage, an interpretation that attempts to evoke "the patient's picture of the analyst" is inevitably perceived as an attack on the patient's mind and sanity. While often not consciously aware of this, we respect it by entering the patient's reality and accepting the role of the "unprofessional, uncaring bastard." Patients get into trouble because other people they come into contact with have far more difficulty, which is why they need analysis.

> This rigidity of perspective did not just occur within the transference relationship. It clearly caused very frequent difficulties for the patient in his dealings with people outside. Early in his analysis he reported a very acrimonious argument between himself and a shop assistant about the change he was given. "*I knew* she was trying to trick me—I gave her five pounds, and the stupid woman only gave me 30p change, when she should have given me 80p. She kept saying that she had given me 80p but I knew that she had deliberately kept 50p." What was interesting from an analytic standpoint in his account was not simply the obvious sense of omnipotence in his understanding of her (i.e., he *knew*) and the sense of betrayal by the analyst in the transference, but his inability to contemplate any other point of view. Reflecting on this episode, some years into his analysis, he said: "I just could not see any possibility, other than I was right; it's not that I did not want to see it, it simply did not exist."

THE REDISCOVERY OF PSYCHOANALYTIC IDEAS IN ATTACHMENT THEORY

It is inevitably a risky enterprise to draw parallels between concepts that emerge independently in different subject areas. The concept of *attachment* in sociology (Hirschi 1969) refers to integration of the individual with a social structure, and can only with difficulty be reduced to qualities of interpersonal relationships (Fonagy et al. 1997d). The same problem is encountered in linking concepts developed in studies of attachment to psychoanalytic ideas based on clinical observations. The problem is compounded by the polymorphous nature of most psychoanalytic ideas (Sandler 1983) and their complex relations with the clinical evidence upon which they are based (Hamilton 1996). There are other problems. Observations of attachment theorists are made based on experimental studies, at least in infancy, and relatively structured situations (interviews or questionnaires) in adulthood. It is not yet proven, and it is unlikely ever to be, that the parameters determining human behavior during free association in the consulting room are the same as those which pertain under conditions of controlled experimentation (Fonagy 1982). The analogy between laboratory and clinically observed behavioral phenomena can therefore only be made at the level of mental processes: laboratory studies may help us identify the psychological mechanisms generating phenomena that become observable under clinical conditions. This principle applies to links between attachment and psychoanalytic theory. Are there any observations from the consulting room that may be helpfully elaborated in terms of constructs developed by attachment researchers? Conversely, are there observations made by attachment theorists that can be given usefully expanded on the basis of psychoanalytic ideas generated in the clinical setting? Let us explore two possible instances of correspondence.

The Concept of Attachment

Not surprisingly, attachment behaviors have been described by psychoanalysts using alternative terms but depicting comparable phenomena. Perhaps the best example is Erikson's (1950) discussion of "basic trust." Based in drive theory, Erikson described the "incorporative" approach to life that led the individual to establish patterns centered on the social modality of taking and holding on to objects physical and psychic. Erikson (1950) defined basic trust as the capacity "to receive and accept what is given" (p. 58). Careful reading of Erikson (1959) allows us to restate the classification of attachment security in Eriksonian terms. He ponders the determinants of basic trust and discusses its dependence on the reception and acceptance of comforting from the primary caretaker. Mistrust (insecure attachment) may be due to the inability to accept comfort and reassurance (resistance) or the withdrawing and in the extreme "closing up, refusing food and comfort and becoming oblivious to companionship" (p. 56) (avoidance). There are several further indications that "basic trust" is basically attachment: 1) Basic trust is derived from infantile experience, not mediated by oral gratification or demonstrations of love—rather the quality of maternal relationships (Erikson 1959, p. 63); 2) the failure of basic trust is the antecedent of whatever is the opposite of the "healthy personality" (Erikson 1964); 3) the notion of coherence of mental representation is the key to the way that basic trust may be transmitted across generations ("the experience of the caretaking person as a coherent human being" [Erikson 1964, p. 117]); 4) maternal sensitivity was seen as a key determinant of basic trust (Erikson 1950); 5) interactional synchrony (Isabella and Belsky 1991) is similar to the Eriksonian description of "reciprocity or mutual regulation" (p. 58), while nonintrusive parenting (Malatesta et al. 1986) was described by Erikson in terms of the degree of control the mother exerted.

There is a clear overlap between Erikson's thinking and Bowlby's observation. But Erikson is by no means the only psychoanalyst to arrive at the attachment construct. Anna Freud, a sworn enemy of attachment theory, clearly described attachment behaviors in her accounts of the impact of wartime separations on children (A. Freud 1941–1945, A. Freud and Burlingham 1944). More recently, Sandler's (1960a, 1985) description of an inborn wish to maintain safety is analogous to Bowlby's emphasis on the innate propensity for attachment; the background of safety appears to be a phenomenological counterpart of the secure base concept. The abused child seeks contact with the abusing caretaker because paradoxically the predictable, familiar, but adverse experience has the potential to generate a greater sense of safety than an unfamiliar, non-abusive one.

A less obvious and potentially quite contentious analogy could be proposed between Klein's (1935) concept of the paranoid-schizoid position and insecurity of attachment. In the paranoid-schizoid position the relationship to the caregiver is represented as fragmented, split into persecutory and idealized relationships, and similarly the ego (the self) is assumed to be split. Only in the depressive position is the child thought to develop an integrated image of both loved and hated aspects of the parent and correspondingly do we see an integration of the self. Facets of the description of insecure adult attachment (Main and Goldwyn 1995) bring this category close to Klein's description of the paranoid-schizoid position. Among these are: 1) the splitting of semantic and episodic memory, particularly in the dismissing category characterized by idealization, and/or denigration of attachment figures;

2) lack of coherence or inconsistencies in relationship descriptions may be indicative of the lability of mental representation that marks the paranoid-schizoid position (Klein 1935); 3) the balance of love and hate and the recognition and acceptance of imperfection in the caregiver is indicative of secure attachment and describes the state of mind characteristic of whole object perception in the depressive position (Klein 1935); 4) secure attachment is marked by the individual's recall and recognition in bringing about interpersonal conflict, and the generally enhanced capacity to monitor thoughts and feelings as these emerge in the narrative. Analogously in Klein's view, the onset of the depressive position is the child's discovery of his capacity to love and hate the parent, which opens the child to experiences of guilt (Klein 1929); 5) the speech and discourse of secure individuals reflects superior symbolic capacity, and this may be linked to the association of symbolization to depressive reparation (Segal 1957); 6) modern Kleinian writers see the critical aspect of the depressive position as the child's achievement of mental separateness and linked to this the perception of the object as independent (Quinodoz 1991, Spillius 1992, Steiner 1992). The same observation concerning the child's perception of the caregiver's independent functioning is made by Bowlby (1973).

This list should not suggest any kind of isomorphism between the concept of insecure attachment and the concept of a paranoid-schizoid state, but rather that the thinking of insecure adults may more frequently show features that have been described by Kleinian clinicians as paranoid-schizoid. Important implications may follow. For example, if it is accepted that paranoid-schizoid thinking is more prominent in insecure adults, this might imply that insecurity rather than security is the basic attachment position. The Kleinian perspective highlights an approach to attachment security as "a mode of mental functioning" with perhaps sometimes rapid cycling between secure and insecure modes (Bion 1962b).

The Attachment Classification

Psychoanalytic clinicians have described patterns of behavior and interpersonal relationship representations that correspond closely to classifications of adult attachment. Once again, such potential correspondences are important because of the alternative perspective psychoanalytic models cast on the mechanisms that could be mediating these individual differences.

Rosenfeld (1964, 1971a, 1971b) distinguished between "thin skinned" and "thick skinned" narcissistic patterns. The clinical detail of his description resembles the preoccupied versus dismissing adult attachment categories. Using Rosenfeld's formulation we could see dismissing patterns of attachment as characterized by the tendency to deposit perceived inadequacies into others, who are then experienced as under the control of the self, given the assistance of projective identification. Preoccupied attachment could be identified psychoanalytically as associated with a sense of dependency that causes the individual to feel intolerable vulnerability to the other warded off through continuous angry attacks on those whose very dependability appears to mock the individual's feelings of helplessness. Those familiar with attachment classification will note that these descriptions cover only the angry resentful (E2) and the denigrating (Ds2) subcategories of the preoccupied and dismissing classifications, respectively.

Balint (1959) offered an alternative model for understanding the avoidant dismissing versus the resistant preoccupied patterns in his description of the "ocnophilic" and "philobatic" attitudes. In this formulation, the dismissing philobat is seen as the person who dislikes attachments but loves the spaces between them, and prefers to invest in his own ego skills at the expense of investing in his object. The preoccupied ocnophile defends against anxiety by enhancing his dependency on the newly emerging objects leading to an intensification of ambivalence. The Ds attachment category may be similarly illuminated by Modell's (1975, 1984) formulation of narcissistic personality disorder.

Psychoanalytic ideas may also help elaborate upon our understanding of the disorganized attachment pattern of infancy (Main and Solomon 1990). These children manifested extraordinary controlling behavior in relation to their caregivers at pre-school age (Cassidy et al. 1989) and in the early school years (Main and Cassidy 1988). Children who were disorganized in their attachment in infancy, in separation-reunion situations, appear to take control of the relationship with their object, sometimes treating the parent in an apparently condescending or humiliating manner. Disorganized attachment has been shown to be associated with unresolved trauma in the parents (Main and Hesse 1990), a history of maltreatment in the child (Carlsson et al. 1989), maternal depression (Radke-Yarrow et al. 1985), and parental substance abuse (Rodning et al. 1991).

We would argue that children exposed to such deprivation are repeatedly confronted with intolerable levels of confusing and hostile caregiving and commonly internalize images of the caregiver that they are incapable of integrating. The self-structure is thus formed incorporating fragmented and flawed images of the other that the child is forced to externalize in order to retain an experience of coherence. This idea certainly dates back to Edith Jacobson, if not to earlier contributors (Jacobson 1964). The process of projective identification well describes the behavior of such children as they attempt to experience themselves as coherent selves and force unassimilable, "alien" parts of themselves into the other. They confirm this illusion by more or less subtle manipulative control over the other's behavior, ensuring that the perception of these alien aspects of the self as being external can be maintained (Fonagy and Target 1997).

13

How Can Attachment Theory
Benefit from Psychoanalytic Insights?

It would be foolhardy to maintain that psychoanalytic critiques of attachment theory are altogether misguided. In important respects psychoanalytic formulations are significantly in advance of the understanding that attachment theory is able to provide. A more complete integration of psychoanalytic and attachment theory would demand that attachment researchers address these areas of discrepancy and elaborate on their formulations in the direction of making them more compatible with a psychoanalytic framework.

What are the shortcomings of current attachment theory from a psychoanalytic standpoint? First, attachment theory should pay more attention to systematic distortions in the child's perceptions of the external world. The relationship of actual experience and its representation is greatly complicated by the fact that comparable caregiver behavior may be experienced and encoded differently by different infants (Eagle 1997). While contextual factors, for example, small differences between the caregiver's behavior towards two siblings (nonshared environment), may account for some of these effects, distortions in the child's perception due to internal states of fantasies, affects, and conflicts are also likely to play a part.

Second, internal working models are probably often in conflict, vying for dominance for organization of a particular relationship. They are also likely to exist in a hierarchy, some with greater access to consciousness than others. Even if these models are solely encoded as procedures, that is, are implicit rather than explicit, it is probable that they will vary in terms of their developmental appropriateness, some appearing to be age-appropriate while others represent immature, regressive ways of relating. Interestingly, the developmental dimension of attachment theory is limited. While it is self-evident that adult manifestations of, say, avoidance must be different from the manifestation of this class of attachments in adolescence, work thus far has focused on the identification of continuities between these manifestations rather than expectable developmental changes that are likely to accompany the maturational differentiation of the child's representational system. Since Freud (1900), psychoanalytic developmentalists have always been concerned by how self, object, and object relationship representations evolve with development (Freud 1965, Jacobson 1964, Mahler et al. 1975). Internal working models are likely to become marked by the mode and level of functioning prevalent at the time of their construction. The amount of interpersonal awareness or self–other differentiation shown by an individual may be a factor of attachment class but also it may indicate the developmental level of the representational model.

A third and related developmental issue concerns discontinuities of attachment classification. Attachment theorists prefer to conceive of such discontinuities in terms of environmental changes. They rarely ask why environmental changes do not invariably impact on the attachment system. Psychoanalysts have also shown considerable sophistication in the way that the same developmental influence, for example, sensitivity, may have quite a different impact on relationship representations at different developmental stages.

Fourth, psychoanalytic objections to attachment theory often focus on the allegedly simplistic categorical system attachment theory offers. This is a misunderstanding and reflects the conflation in the mind of critics of the operationalization of a theory with the theory itself. The criticism, however, is warranted to the extent that attachment researchers often appear to reify attachment categories, considering them as theoretical entities rather than observed clusters of behavior. A problem arises if researchers cease to concern themselves with the mechanisms or psychic processes that may underlie such behavioral clusters. Beginning to think about these groupings more in psychoanalytic terms, whether as habitual modes of defense or as manifestations of a representational system overinfluenced by paranoid-schizoid modes of functioning, might reduce the danger of the reification of attachment categories. The psychoanalytic perspective might encourage us to think less categorically and more dimensionally about attachment security. The potential for both security and insecurity is likely to be present in all of us.

Fifth, psychoanalytic concern with the development of the child's awareness of the integrity of his object could direct the attachment researcher's attention to the biological role of attachment. Bowlby's classical assumption, that attachment behavior has a selective advantage as it promotes the survival of the species, is inconsistent with the advances of sociobiology and behavior genetics. "The survival of the species" is not what drives evolution. It is the survival of the genetic code carried by a particular individual that is at an evolutionary premium. So what is the selection advantage of a social protective mechanism based on the expression of distress in the infant? The answer is not obvious, since we now recognize that the expression of distress carries a high risk for the infant. The work of Bruce Perry (1997) illustrates how neglect, in arousing a chronic fright–flight reaction, has the potential to cause significant neurodevelopmental anomalies (because of the presence of excessive cortisol in the brain). The fright–flight reaction in such infants is thus evolutionarily a high-risk strategy, the purpose of which is unclear since the infant is unable to respond to threat by either of these methods. Surely, a simpler, less distressing, and therefore less risky method of signaling danger could have evolved. The caregiver's attachment system could be activated by an innate releasing mechanism that was neutral to the infant's well-being. Taking a psychoanalytic perspective might illuminate this evolutionary puzzle. The infant's distress not only brings the caregiver physically close to the child but also creates comparable distress in the object. Thus, an ideal situation is created for the infant to experience containment (Bion

1962a), accurate mirroring (Winnicott 1967), in other words, a context within which internalization processes essential to self-development can take place. The evolutionary function of the attachment system thus may not be the eliciting of a protective response from a human adult, as Bowlby thought. Rather the survival risks to the organism entailed in the processes of attachment are justified by the benefit that the ex-perience of psychic containment brings in terms of the development of a coherent and symbolizing self. There is evidence that secure attach-ment in infancy and the experience of sensitive caregiving upon which this is likely to be based predicts superior capacity to understand the nature of mental states (Fonagy et al. 1997a, submitted). It is therefore at least plausible to argue that at least one biological function of the process of attachment is the creation of a particular intersubjective en-vironment. Here the proximity of the caregiver, in the state of arousal concordant with that of the child, permits an internalization of that mental state that can become the root of a second-order representation of this state of distress and ultimately permit symbolic understanding of internal states by the human mind (Gergely and Watson 1996).

Finally, complementary to the addition of a psychoanalytic per-spective to developmental attachment theory, psychoanalytic ideas could greatly enrich attachment theory formulations of psychopathol-ogy. To take the example of borderline personality disorder, Kernberg's (1975, 1977) description of borderline personality organization could be seen in attachment theory terms as a lack of integration of internal working models, or rather the predominance of internal working mod-els where self and object representations rapidly oscillate.

Attachment theory needs to learn more about the incomplete in-ternal working models with which such individuals function. The rela-tionship representation is not that with an actual other, but rather a small fragment of that person experienced at a moment characterized by overwhelming and diffuse affect. Insecure attachment with accom-panying inadequate affect regulation is bound to increase the likelihood of the creation of such partial internal working models. There is evi-dence from studies of borderline patients, using the adult attachment interview, of a characteristic dominance of confusing and confused in-ternal representations of attachment (Fonagy et al. 1996, Patrick et al. 1994). Kernberg's clinical formulation implies the presence of easily activated, poorly structured, highly distorted, partial, and unstable internal working models in such individuals with characteristically loose assignments of objects and subjects. Rapid alteration between working models, as well as the absence of coherence within them, may be associated with an inhibition of a metacognitive or reflective capacity that normally serves the function of self-organization (Fonagy and Target 1997). The abandonment of reflective function may be seen as constitutional or as an extreme defensive response of children confronted with traumatic situations where they might find overwhelming the contemplation of mental states in their caregiver or themselves. They thus voluntarily abandon this crucial psychological capacity, with sometimes disastrous consequences.

14

Conclusion

Attachment theory and psychoanalytic theory have common roots but have evolved in epistemologically distinct ways. Attachment theory, far closer to empirical psychology with its positivist heritage, has been in some ways method bound over the past fifteen years. Its scope was determined less by what fell within the domain defined by relationship phenomena involving a caretaking–dependent dyad and more by the range of groups and behaviors to which the preferred mode of observation, the strange situation, the Adult Attachment interview, and so on, could be productively applied. This sheltered the theory from a range of ideas that clinical psychoanalysts evolved, particularly in the context of analytic work with increasingly severely disturbed, chronic personality-disordered individuals. Psychoanalytic ideas have rarely taken into consideration relevant observations from the field of attachment and, conversely, a paradigm-bound attachment theory has felt it had little to benefit from the clinical discoveries of psychoanalysts. Yet both bodies of knowledge are progressing towards the same endpoint, which is perhaps still some way off: a developmental understanding of personality and psychological disorder. This book has attempted to illustrate that distinctions made by attachment theorists are frequently closely linked to distinctions generally accepted within particular psychoanalytic traditions. Attachment theory may share more with some psychoanalytic traditions than others but this does not mean that even "distant cousins" of attachment theory (e.g., modern Kleinian theory) do not cover similar ground, albeit from a radically different perspective. Taking psychoanalytic theory as a whole, many important discoveries of attachment theory can be seen to have been observed on the couch as well as in the laboratory. There are some areas familiar to psychoanalytic clinicians where attachment theory has not yet ventured. Bringing the two approaches into closer contact, beyond creating lively debate, has the potential greatly to enrich both traditions. Such a dialogue may highlight where attachment theory methodology may be applied for the exploration of psychoanalytic work and ideas. For example, attachment status may be used as a measure of outcome for psychoanalytic treatment. The focus of attachment research may additionally be broadened to incorporate areas beyond its traditional domain of social development in the context of the dyad.

References

Ainsworth, M. D. S. (1963). The development of infant–mother interaction among the Ganda. In *Determinants of Infant Behaviour* vol. 2, ed. B. M. Foss, pp. 67–112. New York: Wiley.

———. (1989). Attachments beyond infancy. *American Psychologist* 44:709–716.

———. (1990). Epilogue: some considerations regarding theory and assessment relevant to attachment beyond infancy. In *Attachment in the Pre-School Years: Theory, Research and Intervention*, ed. M. T. Greenberg, D. Cicchetti, and E. M. Cummings, pp. 463–488. Chicago: University of Chicago Press.

Ainsworth, M. D. S., Blehar, M. C., Waters, E., and Wall, S. (1978). *Patterns of Attachment: A Psychological Study of the Strange Situation.* Hillsdale, NJ: Erlbaum.

Ainsworth, M. D. S., and Bowlby, J. (1991). An ethological aproach to personality development. *American Psychologist* 46:333–341.

Ainsworth, M. D. S., and Wittig, B. A. (1969). Attachment and exploratory behavior of one-year-olds in a strange situation. In *Determinants of Infant Behavior*, ed. B. M. Foss, pp. 113–136. London: Methuen.

Akhtar, S. (1992). *Broken Structures: Severe Personality Disorders and Their Treatment*. Northvale, NJ: Jason Aronson.

Alexander, F., and French, T. (1946). The principle of corrective emotional experience—the case of Jean Valjean. In *Psychoanalytic Theory, Principles and Application*, ed. F. Alexander and T. French, pp. 66–70. New York: Ronald Press.

Allen, J. G. (1995). *Coping with Trauma: A Guide to Self-Understanding*. Washington, DC: American Psychiatric Press.

———. (2000). *Traumatic Attachments*. New York: Wiley.

Allen, J. P., and Hauser, S. T. (1996). Autonomy and relatedness in adolescent-family interactions as predictors of young adults' states of mind regarding attachment. *Development and Psychopathology* 8:793–809.

Allen, J. P., Hauser, S. T., and Borman-Spurrell, E. (1996). Attachment theory as a framework for understanding sequelae of severe adolescent psychopathology: an 11-year follow-up study. *Journal of Consulting and Clinical Psychology* 64:254–263.

Amini, F., Lewis, T., Lannon, R., et al. (1996). Affect, attachment, memory: contributions towards a psychobiologic integration. *Psychiatry* 59:213–239.

Ammaniti, M., Candelori, C., Dazzi, N., et al. (1990). Intervista sull'attaccamento nella latenza: Unpublished.

Ammaniti, M., Speranza, A. M., and Tambelli, R. (in press). Intervista sull'attaccamento nella latenza. *Attachment and Human Development*.

Arlow, J. A., and Brenner, C. (1964). *Psychoanalytic Concepts and the Structural Theory*. New York: International Universities Press.

Armsden, G. C., and Greenberg, M. T. (1987a). The inventory of parent and peer attachment: individual differences and their relationship to psychological well-being in adolescence. *Journal of Youth and Adolescence* 16:427–454.

———. (1987b). The Inventory of Parent and Peer Attachment: relationships to well-being in adolescence. *Journal of Youth and Adolescence* 16:427–454.

Atkinson, L., and Zucker, K. J., eds. (1997). *Attachment and Psychopathology*. New York: Guilford.

Auerbach, J. S. (1993). The origins of narcissism and narcissistic personality disorder: A theoretical and empirical reformulation. In *Psychoanalytic Perspectives on Psychopathology*, ed. J. M. Masling and R. F. Bornstein, pp. 43–110. Washington, D.C.: American Psychological Association.

Auerbach, J. S., and Blatt, S. J. (1996). Self-representation in severe psychopathology: the role of reflexive self-awareness. *Psychoanalytic Psychology* 13:297–341.

Bahrick, L. R., and Watson, J. S. (1985). Detection of intermodal proprioceptive-visual contingency as a potential basis of self-perception in infancy. *Developmental Psychology* 21:963–973.

Bakermans-Kranenburg, M. J., and van Ijzendoorn, M. H. (1993). A psychometric study of the Adult Attachment Interview: reliability and discriminant validity. *Developmental Psychology* 29: 870–879.

Baldwin, M. W. (1992). Relational schemas and the processing of social infrmation. *Psychological Bulletin* 112:461–484.

Balint, M. (1952). On love and hate. *International Journal of Psycho-Analysis* 33:355–362.

———. (1959). *Thrills and Regressions*. London: Hogarth.

———. (1965). *Primary Love and Psycho-analytic Technique*. London: Tavistock.

———. (1968). *The Basic Fault*. London: Tavistock.

Barnett, D., Ganiban, J., and Cicchetti, D. (1999). Maltreatment, emotional reactivity and the development of Type D attachments from 12 to 24 months of age. *Monographs of the Society for Research in Child Development*.

Baron-Cohen, S. (1995). *Mindblindness: An Essay on Autism and Theory of Mind*. Cambridge, MA: MIT Press.

Baron-Cohen, S., Tager-Flusberg, H., and Cohen, D. J. (1993). *Understanding Other Minds: Perspectives from Autism*. Oxford: Oxford University Press.

Bartholomew, K., and Horowitz, L. M. (1991). Attachment styles among young adults: a test of a four-category model. *Journal of Personality and Social Psychology* 61:226–244.

Bateman, A. (1996). *The concept of enactment and "thick-skinned" and "thin-skinned" narcissism*. Paper presented at the European Conference of English Speaking Psychoanalysts, London, July.

Beck, A. T. (1987). Cognitive models of depression. *Journal of Cognitive Psychotherapy, An International Quarterly* 1:5–37.

Beck, A. T., and Freeman, A. (1990). *Cognitive Therapy of Personality Disorders*. New York: Guilford.

Beebe, B., Lachmann, F., and Jaffe, J. (1997). Mother–infant interaction structures and presymbolic self and object representations. *Psychoanalytic Dialogues* 7:113–182.

Belsky, J. (1999a). Interactional and contextual determinants of attachment security. In *Handbook of Attachment: Theory, Research and Clinical Applications*, ed. J. Cassidy and P. R. Shaver, pp. 249–264. New York: Guilford.

———. (1999b). Modern evolutionary theory and patterns of attachment. In *Handbook of Attachment: Theory, Research and Clinical Applications*, ed. J. Cassidy and P. R. Shaver, pp. 141–161. New York: Guilford.

Belsky, J., Campbell, S., Cohn, J., and Moore, G. (1996a). Instability of attachment security. *Developmental Psychology* 32:921–924.

Belsky, J., and Cassidy, J. (1994). Attachment: theory and evidence. In *Development through Life: A Handbook for Clinicians*, ed. M. Rutter and D. Hay, pp. 373–402. Oxford: Blackwell.

Belsky, J., Rovine, M., and Taylor, D. G. (1984). The Pennsylvania Infant and Family Development Project. III: The origins of individual differences in infant–mother attachment: maternal and infant contributions. *Child Development* 55:718–728.

Belsky, J., Spritz, B., and Crnic, K. (1996). Infant attachment security and affective-cognitive information processing at age 3. *Psychological Science* 7:111–114.

Belsky, J., Steinberg, L., and Draper, P. (1991). Childhood experience, interpersonal development, and reproductive strategy: an evolutionary theory of socialisation. *Child Development* 55:718–728.

Berlin, L. J., Cassidy, J., and Belsky, J. (1995). Loneliness in young children and infant–mother attachment: a longitudinal study. *Merrill-Palmer Quarterly* 41:91–103.

Bierman, K. L., Smoot, D. L., and Aumiller, K. (1993). Characteristics of aggressive-rejected, aggressive (nonrejected) and rejected (nonaggressive) boys. *Child Development* 64:139–151.

Bierman, K. L., and Wargo, J. (1995). Predicting the longitudinal course associated with aggressive-rejected, aggressive (non-rejected) and rejected (non-aggressive) status. *Development and Psychopathology* 7:669–682.

Bion, W. R. (1959). Attacks on linking. *International Journal of Psycho-Analysis* 40:308–315.

———. (1962a). *Learning from Experience*. London: Heinemann.

———. (1962b). A theory of thinking. *International Journal of Psycho-Analysis* 43:306–310.

———. (1963). *Elements of Psycho-analysis*. London: Heinemann.

———. (1967). *Second Thoughts*. London: Heinemann.

Blatt, S., and Ford, T. Q. (1994). *Therapeutic Change: An Object Relations Approach*. New York: Plenum.

Blatt, S. J., and Bers, S. A. (1993). The sense of self in depression: a psychodynamic perspective. In *Self Representation and Emotional Disorders: Cognitive and Psychodynamic Perspectives*, ed. Z. V. Segal and S. J. Blatt, pp. 171–210. New York: Guilford.

Blatt, S. J., and Blass, R. (1996). Relatedness and self definition: a dialectic model of personality development. In *Development and Vulnerabilities in Close Relationships*, ed. G. G. Noam and K. W. Fischer, pp. 309–338. New York: Erlbaum.

Blatt, S. J., and Blass, R. B. (1990). Attachment and separateness: a dialectical model of the products and processes of development throughout the life cycle. *Psychoanalytic Study of the Child* 45:107–127. New Haven, CT: Yale University Press.

Blatt, S. J., Quinlan, D. M., Pilkonis, P. A., and Shea, M. T. (1995). Impact of perfectionism and need for approval on the brief treatment of depression: the National Institute of Mental Health Treatment of Depression Collaborative Research Program revisited. *Journal of Consulting and Clinical Psychology* 63:125–132.

Blatt, S. J., Zuroff, D. C., Bondi, C. M., Sanislow, C. A., and Pilkonis, P. A. (1998). When and how perfectionism impedes the brief treatment of depression: further analyses of the National Institute of Mental Health treatment of depression collaborative research program. *Journal of Consulting and Clinical Psychology* 66:423–428.

Bleiberg, E., Fonagy, P., and Target, M. (1997). Child psychoanalysis: critical overview and a proposed reconsideration. *Psychiatric Clinics of North America* 6:1–38.

Blos, P. (1979). *The Adolescent Passage*. New York: International Universities Press.

Boesky, D. (1989). A discussion of evidential criteria for therapeutic change. In *How Does Treatment Help? Models of Therapeutic Action of Psychoanalytic Therapy*, ed. A. Rothstein, pp. 171–180. Madison, CT: International Universities Press.

Bollas, C. (1987). *The Shadow of the Object: Psychoanalysis of the Unthought Known*. New York: Columbia University Press.

Bolton, D., and Hill, J. (1996). *Mind, Meaning and Mental Disorder*. Oxford: Oxford University Press.

Bouvet, M. (1958). Technical variations and the concept of distance. *International Journal of Psycho-Analysis* 39:211–221.

Bowlby, J. (1944). Forty-four juvenile thieves: their characters and home life. *International Journal of Psycho-Analysis* 25:19–52.

———. (1951). *Maternal Care and Mental Health*. WHO Monograph Series, No. 2. Geneva: WHO.

———. (1956). The growth of independence in the young child. *Royal Society of Health Journal* 76:587–591.

———. (1958). The nature of the child's tie to his mother. *International Journal of Psycho-Analysis* 39:350–373.

———. (1959). Separation anxiety. *International Journal of Psycho-Analysis* 41:1–25.

———. (1960). Grief and mourning in infancy and early childhood. *Psychoanalytic Study of the Child* 15:3–39. New York: International Universities Press

———. (1969). *Attachment and Loss, Vol. 1: Attachment*. London: Hogarth Press and the Institute of Psycho-Analysis.

———. (1973). *Attachment and Loss, Vol. 2: Separation: Anxiety and Anger*. London: Hogarth Press and Institute of Psycho-Analysis.

———. (1977). The making and breaking of affectional bonds II: Some principles of psychotherapy. *British Journal of Psychiatry* 130:421–431.

———. (1979). The making and breaking of affectional bonds. *British Journal of Psychiatry* 130:201–210, 421–431.

———. (1980a). *Attachment and Loss, Vol. 3: Loss: Sadness and Depression*. London: Hogarth Press and Institute of Psycho-Analysis.

———. (1980b). By ethology out of psychoanalysis: an experiment in interbreeding. *Animal Behaviour* 28:649–656.

———. (1980c). Epilogue. In *The Place of Attachment in Human*

Behaviour, ed. C. M. Parks and J. Stevenson-Hinde, pp. 301–312. New York: Basic Books.

———. (1981). Psychoanalysis as natural science. *International Review of Psycho-Analysis* 8:243–255.

———. (1987). Attachment. In *The Oxford Companion to the Mind*, ed. R. Gregory, pp. 57–58. Oxford: Oxford University Press.

———. (1988). *A Secure Base: Clinical Applications of Attachment Theory*. London: Routledge.

Brenner, C. (1982). *The Mind in Conflict*. New York: International Universities Press.

Bretherton, I. (1980). Young children in stressful situations: the supporting role of attachment figures and unfamiliar caregivers. In *Uprooting and Development*, ed. G. V. Coehlo and P. I. Ahmed, pp. 179–210. New York: Plenum.

———. (1987). New perspectives on attachment relationships: security, communication and internal working models. In *Handbook of Infant Development*, ed. J. D. Osofsky, pp. 1061–1100. New York: Wiley.

———. (1990). Open communication and internal working models: their role in the development of attachment relationships. In *Socioemotional Development: Nebraska Symposium on Motivation*, 1988, ed. R. A. Thompson, vol. 36, pp. 57–113. Lincoln: University of Nebraska Press.

———. (1991). Pouring new wine into old bottles: the social self as internal working model. In *Self Processes and Development: Minnesota Symposia on Child Psychology*, ed. M. R. Gunnar and L. A. Sroufe, vol. 23, pp. 1–41. Hillsdale, NJ: Erlbaum.

———. (1995). Internal working models: cognitive and affective aspects of attachment representations. In *4th Rochester Symposium on Developmental Psychopathology on 'Emotion, Cognition, and Representation,'* ed. D. Cicchetti and S. Toth, pp. 231–260. Hillsdale, NJ: Erlbaum.

Bretherton, I., Bates, E., Benigni, L., Camaioni, L., and Volterra, V. (1979). Relationships between cognition, communication, and quality of attachment. In *The Emergence of Symbols*, ed. E. Bates, L. Benigni, I. Bretherton, L. Camaioni, and V. Volterra, pp. 223–269. New York: Academic Press.

Bretherton, I., and Munholland, K. A. (1999). Internal working models in attachment relationships: a construct revisited. In *Handbook of Attachment: Theory, Research and Clinical Applications*, ed. J. Cassidy and P. R. Shaver, pp. 89–114. New York: Guilford.

Bretherton, I., Ridgeway, D., and Cassidy, J. (1990). Assessing internal working models of the attachment relationship: an attachment story completion task. In *Attachment in the Preschool Years: Theory, Research and Intervention*, ed. M. T. Greenberg, D. Cicchetti, and E. M. Cummings, pp. 273–308. Chicago: University of Chicago Press.

Britton, R. (1989). The missing link: parental sexuality in the Oedipus complex. In *The Oedipus Complex Today: Clinical Implications*, ed. R. Britton, M. Feldman, and E. O'Shaughnessy, pp. 83–102. London: Karnac.

———. (1992). The Oedipus situation and the depressive position. In *Clinical Lectures on Klein and Bion*, ed. R. Anderson, pp. 34–45. London: Routledge.

Bromberg, P. M. (1998). *Standing in the Spaces*. Hillsdale, NJ: Analytic Press.

Bruch, H. (1982). Anorexia nervosa: therapy and theory. *American Journal of Psychiatry* 139(12):1531–1538.

Bruner, J. (1990). *Acts of Meaning*. Cambridge: Harvard University Press.

Bucci, W. (1997). *Psychoanalysis and Cognitive Science: A Multiple Code Theory*. New York: Guilford.

Burland, J. A. (1986). The vicissitudes of maternal deprivation. In *Self and Object Constancy: Clinical and Theoretical Perspectives*, ed. R. F. Lax and J. A. Burland, pp. 324–347. New York: Guilford.

Busch, F. (1995). Do actions speak louder than words? A query into an enigma in analytic theory and technique. *Journal of the American Psychoanalytic Association* 43:61–82.

Call, J. D. (1984). From early patterns of communication to the grammar of experience and syntax in infancy. In *Frontiers of Infant Psychiatry*, ed. J. D. Call and R. L. Tyson, pp. 15–29. New York: Basic Books.

Carlson, E. A. (1998). A prospective longitudinal study of attachment disorganization/disorientation. *Child Development* 69:1107–1128.

Carlson, M., Dragomir, C., Earls, F., et al. (1995). Effects of social deprivation on cortisol regulation in institutionalized Romanian infants. *Society for Neuroscience Abstracts* 218:12.

Carlson, M., and Earls, F. (1997). Psychological and neuroendocrino-logical sequelae of early social deprivation in institutionalized children in Romania. *Annals of the New York Academy of Sciences* 807:419–428.

Carlsson, E., and Sroufe, L. A. (1995). Contribution of attachment theory to developmental psychopathology. In *Developmental Psychopathology. Vol. 1: Theory and Methods*, ed. D. Cicchetti and D. J. Cohen, pp. 581–617. New York: Wiley.

Carlsson, V., Cicchetti, D., Barnett, D., and Braunwald, K. (1989). Disorganised/disoriented attachment relationships in maltreated infants. *Developmental Psychology* 25:525–531.

Cassidy, J. (1988). Child–mother attachment and the self in six-year-olds. *Child Development* 59:121–134.

———. (1994). Emotion regulation: influences of attachment relationships. In *The Development of Attachment Regulation. Monograph of the Society for Research in Child Development (Serial No 240)*, ed. N. A. Fox, pp. 228–249.

———. (1995). Attachment and generalized anxiety disorder. In *Rochester Symposium on Developmental Psychopathology: Vol. 6. Emotion, Cognition and Representation*, ed. D. Cicchetti and S. L. Toth, pp. 343–370. Rochester, NY: University of Rochester Press.

———. (1999). The nature of the child's ties. In *Handbook of Attachment: Theory, Research and Clinical Applications*, ed. J. Cassidy and P. R. Shaver, pp. 3–20. New York: Guilford.

Cassidy, J., Kirsh, S. J., Scolton, K. L., and Parke, R. D. (1996). Attachment and representations of peer relationships. *Developmental Psychology* 32:892–904.

Cassidy, J., and Marvin, R. S. (1992). Attachment in preschool children: coding guidelines. Seattle: MacArthur Working Group on Attachment. Unpublished coding manual.

Cassidy, J., Marvin, R. S., and The MacArthur Working Group on Attachment (1989). *Attachment Organization in Three- and Four-Year-Olds: Coding Guidelines*. University of Illinois: Unpublished scoring manual.

Cassidy, J., and Shaver, P. R., eds. (1999). *Handbook of Attachment: Theory, Research and Clinical Applications*. New York: Guilford.

Cavell, M. (1994). *The Psychoanalytic Mind*. Cambridge, MA: Harvard University Press.

Chisolm, K. (1998). A three-year follow-up of attachment and indiscriminate friendliness in children adopted from Russian orphanages. *Child Development* 69:1092–1106.

Cicchetti, D., and Barnett, D. (1991). Attachment organisation in preschool aged maltreated children. *Development and Psychopathology* 3:397–411.

Cicchetti, D., Cummings, E. M., Greenberg, M. T., and Marvin, R. S. (1990). An organizational perspective on attachment beyond infancy. In *Attachment in the Preschool Years: Theory, Research, and Intervention*, ed. M. T. Greenberg and E. M. Cummings, pp. 3–49. Chicago: University of Chicago Press.

Coie, J. D., and Dodge, K. A. (1998). Aggression and antisocial behaviour. In *Handbook of Child Psychology (5th ed.): Vol. 3. Social, Emotional, and Personality Development*, ed. W. Damon, pp. 779–862. New York: Wiley.

Coie, J. D., and Lenox, K. F. (1994). The development of antisocial individuals. In *Psychopathy and Antisocial Personality: A Developmental Perspective*, ed. D. Fowles, P. Sutker, and S. Goodman, pp. 45–72. New York: Springer.

Coie, J. D., Terry, R., Lenox, K., Lochman, J., and Hyman, C. (1996). Childhood peer rejection and aggression as predictors of stable patterns of adolescent disorder. *Development and Psychopathology* 7:697–713.

Cole, P. M., Michel, M. K., and Teti, L. O. (1994). The development of emotion regulation and dysregulation: a clinical perspective. *Monographs of the Society for Research in Child Development* 59: 73–102.

Colin, V. L. (1996). *Human Attachment*. New York: McGraw-Hill.

Collins, N. L., and Read, S. J. (1990). Adult attachment, working models and relationship quality in dating couples. *Journal of Personality and Social Psychology* 58:633–644.

Compton, A. (1981a). On the psychoanalytic theory of instinctual drives: Part III, the complications of libido and narcissism. *Psychoanalytic Quarterly* 50:345–562.

———. (1981b). On the psychoanalytic theory of instinctual drives: Part IV, instinctual drives and the ego-id-superego model. *Psychoanalytic Quarterly* 50:363–392.

Craik, K. (1943). *The Nature of Explanation*. Cambridge: Cambridge University Press.

Crews, F. (1995). *The Memory Wars: Freud's Legacy in Dispute*. London: Granta.

Crick, N. R., and Dodge, K. A. (1994). A review and reformulation of social information-processing mechanisms in children's social adjustment. *Psychological Bulletin* 115:74–101.

Crittenden, P. A. (1992). Quality of attachment in the preschool years. *Development and Psychopathology* 4:209–241.

Crittenden, P. M. (1985). Social networks, quality of child rearing and child development. *Child Development* 56:1299–1313.

———. (1990). Internal representational models of attachment relationships. *Infant Mental Health Journal* 11:259–277.

———. (1994). Peering into the black box: an exploratory treatise on the development of self in young children. In *Disorders and Dysfunctions of the Self. Rochester Symposium on Developmental Psychopathology, vol 5*, ed. D. Cicchetti and S. L. Toth, pp. 79–148. Rochester, NY: University of Rochester Press.

Crnic, K. A., Greenberg, M. T., Ragozin, A. S., Robinson, N. M., and Basham, R. B. (1983). Effects of stress and social support on mothers and premature and full-term infants. *Child Development* 54: 209–217.

Crnic, K. A., Greenberg, M. T., and Slough, N. M. (1986). Early stress and social support influence on mothers' and high-risk infants' functioning in late infancy. *Infant Mental Health Journal* 7:19–33.

Crowell, J. A., Frayley, R. C., and Shaver, P. R. (1999). Measurement of individual differences in adolescent and adult attachment. In *Handbook of Attachment: Theory, Research and Clinical Applications*, ed. J. Cassidy and P. R. Shaver, pp. 434–465. New York: Guilford.

Crowell, J. A., and Owens, G. (1996). Current Relationship Interview and scoring system. State University of New York at Stony Brook, New York. Unpublished manuscript.

Crowell, J. A., Waters, E., Treboux, D., and O'Connor, E. (1996). Discriminant validity of the Adult Attachment Interview. *Child Development* 67:2584–2599.

Cutting, A. L., and Dunn, J. (1999). Theory of mind, emotion understanding, language, and family background: individual differences and interrelations. *Child Development* 70:853–865.

Davies, P. T., and Cummings, E. M. (1995). Marital conflict and child adjustment: An emotional security hypothesis. *Psychological Bulletin* 116:387–411.

———. (1998). Exploring children's security as a mediator of the link between marital relations and child adjustment. *Child Development* 69:124–139.

De Wolff, M. S., and van Ijzendoorn, M. H. (1997). Sensitivity and attachment: a meta-analysis on parental antecedents of infant attachment. *Child Development* 68:571–591.

DeCasper, A. J., and Carstens, A. A. (1981). Contingencies of stimulation: effects on learning and emotion in neonates. *Infant Behavior and Development* 4:19–35.

Del Carmen, R., Pedersen, F., Huffman, L., and Bryan, Y. (1993). Dyadic distress management predicts security of attachment. *Infant Behavior and Development* 16:131–147.

Dishion, T. J., Andrews, D. W., and Crosby, L. (1995). Antisocial boys and their friends in early adolescence. *Child Development* 66:139–151.

Dozier, M. (1990). Attachment organization and treatment use for adults with serious psychopathological disorders. *Development and Psychopathology* 2:47–60.

Dozier, M., Cue, K., and Barnett, L. (1994). Clinicians as caregivers: the role of attachment organisation in treatment. *Journal of Consulting and Clinical Psychology* 62:793–800.

Dozier, M., Stevenson, A. L., Lee, S. W., and Velligan, D. I. (1991). Attachment organization and familiar overinvolvement for adults with serious psychopathological disorders. *Development and Psychopathology* 3:475–489.

Dozier, M., Stovall, K. C., and Albus, K. E. (1999). Attachment and psychopathology in adulthood. In *Handbook of Attachment: Theory, Research and Clinical Applications*, ed. J. Cassidy and P. R. Shaver, pp. 497–519. New York: Guilford.

Dunn, J. (1996). Children's relationships: bridging the divide between cognitive and social development. *Journal of Child Psychology and Psychiatry* 37:507–518.

Eagle, M. (1995). The developmental perspectives of attachment and psychoanalytic theory. In *Attachment Theory: Social, Developmental and Clinical Perspectives*, ed. S. Goldberg, R. Muir, and J. Kerr, pp. 123–150. New York: Analytic Press.

———. (1996). Attachment research and psychoanalytic theory. In *Psychoanalytic Perspectives on Developmental Psychology: Empirical Studies of Psychoanalytic Theories*, ed. J. M. Masling, R. F. Bornstein, et al., vol. 6, pp. 105–149. Washington, DC: American Psychological Association.

———. (1997). Attachment and psychoanalysis. *British Journal of Medical Psychology* 70:217–229.

———. (1998). *The relationship between attachment theory and psychoanalysis*. Paper presented at the American Psychological Association Convention, Washington, DC.

———. (1999). *Attachment research and theory and psychoanalysis*. Paper presented at the Psychoanalytic Association of New York, November 15, 1999.

Eagle, M. N. (1984). *Recent Developments in Psychoanalysis: A Critical Evaluation*. Cambridge, MA: Harvard University Press.

Edelman, G. M. (1987). *Neural Darwinism: The Theory of Neuronal Group Selection*. New York: Basic Books.

Ehrenberg, D. (1993). *The Intimate Edge*. New York: Norton.

Eisenberg, N., and Fabes, R. A. (1992). Emotion, regulation and the development of social competence. In *Review of Personality and Social Psychology: Vol 14. Emotion and Social Behaviour*, ed. M. Clarke, pp. 119–150. Newbury Park, CA: Sage.

Elicker, J., Englund, M., and Sroufe, L. A. (1992). Predicting peer competence and peer relationships in childhood from early parent–child relationships. In *Family-Peer Relationships: Modes of Linkage*, ed. R. Parke and G. Ladd, pp. 77–106. Hillsdale, NJ: Erlbaum.

Elkin, I. (1994). The NIMH treatment of depression collaborative research program: where we began and where we are. In *Handbook of Psychotherapy and Behavior Change*, ed. A. E. Bergin and S. L. Garfield, pp. 114–139. New York: Wiley.

Elman, J. L., Bates, A. E., Johnson, M. H., et al. (1996). *Rethinking Innateness: A Connectionist Perspective on Development*. Cambridge, MA: MIT Press.

Emde, R. N. (1980a). A developmental orientation in psychoanalysis: ways of thinking about new knowledge and further research. *Psychoanalysis and Contemporary Thought* 3:213–235.

———. (1980b). Toward a psychoanalytic theory of affect: Part 1, the organizational model and its propositions. In *The Course of Life: Infancy and Early Childhood*, ed. S. I. Greenspan and G. H. Pollock, pp. 63–83. Washington, DC: DHSS.

———. (1980c). Toward a psychoanalytic theory of affect: Part II, emerging models of emotional development in infancy. In *The Course of Life: Infancy and Early Childhood*, ed. S. I. Greenspan and G. H. Pollock, pp. 85–112. Washington, DC: DHSS.

———. (1981). Changing models of infancy and the nature of early development: remodelling the foundation. *Journal of the American Psychoanalytic Association* 29:179–219.

———. (1983). Pre-representational self and its affective core. *Psychoanalytic Study of the Child* 38:165–192. New Haven, CT: Yale University Press.

———. (1988a). Development terminable and interminable. II. Recent psychoanalytic theory and therapeutic considerations. *International Journal of Psycho-Analysis* 69:283–286.

———. (1988b). Development terminable and interminable. I. Innate and motivational factors from infancy. *International Journal of Psycho-Analysis* 69:23–42.

Engel, G. L. (1971). Attachment behaviour, object relations and the dynamic point of view. A critical review of Bowlby's *Attachment and Loss*. *International Journal of Psycho-Analysis* 52:183–196.

Erel, O., and Burman, B. (1995). Interrelatedness of marital relations and parent–child relations. *Psychological Bulletin* 118:108–132.

Erickson, M. F., Sroufe, L. A., and Egeland, B. (1985). The relationship between quality of attachment and behavior problems in preschool in a high-risk sample. *Monographs of the Society for Research in Child Development* 50(1–2):147–166.

Erikson, E. H. (1950). *Childhood and Society*. New York: Norton.

———. (1956). The problem of ego identity. In *Identity and the Life Cycle*, pp. 104–164. New York: International Universities Press, 1959.

———. (1959). *Identity and the Life Cycle*. New York: International Universities Press.

————. (1964). *Insight and Responsibility*. New York: Norton.

————. (1968). *Identity, Youth and Crisis*. New York: Norton.

Fagot, B. I., and Kavanagh, K. (1990). The prediction of antisocial behavior from avoidant attachment classifications. *Child Development* 61:864–873.

Fairbairn, W. R. D. (1952a). *An Object-Relations Theory of the Personality*. New York: Basic Books, 1954.

————. (1952b). *Psychoanalytic Studies of the Personality*. London: Tavistock.

————. (1954). Observations on the nature of hysterical states. *British Journal of Medical Psychology* 29:112–127.

————. (1963). Synopsis of an object-relations theory of the personality. *International Journal of Psycho-Analysis* 44:224–225.

Feiring, C., and Lewis, M. (1996). Finality in the eye of the beholder: multiple sources, multiple time points, multiple paths. *Development and Psychopathology* 8:721–733.

Ferenczi, S. (1933). A confusion of tongues between adults and the child. In *Final Contributions to the Problems and Methods of Psychoanalysis*, pp. 156–167. London: Hogarth.

Fisher, L., Ames, E. W., Chisholm, K., and Savoie, L. (1997). Problems reported by parents of Romanian orphans adopted to British Columbia. *International Journal of Behavioral Development* 20:67–82.

Fonagy, I., and Fonagy, P. (1995). Communication with pretend actions in language, literature and psychoanalysis. *Psychoanalysis and Contemporary Thought* 18:363–418.

Fonagy, P. (1982). Psychoanalysis and empirical science. *International Review of Psycho-Analysis* 9:125–145.

————. (1991). Thinking about thinking: some clinical and theoretical considerations in the treatment of a borderline patient. *International Journal of Psycho-Analysis* 72:1–18.

————. (1997). Attachment and theory of mind: overlapping constructs? *Association for Child Psychology and Psychiatry Occasional Papers* 14:31–40.

————. (1999a). Male perpetrators of violence against women: an attachment theory perspective. *Journal of Applied Psychoanalytic Studies* 1:7–27.

————. (1999b). Memory and therapeutic action (guest editorial). *International Journal of Psycho-Analysis* 80:215–223.

Fonagy, P., and Cooper, A. (1999). Joseph Sandler's intellectual contributions to theoretical and clinical psychoanalysis. In *Psychoanalysis on the Move: The Work of Joseph Sandler*, ed. P. Fonagy, A. Cooper, and R. Wallerstein, pp. 1–29. London: Routledge.

Fonagy, P., Leigh, T., Steele, M., et al. (1996). The relation of attachment status, psychiatric classification, and response to psychotherapy. *Journal of Consulting and Clinical Psychology* 64:22–31.

Fonagy, P., Moran, G. S., and Target, M. (1993). Aggression and the psychological self. *International Journal of Psycho-Analysis* 74:471–485.

Fonagy, P., Redfern, S., and Charman, T. (1997). The relationship between belief-desire reasoning and a projective measure of attachment security (SAT). *British Journal of Developmental Psychology* 15:51–61.

Fonagy, P., Steele, H., Moran, G., Steele, M., and Higgitt, A. (1991). The capacity for understanding mental states: the reflective self in parent and child and its significance for security of attachment. *Infant Mental Health Journal* 13:200–217.

———. (1992). The integration of psychoanalytic theory and work on attachment: the issue of intergenerational psychic processes. In *Attaccamento E Psiconalis*, ed. D. Stern and M. Ammaniti, pp. 19–30. Bari, Italy: Laterza.

———. (1993). Measuring the ghost in the nursery: An empirical study of the relation between parents' mental representations of childhood experiences and their infants' security of attachment. *Journal of the American Psychoanalytic Association* 41:957–989.

Fonagy, P., Steele, H., and Steele, M. (1991). Maternal representations of attachment during pregnancy predict the organization of infant–mother attachment at one year of age. *Child Development* 62:891–905.

Fonagy, P., Steele, M., Steele, H., Higgitt, A., and Target, M. (1994). Theory and practice of resilience. *Journal of Child Psychology and Psychiatry* 35:231–257.

Fonagy, P., Steele, H., Steele, M., and Holder, J. (in press). Quality of attachment to mother at 1 year predicts belief-desire reasoning at 5 years. *Child Development*.

Fonagy, P., Steele, M., Steele, H., Leigh, T., Kennedy, R., Mattoon, G., and Target, M. (1995a). Attachment, the reflective self, and borderline states: the predictive specificity of the Adult Attachment Interview and pathological emotional development. In *Attachment Theory: Social, Developmental and Clinical Perspectives*, ed. S. Goldberg, R. Muir, and J. Kerr, pp. 233–278. Hillsdale, NJ: Analytic Press.

———. The predictive validity of Mary Main's Adult Attachment Interview: a psychoanalytic and developmental perspective on the transgenerational transmission of attachment and borderline states. In *Attachment Theory: Social, Developmental and Clinical Perspectives*, ed. S. Goldberg, R. Muir, and J. Kerr, pp. 233–278. Hillsdale, NJ: Analytic Press.

Fonagy, P., Steele, M., Steele, H., and Target, M. (1997). *Reflective-Functioning Manual, version 4.1, for Application to Adult Attachment Interviews*. London: University College of London.

Fonagy, P., and Target, M. (1995a). Towards understanding violence: the use of the body and the role of the father. *International Journal of Psycho-Analysis* 76:487–502.

———. (1995b). Understanding the violent patient. *International Journal of Psycho-Analysis* 76:487–502.

———. (1996). Playing with reality: I. Theory of mind and the normal development of psychic reality. *International Journal of Psycho-Analysis* 77:217–233.

———. (1997). Attachment and reflective function: their role in self-organization. *Development and Psychopathology* 9:679–700.

Fonagy, P., Target, M., Steele, M., and Steele, H. (1997). The development of violence and crime as it relates to security of attachment. In *Children in a Violent Society*, ed. J. D. Osofsky, pp. 150–177. New York: Guilford.

Fonagy, P., Target, M., Steele, M., Steele, H., Leigh, T., Levinson, A., and Kennedy, R. (1997). Morality, disruptive behavior, borderline personality disorder, crime, and their relationships to security of attachment. In *Attachment and Psychopathology*, ed. L. Atkinson and K. J. Zucker, pp. 223–274. New York: Guilford.

Fox, N. A. (1994). Dynamic cerebral processes underlying emotion regulation. *Monographs of the Society for Research in Child Development* 59:152–166.

Fraiberg, S. (1980). *Clinical Studies in Infant Mental Health*. New York: Basic Books.

———. (1982). Pathological defenses in infancy. *Psychoanalytic Quarterly* 51:612–635.

Fraiberg, S. H., Adelson, E., and Shapiro, V. (1975). Ghosts in the nursery: a psychoanalytic approach to the problem of impaired infant–mother relationships. *Journal of the American Academy Child Psychiatry* 14:387–422.

Franz, C. E., and White, K. M. (1985). Individuation and attachment in personality development. *Journal of Personality* 53:224–256.

Freud, A. (1926a). Four lectures on child analysis. In *The Writings of Anna Freud, Vol. 1*, pp. 3–69. New York: International Universities Press.

———. (1936). *The Ego and the Mechanisms of Defence*. New York: International Universities Press, 1946.

———. (1941–1945). Reports on the Hampstead Nurseries. In *The Writings of Anna Freud*. New York: International Universities Press, 1974.

———. (1954). The widening scope of indications for psychoanalysis: discussion. *Journal of the American Psychoanalytical Association* 2:607–620.

———. (1955). The concept of the rejecting mother. In *The Writings of Anna Freud*, pp. 586–602. New York: International Universities Press, 1968.

———. (1960). Discussion of Dr. Bowlby's paper, "Grief and mourning in infancy and early childhood." In *The Writings of Anna Freud*, pp. 167–186. New York: International Universities Press, 1969.

———. (1963). The concept of developmental lines. *Psychoanalytic Study of the Child* 18:245–265. New York: International Universities Press.

———. (1965). *Normality and pathology in childhood*. Harmondsworth: Penguin.

———. (1970). Child analysis as a subspecialty of psychoanalysis. In *The Writings of Anna Freud*, pp. 204–219. New York: International Universities Press, 1971.

Freud, A., and Burlingham, D. (1944). *Infants Without Families*. New York: International Universities Press.

Freud, S. (1900). The interpretation of dreams. *Standard Edition* 4,5:1–715.

———. (1905). Three essays on the theory of sexuality. *Standard Edition* 7:123–230.

———. (1906). My views on the part played by sexuality in the aetiology of the neuroses. *Standard Edition* 7:269–280.

———. (1911). Formulations on the two principles of mental functioning. *Standard Edition* 12:213–226.

———. (1915). Mourning and melancholia. *Standard Edition* 14:237–258.

———. (1917). Introductory lectures on psycho-analysis: Part III, general theory of the neuroses. *Standard Edition* 16:243–463.

———. (1920). Beyond the pleasure principle. *Standard Edition* 18:1–64.

———. (1923). The ego and the id. *Standard Edition* 19:1–59.

———. (1926b). Inhibitions, symptoms and anxiety. *Standard Edition* 20:77–172.

———. (1931). Female sexuality. *Standard Edition* 21:221–246.

———. (1933). New introductory lectures on psychoanalysis. *Standard Edition* 22:1–182.

———. (1938). An outline of psychoanalysis. *Standard Edition* 23:139–208.

———. (1939). Moses and monotheism. *Standard Edition* 23:3–137.

Freud, S., and Breuer, J. (1895). Studies on hysteria. *Standard Edition* 2:1–305.

Frosch, A. (1995). The preconceptual organization of emotion. *Journal of the American Psychoanalytic Association* 43:423–447.

Garbarino, J. (1995). *Raising Children in a Socially Toxic Environment.* San Francisco: Jossey Bass.

Garmezy, N., and Masten, A. (1994). Chronic adversities. In *Child and Adolescent Psychiatry: Modern Approaches,* ed. M. Rutter, E. Taylor, and L. Hersov, pp. 191–208. Oxford: Blackwell Scientific Publications.

Garnham, A. (1987). *Mental Models as Representations of Discourse and Text.* Chichester: Ellis Horwood.

George, C., Kaplan, N., and Main, M. (1996). The Adult Attachment Interview Protocol, 3rd Edition. Department of Psychology, University of California at Berkeley. Unpublished manuscript.

George, C., and Solomon, J. (1996). Representational models of relationships: links between caregiving and attachment. In *Defining the Caregiving System* (*Infant Mental Health Journal Volume 17*), ed. C. George and J. Solomon, pp. 198–216. New York: Wiley.

Gergely, G. (1991). Developmental reconstructions: infancy from the point of view of psychoanalysis and developmental psychology. *Psychoanalysis and Contemporary Thought* 14:3–55.

———. (2000). Reapproaching Mahler: new perspectives on normal autism, normal symbiosis, splitting and libidinal object constancy from cognitive developmental theory. *Journal of the American Psychoanalytic Association* 48(4):1197–1228.

Gergely, G., and Watson, J. (1996). The social biofeedback model of parental affect-mirroring. *International Journal of Psycho-Analysis* 77:1181–1212.

Gianino, A. F., and Tronick, E. Z. (1988). The mutual regulation model: the infant's self and interactive regulation and coping and defensive capacities. In *Stress and Coping Across Development*, ed. T. M. Field, P. M. McCabe, and N. Schneiderman, pp. 47–68. Hillsdale, NJ: Erlbaum.

Gill, M. M. (1982). *Analysis of Transference, Vol I: Theory and Technique.* New York: International Universities Press.

Giovacchini, P. (1987). The 'unreasonable' patient and the psychotic transference. In *The Borderline Patient: Emerging Concepts in Diagnosis, Psychodynamics and Treatment*, ed. J. S. Grotstein and J. A. Lang, pp. 59–68. Hillsdale, NJ: Analytic Press.

Goldberg, S. (1995). Introduction. In *Attachment Theory: Social, Developmental and Clinical Perspectives*, ed. S. Goldberg, R. Muir, and J. Kerr, pp. 1–15. New York: Analytic Press.

Goldberg, S., Gotowiec, A., and Simmons, R. J. (1995). Infant–mother attachment and behavior problems in healthy and chronically ill pre-schoolers. *Development and Psychopathology* 7:267–282.

Goldberg, W. A., and Easterbrooks, M. A. (1984). The role of marital quality in toddler development. *Developmental Psychology* 20:504–514.

Goosens, F., and van Ijzendoorn, M. (1990). Quality of infants' attachment to professional caregivers. *Child Development* 61:832–837.

Gopnik, A., and Slaughter, V. (1991). Young children's understanding of changes in their mental states. *Child Development* 62:98–110.

Green, A. (1975). The analyst, symbolisation and absence in the analytic setting: on changes in analytic practice and analytic experience. *International Journal of Psycho-Analysis* 56:1–22.

Green, J. (2000). A new method of evaluating attachment representations in young school-age children: the Manchester Child Evaluation Story Task. *Attachment and Human Development* 2(1):48–70.

Greenacre, P. (1952). Pregenital patterning. *International Journal of Psycho-Analysis* 33:410–415.

Greenberg, J. R., and Mitchell, S. A. (1983). *Object Relations in Psychoanalytic Theory*. Cambridge, MA: Harvard University Press.

Greenberg, M. T. (1999). Attachment and psychopathology in childhood. In *Handbook of Attachment: Theory, Research, and Clinical Applications*, ed. J. Cassidy and P. R. Shaver, pp. 469–496. New York: Guilford.

Greenberg, M. T., Speltz, M. L., DeKlyen, M., and Endriga, M. C. (1991). Attachment security in preschoolers with and without externalizing problems: a replication. *Development and Psychopathology* 3:413–430.

Grice, H. P. (1989). *Studies in the Way of Words*. Cambridge, MA: Harvard University Press.

Griffin, D. W., and Bartholomew, K. (1994). The metaphysics of measurement: the case of adult attachment. In *Advances in Personal Relationships: Vol 5. Attachment Processes in Adulthood*, ed. K. Bartholomew and D. Perlman, pp. 17–52. London: Jessica Kingsley.

Grosskruth, P. (1987). *Melanie Klein: Her World and her Work*. Cambridge, MA: Harvard University Press.

Grossman, K. E., and Grossman, K. (1991). Attachment quality as an organizer of emotional and behavioural responses in a longitudinal perspective. In *Attachment Across the Life Cycle*, ed. C. M. Parkes, J. Stevenson-Hinde, and J. Marris, pp. 93–114. London and New York: Routledge.

Grossman, K. E., Grossman, K., Winter, M., and Zimmerman, P. (in press). Attachment relationships and appraisal of partnership: from early experience of sensitive support to later relationship representation. In *Paths to Succesful Development*, ed. L. Pulkkinen and A. Caspi. Cambridge: Cambridge University Press.

Grossman, K. E., Grossman, K., and Zimmermann, P. (1999). A wider view of attachment and exploration. In *Handbook of Attachment: Theory, Research and Clinical Applications*, ed. J. Cassidy and P. R. Shaver, pp. 760–786. New York: Guilford.

Gunderson, J. G. (1996). The borderline patient's intolerance of aloneness: Insecure attachments and therapist availability. *American Journal of Psychiatry* 153(6):752–758.

Guntrip, H. (1961). *Personality Structure and Human Interaction*. New York: International Universities Press.

———. (1969). *Schizoid Phenomena, Object Relations and the Self*. New York: International Universities Press.

Hamilton, C. E. (in press). Continuity and discontinuity of attachment from infancy through adolescence. *Child Development*.

Hamilton, V. (1996). *The Analyst's Preconscious*. Hillsdale, NJ: Analytic Press.

Hanley, C. (1978). A critical consideration of Bowlby's ethological theory of anxiety. *Psychoanalytic Quarterly* 47:364–380.

Hann, D. M., Castino, R. J., Jarosinski, J., and Britton, H. (1991). *Relating mother-toddler negotiation patterns to infant attachment and maternal depression with an adolescent mother sample*. Paper presented at The Consequences of Adolescent Parenting: Predicting Behavior Problems in Toddlers and Preschoolers. Symposium conducted at the biennial meeting of the Society for Research in Child Development, Seattle, WA, April.

Harlow, H. F. (1958). The nature of love. *American Psychologist* 13:673–678.

Hart, J., Gunnar, M., and Cicchetti, D. (1995). Salivary cortisol in maltreated children: evidence of relations between neuroendocrine activity and social competence. Special issue: emotions in developmental psychopathology. *Development and Psychopathology* 7:11–26.

Hartmann, H. (1950). *Comments on the Psychoanalytic Theory of the Ego*. New York: International Universities Press, 1964.

———. (1952). The mutual influences in the development of ego and id. In *Essays on Ego Psychology*, pp. 155–182. New York: International Universities Press, 1964.

———. (1955). Notes on the theory of sublimation. In *Essays on Ego*

Psychology, pp. 215–240. New York: International Universities Press, 1964.

Hartmann, H., Kris, E., and Loewenstein, R. (1946). Comments on the formation of psychic structure. *Psychoanalytic Study of the Child* 2:11–38. New York International Universities Press.

Hazan, C., and Shaver, P. (1987). Romantic love conceptualized as an attachment process. *Journal of Personality and Social Psychology* 52:511–524.

———. (1990). Love and work: an attachment theoretical perspective. *Journal of Personality and Social Psychology* 59:270–280.

Hegel, G. (1807). *The Phenomenology of Spirit.* Oxford: Oxford University Press.

Heinicke, C., and Westheimer, I. J. (1966). *Brief Separations.* New York: International Universities Press.

Hermann, I. (1923). Zur Psychologie der Chimpanzen. *Internationale Zeitschrift fur Psychoanalyse* 9:80–87.

Hertsgaard, L., Gunnar, M., Erickson, M. F., and Nachmias, M. (1995). Adrenocortical response to the strange situation in infants with disorganized/disoriented attachment relationships. *Child Development* 66:1100–1106.

Hesse, E. (1999). The Adult Attachment Interview. In *Handbook of Attachment: Theory, Research and Clinical Applications*, ed. J. Cassidy and P. R. Shaver, pp. 395–433. New York: Guilford.

Hesse, E., and Main, M. (in press). Disorganization in infant and adult attachment: description, correlates and implications for developmental psychopathology. *Journal of the American Psychoanalytic Association.*

Hirschi, T. (1969). *Causes of Delinquency.* Berkeley, CA: University of California Press.

Hodges, J., and Tizard, B. (1989). Social and family relationships of exinstitutional adolescents. *Journal of Child Psychology and Psychiatry* 30:77–97.

Hofer, M. A. (1990). Early symbiotic processes: hard evidence from a soft place. In *Pleasure Beyond the Pleasure Principle*, ed. R. A. Glick and S. Bone, pp. 13–25. New Haven: Yale University Press.

———. (1995). Hidden regulators: implications for a new understanding of attachment, separation and loss. In *Attachment Theory: So-*

cial, Developmental, and Clinical Perspectives, ed. S. Goldberg, R. Muir, and J. Kerr, pp. 203–230. Hillsdale, NJ: Analytic Press.

———. (1996). On the nature and consequences of early loss. *Psychosomatic Medicine* 58:570–581.

Hoffman, I. Z. (1994). Dialectic thinking and therapeutic action in the psychoanalytic process. *Psychoanalytic Quarterly* 63:187–218.

Holland, R. (1990). Scientificity and psychoanalysis: insights from the controversial discussions. *International Review of Psycho-Analysis* 17:133–158.

Holmes, J. (1993a). Attachment theory: a biological basis for psychotherapy? *British Journal of Psychiatry* 163:430–438.

———. (1993b). *John Bowlby and Attachment Theory.* London: Routledge.

———. (1995). Something there is that does not love a wall: John Bowlby, attachment theory and psychoanalysis. In *Attachment Theory: Social, Developmental and Clinical Perspectives*, ed. S. Goldberg, R. Muir, and J. Kerr, pp. 19–45. New York: Analytic Press.

———. (1996a). *Attachment, Intimacy, Autonomy: Using Attachment Theory in Adult Psychotherapy.* Northville, NJ: Jason Aronson.

———. (1996b). Psychotherapy and memory—an attachment perspective. *British Journal of Psychotherapy* 13(2):204–218.

———. (1997). Attachment, autonomy, intimacy: some clinical implications of attachment theory. *British Journal of Medical Psychology* 70:231–248.

———. (1998a). The changing aims of psychoanalytic psychotherapy: An integrative perspective. *International Journal of Psycho-Analysis* 79:227–240.

———. (1998b). Defensive and creative uses of narrative in psychotherapy: an attachment perspective. In *Narrative and Psychotherapy and Psychiatry*, ed. G. Roberts and J. Holmes, pp. 49–68. Oxford: Oxford University Press.

———. (2000). Manual for Brief Attachment Based Intervention. Devon Health Authority. Unpublished manuscript.

———. (in press). Attachment theory and psychoanalysis: a rapprochement. *International Journal of Psycho-Analysis.*

Holtzworth-Munroe, A., Stuart, A., and Hutchison, G. (1997). Violent vs. non-violent husbands: differences in attachment patterns, dependency and jealousy. *Journal of Family Psychology* 11: 314–331.

Horowitz, L. M., Rosenberg, S. E., and Bartholomew, K. (1996). Interpersonal problems, attachment styles and outcome in brief dynamic psychotherapy. *Journal of Consulting and Clinical Psychology* 61:549–560.

Howes, C., Hamilton, C. E., and Matheson, C. C. (1994). Children's relationships with peers: differential associations with aspects of the teacher–child relationship. *Child Development* 65:253–263.

Hubbs-Tait, L., Osofsky, J., Hann, D., and Culp, A. (1994). Predicting behavior problems and social competence in children of adolescent mothers. *Family relations* 43: 439–446.

Hughes, C., Dunn, J., and White, A. (1998). Trick or treat? Uneven understanding of mind and emotion and executive dysfunction in "hard-to-manage" preschoolers. *Journal of Child Psychology and Psychiatry* 39:981–994.

Insel, T. (1997). A neurobiological basis of social attachment. *American Journal of Psychiatry* 154:726–735.

Isabella, R., and Belsky, J. (1991). Interactional synchrony and the origins of infant-mother attachment: a replication study. *Child Development* 62:373–384.

Jacobovitz, D., and Hazen, N. (1999). Developmental pathways from infant disorganization to childhood peer relationships. In *Attachment Disorganization*, ed. J. Solomon and C. George, pp. 127–159. New York: Guilford Press.

Jacobovitz, D., Hazen, N., and Riggs, S. (1997). *Disorganized mental processes in mothers, frightening/frightened caregiving and disoriented/disorganized behavior in infancy.* Paper presented at the Biennial Meeting of the Society for Research in Child Development, Washington, DC.

Jacobsen, T., Edelstein, W., and Hofmann, V. (1994). A longitudinal study of the relation between representations of attachment in childhood and cognitive functioning in childhood and adolescence. *Developmental Psychology* 30:112–124.

Jacobsen, T., Huss, M., Fendrich, M., Kruesi, M. J. P., and Ziegenhain, U. (1997). Children's ability to delay gratification: longitudinal relations to mother–child attachment. *Journal of Genetic Psychology* 158:411–426.

Jacobson, E. (1954a). Contribution to the metapsychology of psychotic identifications. *Journal of the American Psychoanalytic Association* 2:239–262.

————. (1954b). The self and the object world: vicissitudes of their infantile cathexes and their influence on ideational affective development. *Psychoanalytic Study of the Child* 9:75–127. New York: International Universities Press.

————. E. (1964). *The Self and the Object World.* New York: International Universities Press.

Johnson, J. G., Cohen, P., Brown, J., Smailes, E. M., and Bernstein, D. P. (1999). Childhood maltreatment increases risk for personality disorders during early adulthood. *Archives of General Psychiatry* 56:600–605.

Johnson-Laird, P. N. (1983). *Mental Models: Towards a Cognitive Science of Language, Inference and Consciousness.* Cambridge: Cambridge University Press.

————. (1990). The development of reasoning ability. In *Causes of Development: Interdisciplinary Perspectives*, ed. G. Butterworth and P. Bryant, pp. 85–110. Hillsdale, NJ: Erlbaum.

Johnson-Laird, P. N., and Byrne, R. M. (1991). *Deduction.* Hillsdale, NJ: Erlbaum.

————. (1993). Precis of deduction. *Behavioural and Brain Sciences* 16:323–380.

Joseph, B. (1989). *Psychic Equilibrium and Psychic Change.* London: Routledge.

Kahn, M. (1974). *The Privacy of the Self.* London: Hogarth.

————. (1978). Secret and potential space. In *Hidden Selves.* London: Hogarth, 1983.

Kandel, E. R. (1998). A new intellectual framework for psychiatry. *American Journal of Psychiatry* 155:457–469.

————. (1999). Biology and the future of psychoanalysis: a new intellectual framework for psychiatry revisited. *American Journal of Psychiatry* 156:505–524.

Kaplan, N. (1987). *Individual Differences in 6-Year-Olds' Thoughts about Separation: Predicted from Attachment to Mother at Age 1.* Berkeley: University of California.

Karen, R. (1994). *Becoming Attached.* New York: Warner.

Kellman, P. J., and Spelke, E. S. (1983). Perception of partly occluded objects in infancy. *Cognitive Psychology* 15:483–524.

Kennedy, H., and Moran, G. (1991). Reflections on the aims of child psychoanalysis. *Psychoanalytic Study of the Child* 46:181–198. New Haven, CT: Yale University Press.

Kennedy, H., and Yorke, C. (1980). Childhood neurosis v. developmental deviations: two clinical case histories. *Dialogue: A Journal of Psychoanalytic Perspectives* 4:20–33.

Kernberg, O. F. (1967). Borderline personality organization. *Journal of the American Psychoanalytic Association* 15:641–685.

———. (1975). *Borderline Conditions and Pathological Narcissism*. New York: Jason Aronson.

———. (1976a). *Object Relations Theory and Clinical Psychoanalysis*. New York: Jason Aronson.

———. (1976b). Technical considerations in the treatment of borderline personality organization. *Journal of the American Psychoanalytic Association* 24:795–829.

———. (1977). The structural diagnosis of borderline personality organization. In *Borderline Personality Disorders: The Concept, the Syndrome, the Patient*, ed. P. Nartocollis, pp. 87–121. New York: International Universities Press.

———. (1980). *Internal World and External Reality: Object Relations Theory Applied*. New York: Jason Aronson.

———. (1982). Self, ego, affects and drives. *Journal of the American Psychoanalytic Association* 30:893–917.

———. (1984). *Severe Personality Disorders: Psychotherapeutic Strategies*. New Haven, CT: Yale University Press.

———. (1987). Borderline personality disorder: a psychodynamic approach. *Journal of Personality Disorders* 1:344–346.

———. (1988). Object relations theory in clinical practice. *Psychoanalytic Quarterly* LVII:481–504.

———. (1993). The current status of psychoanalysis. *Journal of the American Psychoanalytic Association* 41:45–62.

Kernberg, O. F., Selzer, M. A., Koenigsberg, H. W., Carr, A. C., and Appelbaum, A. H. (1989). *Psychodynamic Psychotherapy of Borderline Patients*. New York: Basic Books.

Klein, G. S. (1976). Freud's two theories of sexuality. *Psychological Issues* 36:14–70.

Klein, M. (1929). Infantile anxiety-situations reflected in a work of art and in the creative impulse. In *Contributions to Psycho-*

analysis, 1921–1945, pp. 227–235. New York: McGraw-Hill, 1964.

———. (1930). The importance of symbol-formation in the development of the ego. In *Contributions to Psychoanalysis, 1921–1945.* New York: McGraw-Hill, 1964.

———. (1932a). *The Psycho-Analysis of Children.* London: Hogarth.

———. (1932b). The psycho-analysis of children. In *The Writings of Melanie Klein.* London: Hogarth, 1975.

———. (1935). A contribution to the psychogenesis of manic-depressive states. In *The Writings of Melanie Klein,* pp. 236–289. London: Hogarth, 1975.

———. (1936). The psychotherapy of the psychoses. In *Contributions to psychoanalysis, 1921–1945.* New York: McGraw-Hill, 1964.

———. (1945). The Oedipus complex in the light of early anxieties. In *The Writings of Melanie Klein,* pp. 370–419. London: Hogarth, 1975.

———. (1946). Notes on some schizoid mechanisms. In *Developments in Psychoanalysis,* ed. M. Klein, P. Heimann, S. Isaacs, and J. Riviere, pp. 292–320. London: Hogarth.

———. (1957). Envy and gratitude. In *The Writings of Melanie Klein,* vol. 3, pp. 176–235. London: Hogarth.

———. (1959). Our adult world and its roots in infancy. In *The Writings of Melanie Klein,* vol. 3, ed. R. Money-Kyrle, pp. 247–263. London: Hogarth, 1975.

———. (1980). On Mahler's autistic and symbiotic phases: An exposition and evolution. *Psychoanalysis and Contemparary Thought* 4:69–105.

———. (1981). On Mahler's autistic and symbiotic phases: an exposition and evaluation. *Psychoanalysis and Contemporary Thought* 4:69–105.

Kobak, R., and Sceery, A. (1988). Attachment in late adolescence: working models, affect regulation and perceptions of self and others. *Child Development* 59:135–146.

Kohut, H. (1971). *The Analysis of the Self.* New York: International Universities Press.

———. (1972). Thoughts on narcissism and narcissistic rage. *Psychoanalytic Study of the Child* 27:360–400. New Haven, CT: Yale University Press.

——. (1977). *The Restoration of the Self.* New York: International Universities Press.

——. (1984). *How Does Analysis Cure?* Chicago: University of Chicago Press.

Kohut, H., and Wolf, E. S. (1978). The disorders of the self and their treatment: an outline. *International Journal of Psycho-Analysis* 59:413–426.

Kramer, S. (1979). The technical significance and application of Mahler's separation-individuation theory. *Journal of the American Psychoanalytic Association* 27:241–262.

Kramer, S., and Akhtar, S. (1988). The developmental context of internalized preoedipal object relations: clinical applications of Mahler's theory of symbiosis and separation-individuation. *Psychoanalytic Quarterly* LVII:547–576.

Kris, E. (1952). *Psychoanalytic Explorations in Art.* New York: International Universities Press.

Kupersmidt, K. B., Coie, J. D., and Dodge, K. A. (1990). The role of poor peer relationships in the development of disorder. In *Peer Rejection in Childhood*, ed. S. R. Asher and J. D. Coie, pp. 274–305. Cambridge: Cambridge University Press.

Laible, D. J., and Thompson, R. A. (1998). Attachment and emotional understanding in pre-school children. *Developmental Psychology* 34:1038–1045.

Lamb, M. (1987). Predictive implications of individual differences in attachment. *Journal of Consulting Clinical Psychology* 55:817–824.

Lamb, M. E., Thompson, R. A., Gardner, W., and Charnov, E. (1985). *Infant–Mother Attachment: The Origins and Developmental Significance of Individual Differences in Strange Situation Behavior.* Hillsdale, NJ: Erlbaum.

Lecours, S., and Bouchard, M.-A. (1997). Dimensions of mentalisation: outlining levels of psychic transformation. *International Journal of Psycho-Analysis* 78:855–875.

LeDoux, J. E. (1995). Emotion: clues from the brain. *Annual Review of Psychology* 46:209–235.

Levenson, E. (1972). *The Fallacy of Understanding.* New York: Basic Books.

——. (1983). *The Ambiguity of Change.* New York: Basic Books.

———. (1990). *The Purloined Self*. New York: Contemporary Psychoanalysis Books.

Levinson, A., and Fonagy, P. (in press). Attachment classification in prisoners and psychiatric patients.

Lewin, K. (1952). *Field Theory and Social Science*. London: Tavistock Publications.

Lewis, M., and Feiring, C. (1989). Early predictor of childhood friendship. In *Peer Relationships in Child Development*, ed. T. J. Berndt and G. W. Ladd, pp. 246–273. New York: Wiley.

Lichtenberg, J. (1989). *Psychoanalysis and Motivation*. Hillsdale, NJ: Analytic Press.

Lichtenberg, J. D. (1995). Can empirical studies of development impact on psychoanalytic theory and technique? In *Research in Psychoanalysis: Process, Development, Outcome*, ed. T. Shapiro and R. N. Emde, pp. 261–276. New York: International Universities Press.

Lichtenstein, H. (1961). Identity and sexuality: a study of their interrelationship in man. *Journal of the American Psychoanalytic Association* 9:179–260.

———. (1963). The dilemma of human identity. Notes on self-transformation, self-observation, and metamorphosis. *Journal of the American Psychoanalytic Association* 11:173–223.

Lieberman, A. F. (1991). Attachment theory and infant-parent psychotherapy: Some conceptual, clinical and research issues. In *Rochester Symposium on Developmental Psychopathology: Vol. 3. Models and Integrations*, ed. D. Cicchetti and S. Toth, pp. 261–288. Hillsdale, NJ: Erlbaum.

Lieberman, A. F., and Pawl, J. (1993). Infant-parent psychotherapy. In *Handbook of Infant Mental Health*, ed. C. H. Zeanah, pp. 427–442. New York: Guilford.

Lieberman, A. F., and Zeanah, C. H. (1999). Contributions of attachment theory to infant-parent psychotherapy and other interventions with infants and young children. In *Handbook of Attachment: Theory, Research and Clinical Applications*, ed. J. Cassidy and P. R. Shaver, pp. 555–574. New York: Guilford.

Lilleskov, R. (1992). Review of "Attachment in the Pre-school Years: Theory Research and Intervention." *International Review of Psycho-Analysis* 19:126–130.

Liotti, G. (1995). Disorganized/disorientated attachment in the psycho-therapy of the dissociative disorders. In *Attachment Theory: Social, Developmental, and Clinical Perspectives*, ed. S. Goldberg, R. Muir, and J. Kerr, pp. 343–363. Hillsdale, NJ: Analytic Press.

Loeber, R. (1990). Development and risk factors of juvenile antisocial behaviour and delinquency. *Clinical Psychology Review* 10:1–42.

Lorenz, K. (1935). Der Kumpan in der Umvelt des Vogels [Companionship in Bird Life]. In *Instinctive Behavior*, ed. & trans. C. H. Schiller, pp. 83–128. New York: International Universities Press.

Luquet, P. (1981). Le changement dans la mentalisation. *Revue Francais de Psychoanalyse* 45:1023–1028.

———. (1987). Penser-Parler: un apport psychanalytique a la theorie du langage. In *La Parole Troublee*, ed. R. Christie, M. M. Christie-Luterbacher, and P. Luquet, pp. 161–300. Paris: Presses Universitaire de France.

———. (1988). Langage, pensee et structure psychique. *Revue Francais de Psychoanalyse* 52:267–302.

Lyons-Ruth, K. (1991). Rapprochement or approchement: Mahler's theory reconsidered from the vantage point of recent research in early attachment relationships. *Psychoanalytic Psychology* 8:1–23.

———. (1995). Broadening our conceptual frameworks: can we re-introduce relational strategies and implicit representational systems to the study of psychopathology? *Developmental Psychology* 31:432–436.

———. (1996a). Attachment relationships among children with aggressive behavior problems: the role of disorganized early attachment patterns. *Journal of Consulting and Clinical Psychology* 64:32–40.

———. (1996b). Attachment relationships among children with aggressive behavior problems: the role of disorganized early attachment patterns. *Journal of Consulting and Clinical Psychology* 64:64–73.

———. (1999). The two person unconscious: intersubjective dialogue, enactive relational representation and the emergence of new forms of relational organization. *Psychoanalytic Inquiry* 19(4):576–617.

Lyons-Ruth, K., Alpern, L., and Repacholi, B. (1993). Disorganized infant attachment classification and maternal psychosocial problems as predictors of hostile-aggressive behavior in the preschool classroom. *Child Development* 64:572–585.

Lyons-Ruth, K., and Block, D. (1996). The disturbed caregiving system: relations among childhood trauma, maternal caregiving and infant affect and attachment. *Infant Mental Health Journal* 17:257–275.

Lyons-Ruth, K., Bronfman, E., and Atwood, G. (1999). A relational diathesis model of hostile-helpless states of mind: expressions in mother–infant interaction. In *Attachment Disorganization*, ed. J. Solomon and C. George, pp. 33–70. New York: Guilford.

Lyons-Ruth, K., Bronfman, E., and Parsons. (1999). Atypical attachment in infancy and early childhood among children at developmental risk. IV. Maternal frightened, frightening, or atypical behavior and disorganized infant attachment patterns. In *Typical Patterns of Infant Attachment: Theory, Research and Current Directions*, ed. J. Vondra and D. Barnett, pp. 67–96. Monographs of the Society for Research in Child Development, vol. 64.

Lyons-Ruth, K., Connell, D. B., and Grunebaum, H. U. (1990). Infants at social risk: maternal depression and family support services as mediators of infant development and security of attachment. *Child Development* 61:85–98.

Lyons-Ruth, K., Easterbrooks, A., and Cibelli, C. (1997). Infant attachment strategies, infant mental lag, and maternal depressive symptoms: predictors of internalizing and externalizing problems at age 7. *Developmental Psychology* 33:681–692.

Lyons-Ruth, K., and Jacobovitz, D. (1999). Attachment disorganization: unresolved loss, relational violence and lapses in behavioral and attentional strategies. In *Handbook of Attachment Theory and Research*, ed. J. Cassidy and P. R. Shaver, pp. 520–554. New York: Guilford.

Lyons-Ruth, K., Repacholi, B., McLeod, S., and Silver, E. (1991). Disorganized attachment behavior in infancy: short-term stability, maternal and infant correlates, and risk-related sub-types. *Development and Psychopathology* 3:377–396.

Lyons-Ruth, K., Zoll, D., Connell, D., and Grunebaum, H. U. (1986). The depressed mother and her one-year-old infant: environment, interaction, attachment, and infant development. In *Maternal Depression and Infant Disturbance*, ed. E. Z. Tronick and T. Field, pp. 61–82. San Francisco: Jossey-Bass.

———. (1989). Family deviance and family disruption in childhood: associations with maternal behavior and infant maltreatment during the first two years of life. *Development and Psychopathology* 1:219–216.

Maccoby, E. E. (2000). Parenting and its effects on children: on reading and misreading behaviour genetics. *Annual Review of Psychology* 51:1–27.

Mace, C., and Margison, R. (1997). Attachment and psychotherapy: an overview. *British Journal of Medical Psychology* 70:209–215.

Mahler, M. S. (1967). On human symbiosis and the vicissitudes of individuation. *Journal of the American Psychoanalytic Association* 15:740–763.

———. (1971). A study of separation-individuation process and its possible application to borderline phenomena in the psychoanalytic situation. *Psychoanalytic Study of the Child* 26:403–424. New Haven, CT: Yale University Press.

———. (1972a). On the first three subphases of the separation-individuation process. *International Journal of Psycho-Analysis* 53:333–338.

———. (1972b). Rapprochement subphase of the separation-individuation process. *Psychoanalytic Quarterly* 41:487–506.

———. (1975). On human symbiosis and the vicissitudes of individuation. *Journal of the American Psychoanalytic Association* 23:740–763.

Mahler, M. S., and Furer, M. (1968). *On human symbiosis and the vicissitudes of individuation. Vol. 1: Infantile psychosis.* New York: International Universities Press.

Mahler, M. S., and Kaplan, L. (1977). Developmental aspects in the assessment of narcissistic and so-called borderline personalities. In *Borderline Personality Disorders: The Concept, the Syndrome, the Patient*, ed. P. Hartocollis, pp. 71–86. New York: International Universities Press.

Mahler, M., and McDevitt, J. F. (1980). The separation-individuation process and identity formation. In *Infancy and Early Childhood, Vol. 1 of The Course of Life, Psychoanalytic Contributions toward Understanding Personality Development*, ed. S. I. Greenspan and G. H. Pollock, pp. 395–406. Washington, DC: Publication No. (ADM) 80-786. National Institute of Mental Health.

Mahler, M. S., Pine, F., and Bergman, A. (1975). *The Psychological Birth of the Human Infant: Symbiosis and Individuation.* New York: Basic Books.

Main, M. (1991). Metacognitive knowledge, metacognitive monitoring, and singular (coherent) vs. multiple (incoherent) model of attachment: Findings and directions for future research. In *Attachment Across the Life Cycle*, ed. C. M. Parkes, J. Stevenson-Hinde, and P. Marris, pp. 127–159. London: Tavistock/Routledge.

————. (1995). Recent studies in attachment: overview, with selected implications for clinical work. In *Attachment Theory: Social, Developmental, and Clinical Perspectives*, ed. S. Goldberg, R. Muir, and J. Kerr, pp. 407–474. Hillsdale, NJ: Analytic Press.

Main, M., and Cassidy, J. (1988). Categories of response to reunion with the parent at age 6: Predictable from infant attachment classifications and stable over a 1-month period. *Developmental Psychology* 24:415–426.

————. (1995). Adult attachment classification system. In *Behavior and the Development of Representational Models of Attachment: Five Methods of Assessment*, ed. M. Main. Cambridge University Press.

————. (1998). Adult attachment scoring and classification system. University of California at Berkeley. Unpublished Manuscript.

————. (1998a). Adult attachment scoring and classification systems. University of California at Berkeley. Unpublished manuscript.

————. (1998b). Interview-based adult attachment classifications: related to infant–mother and infant–father attachment. University of California at Berkeley. Unpublished manuscript.

————. (in press). Adult attachment rating and classification systems. In *A Typology of Human Attachment Organization Assessed in Discourse, Drawings and Interviews* (working title), ed. M. Main. New York: Cambridge University Press.

Main, M., and Hesse, E. (1990). Parents' unresolved traumatic experiences are related to infant disorganized attachment status: Is frightened and/or frightening parental behavior the linking mechanism? In *Attachment in the Preschool Years: Theory, Research and Intervention*, ed. M. Greenberg, D. Cicchetti, and E. M. Cummings, pp. 161–182. Chicago: University of Chicago Press.

————. (1992). Disorganized/disoriented infant behaviour in the Strange Situation, lapses in the monitoring of reasoning and discourse during the parent's Adult Attachment Interview, and dissociative states. In *Attachment and Psychoanalysis*, ed. M. Ammaniti and D. Stern, pp. 86–140. Rome: Gius, Latereza and Figli.

Main, M., Kaplan, N., and Cassidy, J. (1985a). Security in infancy, childhood and adulthood: a move to the level of representation. In *Growing Points of Attachment Theory and Research. Monographs of the Society for Research in Child Development*, vol. 50, ed. I. Bretherton and E. Waters, pp. 66–104. Chicago: University of Chicago Press.

———. (1985b). Security in infancy, childhood, and adulthood: a move to the level of representation. *Monographs of the Society for Research in Child Development* 50(1–2):66–104.

Main, M., and Solomon, J. (1986). Discovery of an insecure-disorganized/disoriented attachment pattern. In *Affective Development in Infancy*, ed. T. B. Brazelton and M. W. Yogman, pp. 95–124. Norwood, NJ: Ablex.

———. (1990). Procedures for identifying infants as disorganized/disoriented during the Ainsworth Strange Situation. In *Attachment During the Preschool Years: Theory, Research and Intervention*, ed. M. Greenberg, D. Cicchetti, and E. M. Cummings, pp. 121–160. Chicago: University of Chicago Press.

Main, T. (1957). The ailment. *British Journal of Medical Psychology* 30:129–145.

Malatesta, C. Z., Culver, C., Tesman, J. R., and Shepard, B. (1989). The development of emotion expression during the first two years of life. *Monographs of the Society for Research in Child Development* 54:1–104.

Malatesta, C. Z., Grigoryev, P., Lamb, C., Albin, M., and Culver, C. (1986). Emotional socialisation and expressive development in pre-term and full-term infants. *Child Development* 57:316–330.

Marcovitch, S., Goldberg, S., Gold, A., et al. (1997). Determinants of behavioral problems in Romanian children adopted in Ontario. *International Journal of Behavioral Development* 20:17–31.

Marr, D. (1982). *Vision: A Computational Investigation into the Human Representation and Processing of Visual Information*. San Francisco: W. H. Freeman.

Marrone, M. (1998). *Attachment and Interaction*. London: Jessica Kingsley.

Martin, C. S., Earleywine, M., Blackson, T. C., et al. (1994). Aggressivity, inattention, hyperactivity, and impulsivity in boys at high and low risk for substance abuse. *Journal of Abnormal Child Psychology* 22:177–203.

Marty, P. (1968). A major process of somatization: the progressive disorganization. *International Journal of Psycho-Analysis* 49:246–249.
———. (1990). *La Psychosomatique de l'Adulte*. Paris: Presses Universitaire de France.
———. (1991). *Mentalisation et Psychosomatique*. Paris: Laboratoire Delagrange.
Marvin, R. S., and Britner, P. A. (1999). Normative development: the ontogeny of attachment. In *Handbook of Attachment: Theory, Research and Clinical Applications*, ed. J. Cassidy and P. R. Shaver, pp. 44–67. New York: Guilford.
Maslin, C. A., and Bates, J. E. (1983). *Precursors of anxious and secure attachments: a multivariant model at age 6 months*. Paper presented at the Biennial meeting of the Society for Research in Child Development, Detroit, MI.
Masson, J. (1984). *The Assault on Truth: Freud's Suppression of the Seduction Theory*. New York: Farrar, Straus and Giroux.
Masterson, J. F. (1972). *Treatment of the Borderline Adolescent: A Developmental Approach*. New York: Wiley Interscience.
———. (1976). *Psychotherapy of the Borderline Adult: A Developmental Approach*. New York: Brunner/Mazel.
Masterson, J. F., and Rinsley, D. (1975). The borderline syndrome: the role of the mother in the genesis and psychic structure of the borderline personality. *International Journal of Psycho-Analysis* 56:63–177.
Matthys, W., Cuperus, J. M., and van Engeland, H. (1999). Deficient social problem-solving in boys with ODD/CD, with ADHD, and with both disorders. *Journal of the American Academy of Child and Adolescent Psychiatry* 38:311–321.
Mayes, L. C., and Spence, D. P. (1994). Understanding therapeutic action in the analytic situation: a second look at the developmental metaphor. *Journal of the American Psychoanalytic Association* 42:789–816.
McDougall, J. (1978). *Plea for a Measure of Abnormality*. New York: International Universities Press.
———. (1989). *Theaters of the Body: A Psychoanalytic Approach to Psychosomatic Illness*. New York: Norton.
McGinn, C. (1989). *Mental Content*. Basil Blackwell.

McLaughlin, J. (1991). Clinical and theoretical aspects of enactment. *Journal of the American Psychoanalytic Association* 39:595–614.

Meins, E., Fernyhough, C., Russel, J., and Clark-Carter, D. (1998). Security of attachment as a predictor of symbolic and mentalising abilities: a longitudinal study. *Social Development* 7:1–24.

Meltzer, D. (1974). Mutism in infantile autism, schizophrenia and manic-depressive states. *International Journal of Psycho-Analysis* 55:397–404.

Meltzoff, A. N. (1995). Understanding the intentions of others: re-enactment of intended acts by 18-month-old children. *Developmental Psychology* 31:838–850.

Meltzoff, A. N., and Moore, M. K. (1977). Imitation of facial and manual gestures by human neonates. *Science* 198:75–78.

———. (1983). Newborn infants imitate adult facial gestures. *Child Development* 54:702–709.

———. (1989). Imitation in newborn infants: exploring the range of gestures imitated and the underlying mechanisms. *Developmental Psychology* 25:954–962.

Migone, P., and Liotti, G. (1998). Psychoanalysis and cognitive-evolutionary psychology: an attempt at integration. *International Journal of Psycho-Analysis* 79:1071–1095.

Mitchell, S. (1998). Attachment theory and the psychoanalytic tradition: reflections on human relationality. *British Journal of Psychotherapy* 15:177–193.

Mitchell, S. A. (1986). The wings of Icarus: Illusion and the problem of narcissism. *Contemporary Psychoanalysis* 22:107–132.

———. (1988). *Relational Concepts in Psychoanalysis: An Integration.* Cambridge, MA: Harvard University Press.

———. (1993a). Aggression and the endangered self. *Psychoanalytic Quarterly* 62:351–382.

———. (1993b). *Hope and Dread in Psychoanalysis.* New York: Basic Books.

———. (1995). Interaction in the Kleinian and interpersonal traditions. *Contemporary Psychoanalysis* 31:65–91.

———. (1996). Merton Gill: in appreciation. *Contemporary Psychoanalysis* 32:177–190.

———. (1997). *Influence and Autonomy in Psychoanalysis.* Hillsdale, NJ: Analytic Press.

Mitchell, S. A., and Black, M. (1995). *Freud and Beyond*. New York: Basic Books.

Modell, A. (1963). Primitive object relationships and the predisposition to schizophrenia. *International Journal of Psycho-Analysis* 44:282–292.

———. (1968). *Object Love and Reality*. New York: International Universities Press.

———. (1975). A narcissistic defense against affects and the illusion of self-sufficiency. *International Journal of Psycho-Analysis* 56:275–282.

———. (1984). *Psychoanalysis in a New Context*. New York: International Universities Press.

———. (1985). Object relations theory. In *Models of the Mind: Their Relationships to Clinical Work*, ed. A. Rothstein, pp. 85–100. New York: International Universities Press.

Morgan, A. C. (1998). Moving along to things left undone. *Infant Mental Health Journal* 19:324–332.

Morton, J., and Frith, U. (1995). Causal modeling: a structural approach to developmental psychology. In *Developmental psychopathology. Vol. 1: Theory and methods*, ed. D. Cicchetti and D. J. Cohen, pp. 357–390. New York: Wiley.

Moss, E., Parent, S., and Gosselin, C. (1995). *Attachment and theory of mind: cognitive and metacognitive correlates of attachment during the preschool period.* Paper presented at the biennial meeting of the Society for Research in Child Development, Indianapolis, Indiana, March-April.

Moss, E., Parent, S., Gosselin, C., Rousseau, D., and St.-Laurent, D. (1996). Attachment and teacher-reported behavior problems during the preschool and early school-age period. *Development and Psychopathology* 8:511–525.

Moss, E., Rousseau, D., Parent, S., St.-Laurent, D., and Saintong, J. (1998). Correlates of attachment at school-age: maternal reported stress, mother–child interaction and behavior problems. *Child Development* 69:1390–1405.

Moss, E., and St. Laurent, D. (1999). Disorganized attachment and developmental risk at school age. In *Attachment Disorganization*, ed. J. Solomon and C. George, pp. 160–186. New York: Guilford.

Murphy, L. B., and Moriarty, A. E. (1976). *Vulnerability, Coping, and*

Growth: From Infancy to Adolescence. New Haven, CT: Yale University Press.

Murray, L., and Cooper, P. J. (1997). The role of infant and maternal factors in postpartum depression, mother–infant interactions and infant outcome. In *Postpartum Depression and Child Development*, ed. L. Murray and P. J. Cooper, pp. 111–135. New York: Guilford.

Nesse, R. M. (1990). The evolutionary functions of repression and the ego defences. *Journal of the American Academy of Psychoanalysis* 18:260–285.

Nesse, R. M., and Lloyd, A. T. (1992). The evolution of psychodynamic mechanisms. In *The Adapted Mind*, ed. J. H. Barkow, L. Cosmides, and J. Tooby, pp. 601–624. New York: Oxford University Press.

NICHD Early Child Care Research Network (1997). The effects of infant child care on infant–mother attachment: security: results of the NICHD study of early child care. *Child Development* 68: 860–879.

O'Connor, M. J., Sigman, M., and Brill, N. (1987). Disorganization of attachment in relation to maternal alcohol consumption. *Journal of Consulting and Clinical Psychology* 55:831–836.

O'Connor, T. G., Rutter, M., and Kreppner, J. (2000). The effects of global severe privation of cognitive competence: extension and longitudinal follow-up. *Child Development* 71(2):376–390.

Ogawa, J. R., Sroufe, L. A., Weinfield, N. S., Carlson, E. A., and Egeland, B. (1997). Development and the fragmented self: longitudinal study of dissociative symptomatology in a nonclinical sample. *Development and Psychopathology* 9:855–879.

Ogden, T. (1994). The analytic third: working with intersubjective clinical facts. *International Journal of Psycho-Analysis* 75:3–19.

Ogden, T. H. (1989). *The Primitive Edge of Experience*. New York: Jason Aronson.

Oppenheim, D., Emde, R., and Warren, S. (1997). Children's narrative representations of mothers: their development and associations with child and mother adaptation. *Child Development* 68: 127–138.

Orbach, S. (1978). *Fat is a Feminist Issue*. London: Paddington Press.
———. (1986). *Hunger Strike*. London: Faber and Faber.

O'Shaughnessy, E. (1989). The invisible Oedipus complex. In *The Oedipus Complex Today*, ed. J. Steiner, pp. 129–150. London: Karnac.

Owen, M. T., and Cox, M. J. (1997). Marital conflict and the development of infant-parent attachment relationships. *Journal of Family Psychology* 11:152–164.

Parens, H. (1979). *The Development of Aggression in Early Childhood.* New York: Jason Aronson.

———. (1980). An exploration of the relations of instinctual drives and the symbiosis/separation-individuation process. *Journal of the American Psychoanalytic Association* 28:89–114.

Patrick, M., Hobson, R. P., Castle, D., Howard, R., and Maughan, B. (1994). Personality disorder and the mental representation of early social experience. *Developmental Psychopathology* 6:375–388.

Pawl, J., and Lieberman, A. F. (1997). Infant–parent psychotherapy. In *Handbook of Child and Adolescent Psychiatry*, vol. 1, ed. J. Noshpitz, pp. 339–351. New York: Basic Books.

Pederson, D. R., Gleason, K. E., Moran, G., and GBento, S. (1998). Maternal attachment representations, maternal sensitivity and the infant–mother attachment relationship. *Developmental Psychology* 34:925–933.

Perry, B. (1997). Incubated in terror: neurodevelopmental factors in the "cycle of violence." In *Children in a Violent Society*, ed. J. Osofsky, pp. 124–149. New York: Guilford.

Perry, D. G., Perry, L. C., and Kennedy, E. (1992). Conflict and the development of antisocial behavior. In *Conflict in Child and Adolescent Development*, ed. C. U. Shantz and W. W. Hartup, pp. 301–329. Cambridge: Cambridge University Press.

Peterfreund, E. (1978). Some critical comments on psychoanalytic conceptualizations of infancy. *International Journal of Psycho-Analysis* 59:427–441.

Polan, H. J., and Hofer, M. (1999). Psychobiological origins of infant attachment and separation responses. In *Handbook of Attachment: Theory, Research and Clinical Applications*, ed. J. Cassidy and P. R. Shaver, pp. 162–180. New York: Guilford.

Pope, A. W., and Bierman, K. L. (1999). Predicting adolescent peer problems and antisocial activities: the relative roles of aggression and dysregulation. *Developmental Psychology* 35:335–346.

Posada, G., Gao, Y., Wu, F., et al. (1995). The secure based phenomenon across cultures: children's behavior, mothers' preferences and experts' concepts. *Monographs of the Society for Research in Child Development* 60:27–48.

Pottharst, K. (1990). *Explorations in Adult Attachment.* New York: Peter Lang.

Quinodoz, J. M. (1991). Accepting fusion to get over it. *Review Francais de Psychoanalyse* 55:1697–1700.

Radke-Yarrow, M., Cummings, E. M., Kuczynski, L., and Chapman, M. (1985). Patterns of attachment in two- and three-year-olds in normal families and families with parental depression. *Child Development* 56:884–893.

Rajecki, D. W., Lamb, M., and Obmascher, P. (1978). Toward a general theory of infantile attachment: a comparative review of aspects of the social bond. *Behavioral and Brain Sciences* 3:417–464.

Rapaport, D., and Gill, M. M. (1959). The points of view and assumptions of metapsychology. *International Journal of Psycho-Analysis* 40: 153–162.

Rayner, E. (1991). *The Independent Mind in British Psychoanalysis.* London: Free Association Books.

Reiss, D., Hetherington, E. M., Plomin, R., et al. (1995). Genetic questions for environmental studies: differential parenting and psychopathology in adolescence. *Archives of General Psychiatry* 52:925–936.

Renik, O. (1993). Analytic interaction: conceptualizing technique in the light of the analyst's irreducible subjectivity. *Psychoanalytic Quarterly* 62:553–571.

Richters, J., and Walters, E. (1991). Attachment and socialization: the positive side of social influence. In *Social influences and socialization in infancy*, ed. M. Lewis and S. Feinman, pp. 185–213. New York: Plenum.

Rinsley, D. B. (1977). An object relations view of borderline personality. In *Borderline Personality Disorders: The Concept, the Syndrome, the Patient*, ed. P. Hartocollis, pp. 47–70. New York: International Universities Press.

———. (1978). Borderline psychopathology: a review of etiology dynamics and treatment. *International Review of Psycho-Analysis* 5:45–54.

———. (1982). *Borderline and Other Self Disorders: A Developmental and Object Relations Perspective.* New York: Jason Aronson.

Riviere, J. (1927). Contribution to symposium on child analysis. *International Journal of Psycho-Analysis* 8:373–377.

Robertson, J. (1962). *Hospitals and Children: A Parent's Eye View*. New York: Gollancz.

Rochlin, G. (1971). Review of Bowlby, J., *Attachment and Loss: Attachment*. *Psychoanalytic Quarterly* 50:504–506.

Rodning, C., Beckwith, L., and Howard, J. (1991). Quality of attachment and home environment in children prenatally exposed to PCP and cocaine. *Development and Psychopathology* 3:351–366.

Rogers, J. H., Widiger, T., and Krupp, A. (1995). Aspects of depression associated with borderline personality disorder. *American Journal of Psychiatry* 152:168–270.

Roiphe, H. (1976). Review of J. Bowlby, *Attachment and Loss. II: Separation, Anxiety and Anger*. *Psychoanalytic Quarterly* 65:307–309.

Rosenblatt, A. D., and Thickstun, J. T. (1977). *Modern Psychoanalytic Concepts in a General Psychology. Part 1: General Concepts and Principles. Part 2: Motivation*. New York: International Universities Press.

Rosenblum and Coplan. (1994). Adverse early experiences, affect, noradrenergic and serotonergic functioning in adult primates. *Biological Psychiatry* 3:221–227.

Rosenfeld, H. (1964). On the psychopathology of narcissism: a clinical approach. *International Journal of Psycho-Analysis* 45:332–337.

———. (1965). *Psychotic States: A Psychoanalytic Approach*. New York: International Universities Press.

———. (1971a). A clinical approach to the psychoanalytic theory of the life and death instincts: an investigation into to the aggressive aspects of narcissism. *International Journal of Psycho-Analysis* 52:169–178.

———. (1971b). Contribution to the psychopathology of psychotic states: the importance of projective identification in the ego structure and object relations of the psychotic patient. In *Melanie Klein Today*, ed. E. B. Spillius, pp. 117–137. London: Routledge, 1988.

Roy, P. R., and Pickles, A. (2000). Institutional care: risk from family background or pattern of rearing? *Journal of Child Psychology and Psychiatry* 41(2):139–149.

Rumelhart, D. E., and McClelland, J. L. (1986). *Parallel Distributed Processing*. Cambridge, Mass: MIT Press.

Rutter, M. (1971). *Maternal Deprivation Reassessed*. Harmondsworth, Middlesex: Penguin.

————. (1999). Psychosocial adversity and child psychopathology. *British Journal of Psychiatry* 174:480–493.

Rutter, M., and O'Connor, T. (1999). Implications of attachment theory for child care policies. In *Handbook of Attachment*, ed. J. Cassidy and P. R. Shaver, pp. 823–844. New York: Guilford.

Sagi, A., van Ijzendoorn, M. H., Scharf, M., et al. (1994). Stability and discriminant validity of the Adult Attachment Interview: a psychometric study in young Israeli adults. *Developmental Psychology* 30:771–777.

Sander, L. (in press). Interventions that effect therapeutic change. *Infant Mental Health Journal*.

Sander, L. W. (1962). Issues in early mother–child interaction. *Journal of the American Academy of Child Psychiatry* 1:141–166.

Sandler, J. (1960a). The background of safety. In *From Safety to Superego: Selected Papers of Joseph Sandler*, pp. 1–8. London: Karnac, 1987.

————. (1960b). The background of safety. In *From Safety to Superego: Selected Papers of Joseph Sandler*. London: Karnac, 1975.

————. (1960c). On the concept of superego. *Psychoanalytic Study of the Child* 15:128–162. New York: International Universities Press.

————. (1962). The Hampstead Index as an Instrument of Psychoanalytic Research. *Internal Journal of Psycho-Analysis* 43:287–291.

————. (1974). Psychological conflict and the structural model: some clinical and theoretical implications. *International Journal of Psycho-Analysis* 55:53–72.

————. (1976a). Actualization and object relationships. *Journal of the Philadelphia Association of Psychoanalysis* 3:59–70.

————. (1976b). Countertransference and role-responsiveness. *International Review of Psycho-Analysis* 3:43–47.

————. (1981). Character traits and object relationships. *Psychoanalytic Quarterly* 50:694–708.

————. (1983). Reflections on some relations between psychoanalytic concepts and psychoanalytic practice. *International Journal of Psycho-Analysis* 64:35–45.

————. (1985). Towards a reconsideration of the psychoanalytic theory of motivation. *Bulletin of the Anna Freud Centre* 8:223–243.

————. (1987a). The concept of projective identification. In *Projection, Identification, Projection Identification*, pp. 13–26. Madison, CT: International Universities Press.

———. (1987b). *From Safety to Superego: Selected Papers of Joseph Sandler*. New York: Guilford.

———. (1987c). *Projection, Identification, Projective Identification*. London: Karnac.

———. (1990). On the structure of internal objects and internal object relationships. *Psychoanalytic Inquiry* 10(2):163–181.

———. (1992). Reflections on developments in the theory of psychoanalytic technique. 37th Congress of the International Psychoanalytical Association: Psychic change: Developments in the theory of psychoanalytic technique (1991, Buenos Aires, Argentina). *International Journal of Psycho-Analysis* 73(2):189–198.

———. (1993). Communication from patient to analyst: not everything is projective identification. *British Psycho-Analytical Society Bulletin* 29:8–16.

Sandler, J., Holder, A., Dare, C., and Dreher, A. U. (1997). *Freud's Models of the Mind: An Introduction*. London: Karnac.

Sandler, J., and Rosenblatt, B. (1962). The representational world. In *From Safety to Superego: Selected Papers of Joseph Sandler*, pp. 58–72. London: Karnac, 1987.

Sandler, J., and Sandler, A.-M. (1978). On the development of object relationships and affects. *International Journal of Psycho-Analysis* 59:285–296.

——— (1998). *Object Relations Theory and Role Responsiveness*. London: Karnac.

Sapolsky, R. M. (1996). Why stress is bad for your brain. *Science* 273:749–750.

Schachter, D. L. (1992). Understanding implicit memory: a cognitive neuroscience approach. *American Psychologist* 47:559–569.

Schafer, R. (1974). Problems in Freud's psychology of women. *Journal of the American Psychoanalytic Association* 22:459–485.

———. (1983). *The Analytic Attitude*. New York: Basic Books.

Schore, A. N. (1997). Early organization of the nonlinear right brain and development of a predisposition to psychiatric disorders. *Development and Psychopathology* 9:595–631.

Schuengel, C., Bakermans-Kranenburg, M., and van Ijzendoorn, M. (1999a). Frightening maternal behaviour linking unresolved loss and disorganised infant attachment. *Journal of Consulting and Clinical Psychology* 67:54–63.

Schuengel, C., Bakermans-Kranenburg, M. J., van Ijzendoorn, M. H., and Blom, M. (1999b). Unresolved loss and infant disorganisation: links to frightening maternal behavior. In *Attachment Disorganization*, ed. J. Solomon and C. George, pp. 71–94. New York: Guilford.

Schur, M. (1960). Discussion of Dr. John Bowlby's paper. *Psychoanalytic Study of the Child* 15:63–84. New York: International Universities Press.

Searles, H. F. (1986). *My Work with Borderline Patients*. Northvale, NJ: Jason Aronson.

Segal, H. (1957). Notes on symbol formation. *International Journal of Psycho-Analysis* 38:391–397.

Settlage, C. F. (1977). The psychoanalytic understanding of narcissistic and borderline personality disorders: advances in developmental theory. *Journal of the American Psychoanalytic Association* 25:805–833.

———. (1980). The psychoanalytic theory and understanding of psychic development during the second and third years of life. In *The Course of Life*, ed. S. I. Greenspan and G. H. Pollock, pp. 523–539. Washington, D.C.: NIMH.

Shane, M., Shane, E., and Gales, M. (1997). *Intimate Attachments: Toward a New Self Psychology*. New York: Guilford.

Shaw, D., and Bell, R. Q. (1993). Developmental theories of parental contributors to antisocial behavior. *Journal of Abnormal Child Psychology* 21: 493–518.

Shaw, D. S., Owens, E. B., Vondra, J. I., Keenan, K., and Winslow, E. B. (1996). Early risk factors and pathways in the development of early disruptive behavior problems. *Development and Psychopathology* 8:679–699.

———. (1997). Early risk factors and pathways in the development of early disruptive behavior problems. *Development and Psychopathology* 8:679–700.

Shaw, D. S., and Vondra, J. I. (1995). Infant attachment security and maternal predictors of early behavior problems: a longitudinal study of low-income families. *Journal of Abnormal Child Psychology* 23:335–357.

Shelton, T. L., Barkley, R. A., Crosswait, C., et al. (1998). Psychiatric and psychological morbidity as a function of adaptive disability in preschool children with aggressive and hyperactive-impulsive-inattentive behavior. *Journal of Abnormal Child Psychology* 26: 475–494.

Silverman, R., Lieberman, A. F., and Pekarsky, J. H. (1997). Anxiety disorders. In *Casebook of the Zero to Three Diagnostic Classification of Mental Health and Developmental Disorders of Infancy and Early Childhood*, ed. A. F. Lieberman, S. Wieder, and E. Fenichel, pp. 47–59. Arlington, VA: Zero to Three.

Simpson, J. A., Rholes, W. S., and Nelligan, J. S. (1992). Support seeking and support giving within couples in an anxiety provoking situation: the role of attachment styles. *Journal of Personality and Social Psychology* 60:434–446.

Slade, A. (1987). Quality of attachment and early symbolic play. *Developmental Psychology* 17:326–335.

———. (1996). A view from attachment theory and research. *Journal of Clinical Psychoanalysis* 5:112–123.

———. (1999a). Attachment theory and research: implications for the theory and practice of individual psychotherapy with adults. In *Handbook of Attachment: Theory, Research and Clinical Applications*, ed. J. Cassidy and P. R. Shaver, pp. 575–594. New York: Guilford.

———. (1999b). Representation, symbolization and affect regulation in the concomitant treatment of a mother and child: attachment theory and child psychotherapy. *Psychoanalytic Inquiry* 19:824–857.

———. (in press). The development and organisation of attachment: implications for psychoanalysis. *Journal of the American Psychoanalytic Association*.

Slade, A., Belsky, J., Aber, J. L., and Phelps, J. L. (1999a). Mothers' representation of their relationships with their toddlers links to adult attachment and observed mothering. *Developmental Psychology* 35:611–619.

——— (1999b). Maternal representations of their toddlers: links to adult attachment and observed mothering. *Developmental Psychology* 35:611–619.

Slough, N. M., and Greenberg, M. T. (1990). 5-year-olds' representations of separations from parents: responses from the perspective of self and other. *New Directions for Child Development* 48:67–84.

Solomon, J., and George, C. (1999a). *Attachment Disorganization*. New York: Guilford.

———. (1999b). The measurement of attachment security in infancy and childhood. In *Handbook of Attachment: Theory, Research and Clinical Applications*, ed. J. Cassidy and P. R. Shaver, pp. 287–316. New York: Guilford.

Solomon, J., George, C., and Dejong, A. (1995). Children classified as controlling at age six: evidence of disorganized representational strategies and aggression at home and at school. *Development and Psychopathology* 7:447–463.

Spangler, G., and Grossman, K. E. (1993). Biobehavioral organization in securely and insecurely attached infants. *Child Development* 64:1439–1450.

Spangler, G., and Schieche, M. (1998). Emotional and adrenocortical responses of infants to the strange situation: the differential function of emotional expression. *International Journal of Behavioral Development* 22:681–706.

Spelke, E. S. (1985). Preferential looking methods as tools for the study of cognition in infancy. In *Measurement of Audition and Vision in the First Year of Post-Natal Life*, ed. G. Gottlieb and N. Krasnegor, pp. 323–363. Hillsdale, NJ: Erlbaum.

———. (1990). Principles of object perception. *Cognitive Science* 14: 29–56.

Speltz, M. L., Greenberg, M. T., and DeKlyen, M. (1990). Attachment in preschoolers with disruptive behavior: a comparison of clinic-referred and non-problem children. *Development and Psychopathology* 2:31–46.

Spemann, H. (1938). *Embryonic Development and Induction*. New Haven: Yale University Press.

Spillius, E. B. (1992). *Discussion of "Aggression and the Psychological Self."* Given at scientific meeting 'Psychoanalytic Ideas & Developmental Observation' in honour of George S. Moran, London, June.

———. (1994). Developments in Kleinian thought: overview and personal view. *Psychoanalytic Inquiry* 14:324–364.

Spitz, R. (1945). Hospitalism: an inquiry into the genesis of psychiatric conditions in early childhood. *Psychoanalytic Study of the Child* 1:53–73. New York: International Universities Press.

————. (1959). *A Genetic Field Theory of Ego Formation: Its Implications for Pathology.* New York: International Universities Press.

————. (1960). Discussion of Dr. John Bowlby's paper. *Psychoanalytic Study of the Child* 15:85–94. New York: International Universities Press.

————. (1965). *The First Year of Life.* New York: International Universities Press.

Sroufe, L. A. (1986). Bowlby's contribution to psychoanalytic theory and developmental psychopathology. *Journal of Child Psychology and Psychiatry* 27:841–849.

————. (1990). An organizational perspective on the self. In *The Self in Transition: Infancy to Childhood*, ed. D. Cicchetti and M. Beeghly, pp. 281–307. Chicago: University of Chicago Press.

————. (1996). *Emotional Development: The Organization of Emotional Life in the Early Years.* New York: Cambridge University Press.

Sroufe, L. A., and Waters, E. (1977a). Attachment as an organizational construct. *Child Development* 48:1184–1199.

————. (1977b). Heart rate as a convergent measure in clinical and developmental research. *Merrill-Palmer Quarterly* 23:3–28.

Stalker, C., and Davies, F. (1995). Attachment organization and adaptation in sexually abused women. *Canadian Journal of Psychiatry* 40:234–240.

Steele, H., Steele, M., and Fonagy, P. (1996a). Associations among attachment classifications of mothers, fathers, and their infants. *Child Development* 67:541–555.

————. (1996b). Associations among attachment classifications of mothers, fathers, and their infants: evidence for a relationship-specific perspective. *Child Development* 67:541–555.

Stein, H., Jacobs, N. J., Ferguson, K. S., Allen, J. G., and Fonagy, P. (1998). What do adult attachment scales measure? *Bulletin of The Menninger Clinic* 62(1):33–82.

Steiner, J. (1992). The equilibrium between the paranoid-schizoid and the depressive positions. In *Clinical Lectures on Klein and Bion*, ed. R. Anderson, pp. 46–58. London: Routledge.

Stern, D. N. (1977). *The First Relationship: Mother and Infant.* Cambridge: Harvard University Press.

————. (1985). *The Interpersonal World of the Infant: A View from Psychoanalysis and Developmental Psychology.* New York: Basic Books.

————. (1994). One way to build a clinically relevant baby. *Infant Mental Health Journal* 15:36–54.

————. (1998). The process of therapeutic change involving implicit knowledge: some implications of developmental observations for adult psychotherapy. *Infant Mental Health Journal* 19:300–308.

Stern, D. N., Barnett, R. K., and Spieker, S. (1983). Early transmission of affect: some research issues. In *Frontiers of Infant Psychiatry*, ed. J. D. Call and R. L. Tyson, pp. 74–85. New York: Basic Books.

Stolorow, R., and Atwood, G. (1991). The mind and the body. *Psychoanalytic Dialogues* 1:190–202.

Stolorow, R., Brandchaft, B., and Atwood, G. (1987). *Psychoanalytic treatment: an intersubjective approach*. Hillsdale, NJ: Analytic Press.

Sullivan, H. S. (1953). *The Interpersonal Theory of Psychiatry*. New York: Norton.

————. (1964). *The Fusion of Psychiatry and Social Science*. New York: Norton.

Suomi, S. J. (1999). Attachment in rhesus monkeys. In *Handbook of Attachment: Theory, Research and Clinical Applications*, ed. J. Cassidy and P. R. Shaver, pp. 181–197. New York: Guilford.

Susman-Stillman, A., Kalkoske, M., Egeland, B., and Waldman, I. (1996). Infant temperament and maternal sensitivity as predictors of attachment security. *Infant Behavior and Development* 19:33–47.

Target, M., and Fonagy, P. (1996). Playing with reality II: the development of psychic reality from a theoretical perspective. *International Journal of Psycho-Analysis* 77:459–479.

Target, M., Shmueli-Goetz, Y., Fonagy, P., and Datta, A. (in preparation). Attachment representations in school-age children: the development and validity of the Child Attachment Interview (CAI). London: University College. Unpublished manuscript.

Teti, D. M., and Ablard, K. E. (1989). Security of attachment and infant–sibling relationships: a laboratory study. *Child Development* 60:1519–1528.

Teti, D. M., Gelfand, D., and Isabella, R. (1995). Maternal depression and the quality of early attachment: an examination of infants, preschoolers and their mothers. *Developmental Psychology* 31:364–376.

Thompson, C. (1964). Transference and character analysis. In *Inter-

personal Psychoanalysis, ed. M. Green, pp. 22–31. New York: Basic Books.

Thompson, R. A. (1994). Emotion regulation: a theme in search of definition. *Monographs of the Society for Research in Child Development* 59:25–52.

————. (1999). Early attachment and later development. In *Handbook of Attachment: Theory, Research and Clinical Applications*, ed. J. Cassidy and P. R. Shaver, pp. 265–286. New York: Guilford.

Trevarthen, C. (1984). Emotions in infancy: regulators of contacts and relationships with Persons. In *Approaches to Emotion*, ed. K. Scherer and P. Elkman, pp. 129–157. Hillsdale, NJ: Erlbaum.

Trivers, R. L. (1974). Parental–offspring conflict. *American Zoologist* 14:249–264.

Tronick, E. Z. (1998). Dyadically expanded states of consciousness and the process of therapeutic change. *Infant Mental Health Journal* 19:290–299.

Vaillant, G. E. (1992). *Ego Mechanisms of Defense: A Guide for Clinicians and Researchers*. Washington, DC: American Psychiatric Association Press.

van den Boom, D. C. (1994). The influence of temperament and mothering on attachment and exploration: an experimental manipulation of sensitive responsiveness among lower-class mothers with irritable infants. *Child Development* 65:1449–1469.

van Ijzendoorn, M. H. (1995). Adult attachment representations, parental responsiveness, and infant attachment: a meta-analysis on the predictive validity of the Adult Attachment Interview. *Psychological Bulletin* 117:387–403.

van Ijzendoorn, M. H., and DeWolff, M. (1997). In search of the absent father: meta-analysis of infant–father attachment. *Child Development* 68:604–609.

van Ijzendoorn, M. H., Goldberg, S., Kroonenberg, P. M., and Frenkel, O. J. (1992). The relative effects of maternal and child problems on the quality of attachment: a meta-analysis of attachment in clinical samples. *Child Development* 59:147–156.

van Ijzendoorn, M. H., Juffer, F., and Duyvesteyn, M. G. C. (1995). Breaking the intergenerational cycle of insecure attachment: a review of the effects of attachment-based interventions on maternal sensitivity and infant security. *Journal of Child Psychology and Psychiatry* 36:225–248.

van Ijzendoorn, M. H., Scheungel, C., and Bakermanns-Kranenburg, M. J. (in press). Disorganized attachment in early childhood: Meta-analysis of precursors, concomitants and sequelae. *Development and Psychopathology.*

van Ijzendoorn, M. H., Vereijken, C. M. and Riksen-Walraven, M. J. (in press). Is the Attachment Q-Sort a valid measure of attachment security in young children? In *Patterns of Secure-base Behavior: Q-sort Perspectives on Attachment and Caregiving,* ed. E. Waters, B. Vaughn, and D. Teti. Mahwah, NJ: Erlbaum.

Vaughn, B. E., and Bost, K. K. (1999). Attachment and temperament. In *Handbook of Attachment: Theory, Research and Clinical Applications,* ed. J. Cassidy and P. R. Shaver, pp. 198–225. New York: Guilford.

Vinamäki, H., Kuikka, J., Tiihonen, J., and Lehtonen, J. (1998). Change in monoamine transporter density related to clinical recovery: a case-control study. *Nordic Journal of Psychiatry* 52:39–44.

Volling, B. L., and Belsky, J. (1992). The contribution of mother–child and father–child relationships to the quality of sibling interaction: a longitudinal study. *Child Development* 63:1209–1222.

Vondra, J. I., Hommerding, K. D., and Shaw, D. S. (1999). A typical attachment in infancy and early childhood among children at developmental risk. VI. Stability and change in infant attachment in a low income sample. *Monographs of the Society for Research in Child Development* 64:119–144. Chicago: University of Chicago Press.

Waddington, C. H. (1966). *Principles of Development and Differentiation.* New York: Macmillan.

Warren, S. L., Huston, L., Egeland, B., and Sroufe, L. A. (1997). Child and adolescent anxiety disorders and early attachment. *Journal of the American Academy of Child and Adolescent Psychiatry* 36:637–644.

Wartner, U. G., Grossman, K., Fremmer-Bombrik, E., and Suess, G. (1994). Attachment patterns at age six in South Germany: predictability from infancy and implications for pre-school behaviour. *Child Development* 65:1014–1027.

Waters, E. (1995). The attachment Q-Set. *Monographs of the Society for Research in Child Development* 60:247–254.

Waters, E., and Deane, K. E. (1985). Defining and assessing individual differences in attachment relationships: Q-methodology and organization of behavior in infancy and early childhood. *Monographs of the Society for Research in Child Development* 50:41–65.

Waters, E., Merrick, S. K., Treboux, D., Crowell, J., and Albersheim, L. (in press). Attachment security from infancy to early adulthood: a 20-year longitudinal study. *Child Development*.

Watson, J. S. (1994). Detection of self: the perfect algorithm. In *Self-Awareness in Animals and Humans: Developmental Perspectives*, ed. S. Parker, R. Mitchell, and M. Boccia, pp. 131–149. Cambridge: Cambridge University Press.

Weil, A. P. (1970). The basic core. *Psychoanalytic Study of the Child* 25:442–460. New York: International Universities Press.

———. (1978). Maturational variations and genetic-dynamic issues. *Journal of the American Psychoanalytic Association* 26:461–491.

Weinfield, N., Sroufe, L. A., and Egeland, B. (in press). Attachment from infancy to early adulthood in a high risk sample: continuity, discontinuity and their correlates. *Child Development*.

Weinfield, N. S., Sroufe, L. A., Egeland, B., and Carlson, A. E. (1999). The nature of individual differences in infant-caregiver attachment. In *Handbook of Attachment: Theory, Research and Clinical Applications*, ed. J. Cassidy and P. R. Shaver, pp. 68–88. New York: Guilford.

Weiss, B., Dodge, K. A., Bates, J. E., and Pettit, G. S. (1992). Some consequences of early harsh discipline: child aggression and a maladapative social information processing style. *Child Development* 63:1321–1335.

Weiss, J., Sampson, H., and the Mount Zion Psychotherapy Research Group (1986). *The Psychoanalytic Process: Theory, Clinical Observation, and Empirical Research*. New York: Guilford.

West, M., and George, C. (in press). Abuse and violence in intimate adult relationships: new perspectives from attachment theory. In *Treatment of Assaultiveness*, ed. D. G. Dutton. New York: Guilford.

West, M. L., and Seldon-Keller, A. E. (1994). *Patterns of Relating: An Adult Attachment Perspective*. New York: Guilford.

Westen, D. (1991). Social cognition and object relations. *Psychological Bulletin* 109:429–455.

Westen, D., Moses, M. J., Silk, K. R., et al. (1992). Quality of depressive experience in borderline personality disorder and major depression: when depression is not just depression. *Journal of Personality Disorders* 6:383–392.

Whittle, P. (in press). Experimental psychology and psychoanalysis: What we can learn from a century of misunderstanding. *Neuropsychoanalysis* 2.

Winnicott, D. W. (1948). Paediatrics and psychiatry. In *Collected Papers*, pp. 157–173. New York: Basic Books, 1958.

———. (1953). Transitional objects and transitional phenomena. *International Journal of Psycho-Analysis* 34:1–9.

———. (1956). Mirror role of mother and family in child development. In *Playing and Reality*, pp. 111–118. London: Tavistock.

———. (1958a). The capacity to be alone. In *The Maturational Processes and the Facilitating Environment*, pp. 29–36. New York: International Universities Press, 1965.

———. (1958b). *Collected Papers: Through Paediatrics to Psycho-analysis.* London: Tavistock.

———. (1960a). The theory of the parent–infant relationship. *International Journal of Psycho-Analysis* 41:585–595.

———. (1960b). The theory of the parent–infant relationship. In *The Maturational Process and the Facilitating Environment*, pp. 37–55. New York: International Universities Press.

———. (1962a). Ego integration in child development. In *The Maturational Processes and the Facilitating Environment*, pp. 56–63. London: Hogarth, 1965.

———. (1962b). The theory of the parent–infant relationship—further remarks. *International Journal of Psycho-Analysis* 43:238–245.

———. (1963a). Communicating and not communicating leading to a study of certain opposites. In *The Maturational Processes and the Facilitating Environment*, pp. 179–192. New York: International Universities Press, 1965.

———. (1963b). Morals and education. In *The Maturational Processes and the Facilitating Environment*, pp. 93–105. New York: International Universities Press, 1965.

———. (1963c). Psychotherapy of character disorders. In *The Maturational Processes and the Facilitating Environment*, pp. 203–216. London: Hogarth Press, 1965.

———. (1965a). Ego distortion in terms of true and false self. In *The Maturational Processes and the Facilitating Environment*, pp. 140–152. New York: International Universities Press.

———. (1965b). *The Maturational Processes and the Facilitating Environment*. London: Hogarth.

———. (1967). Mirror-role of the mother and family in child development. In *The Predicament of the Family: A Psycho-Analytical Symposium*, ed. P. Lomas, pp. 26–33. London: Hogarth.

———. (1971a). *Playing and Reality*. London: Tavistock.

———. (1971b). Playing: creative activity and the search for the self. In *Playing and Reality*, pp. 62–75. London: Penguin.

Wolf, E. (1988). *Treating the Self*. New York: Guilford.

Wolstein, B. (1977). Psychology, metapsychology, and the evolving American school. *Contemporary Psychoanalysis* 13:128–154.

———. (1994). The evolving newness of interpersonal psychoanalysis—from the vantage point of immediate experience. *Contemporary Psychoanalysis* 30:473–498.

Yehuda, R. (1998). Psychoneuroendocrinology of post-traumatic stress disorder. *Psychiatric Clinics of North America* 21(2):359–379.

Yorke, C. (1971). Some suggestions for a critique of Kleinian psychology. *Psychoanalytic Study of the Child* 26:129–155. New Haven, CT: Yale University Press.

Young, J. E. (1990). *Cognitive Therapy for Personality Disorders: A Schema-Focused Approach*. Sarasota, FL: Professional Resource Exchange.

Youngblade, L. M., and Belsky, J. (1992). Parent–child antecedents of 5-year-olds' close friendships: a longitudinal analysis. *Developmental Psychology* 28:700–713.

Index

Abandonment, threats of, 15
Abuse. *See also* Trauma
   and disorganized attachment, 37,
      43–44, 50
   effects of, 15–16, 80, 174–175
Adolescence, psychopathology in,
   32
Adult Attachment Interview
   (AAI), 23–24, 114
   attachment patterns in, 89–90,
      139
   and attachment security, 29, 142–
      143
   depressive and paranoid-schizoid
      positions in, 85–87
   and quality of parenting, 26–27
   unresolved loss in, 37–38, 43,
      137

Adults, 102
   attachment of, 24–25, 43–44, 61,
      89
   continuity of behavior from
      childhood, 163
   relationships of, 25, 53
   unresolved oedipal conflicts in,
      140–141
Aetiology of Hysteria (Freud), 48
Affect, 106. *See also* Affect
      regulation
   Bowlby accused of renouncing
      richness of, 1–2
   containment of, 88–89
   in development, 56, 170–173
   expressions of, 55
   as motivation, 93–94, 111
   and object representations, 113–114

Affect regulation, 90–91, 166
  and attachment security, 14, 33
  development of, 160, 164–165,
    171–173
  inadequate, 40–42, 188–189
  and use of narratives in therapy,
    151–152
Affectional bonds. See Attachment
Affectionless, juvenile delinquents
    separated from mothers as, 6
Affect-trauma model, 48, 51
Aggression, 32, 74, 106, 116
  and attachment patterns, 39–42
  in attachment theory vs. other
    theories, 57, 91, 129
  causes of, 77, 100–101, 109
  as drive, 83, 111–112
Ainsworth, M. D. S., 11, 14, 20–21,
    70, 155
Akhtar, S., 81–82
Allen, J. G., 4, 19
Ambivalence, 74, 85. See also
    Attachment classifications
  of attachment, 72–73
Anaclitic pathology, 34–35
Analysis. See Psychoanalysis;
    Therapy
Analysts. See Psychoanalysts
Anxiety, 106
  and attachment, 33, 69
  caused by loss, 9, 110, 158
  causes of, 49–50, 72, 90, 113, 158
  Freud's theories on, 48–49, 158
  management of, 95–96
Aron, L., 123
Attachment, 2, 8, 50, 70, 94
  of adults, 24–25, 43–44, 61, 89–
    90
  as affect regulation, 14
  to "bad" objects, 130, 142
  biological role of, 6–7, 187–188

continuity of, 44
definitions of, 10, 95, 145
development of, 2, 67–68
different patterns to parents, 69–
  70
disturbance of, 44
functions of, 16–17, 46, 63, 118
goals of, felt security, 13–14
and identification, 87–88
measurement of, 20–25
need for, 3, 106, 147, 162
and representations, 102, 114
research into, 15–16
therapy as new relationship of,
  132–134
Attachment and Loss (Bowlby), 10–
  12
Attachment behaviors, 7–9, 71, 181
  cognitive mechanisms underlying,
    11–12
  controlling and disorganized
    attachment, 39–40, 46, 87–
    88, 136, 183–184
Attachment classifications, 12, 15,
    45, 182–184. See also
    Disorganized/disoriented
    attachment
  of adults, 23–25, 89–90, 140–141
  avoidant, 106, 116, 130
  continuity of, 28–30, 186
  detached-dismissing, 95–96
  effects of, 15, 32, 144, 167
  functions of, 147, 159
  Mahler's explanations for, 72–73
  measurement of, 19–25
  and relations with caregivers, 60,
    69–70
  as simplistic, 186–187
  and tasks of therapy, 143, 147–
    148
  use of system, 30–31, 151

Attachment figures. *See* Caregivers/
    parents
Attachment Q-sort (AQS), 23
Attachment security, 187
    compared to similar concepts, 97,
        180–181
    continuity of, 29, 61, 91
    determinants of, 12, 20, 25–28,
        44–45, 60–61, 97–98
    effects of, 9, 28–35, 100–101,
        130, 167
    measurement of, 87, 166
    relation to paranoid-schizoid and
        depressive positions, 84–87,
        97, 181–182
    secure *vs.* insecure, 12, 14
    of therapist, 152
Attachment theory, 18, 30, 82,
    120
    compared to ego psychology, 53–
        63
    compared to interpersonal school,
        126–134
    compared to Kleinian model, 84–
        92
    compared to object relations
        theories, 105–116
    compared to similar theories, 71–
        80, 110
    contacts with psychoanalysis, 10,
        17, 49, 95, 135–156, 158–
        163, 179–184
    developmental continuities in,
        68–69
    distance from psychoanalysis, 3–
        4, 17, 50–52, 103
    on present *vs.* past, 128–129
    psychoanalytic critiques of, 1–2,
        185–188
    research in, 19–46, 121
    on sexuality, 128–129

on unconscious, 146–147
use in therapy, 130–133, 147–
    153
Attunement, 119
Atwood, G., 125–126
Autobiographical competency, 142–
    143, 147–149
Autonomous identity, sense of, 34–
    35
Autonomy, striving for, 80–81
Availability, of caregivers, 11–12,
    15

Bahrick, L. R., 76
Balint, M., 93, 95–96, 162, 183
Bartholomew, K., 25
Basic trust, in Erikson's drive model,
    58–59, 161, 180–181
Beebe, B., 121
Behavior, 55, 102, 163. *See also*
    Attachment behaviors
    adapted by autonomous ego, 53–
        54
    and attachment classifications,
        182–184
    as defensive, 155–156
    individual differences in, 19–20
    motivators for, 17, 110
    in strange situations, 15–16, 20
Behavioral system, attachment
    behaviors as, 8, 10–11
Belsky, J., 21, 28, 44
Bierman, K. L., 41
Biological vulnerabilities, 2
Biology, 58, 62, 131–132
    basis of attachment in, 3, 7–9, 12,
        16, 106, 187–188
    in psychoanalysis and attachment
        theory, 145–147, 149
    role in anxiety, 48–49
    of sexuality, 128–129

Bion, W. R., 103, 160, 162
  on containment, 97, 165, 167
  on mirroring, 170–171
  on projective identification, 84,
    88–89
Blass, R. B., 77
Blatt, S., 34–35, 77, 143
Bodily fixations, 57- 58
Body, development of boundaries, 77
Bollas, C., 93
Borderline personalities
  and attachment problems, 34–35,
    44, 188–189
  causes of, 114–116, 174
  Mahler's work on, 74–75
  symptoms of, 145, 173, 177–179
  transitional relatedness of, 106–
    107
Bost, K. K., 25
Bowlby, J., 82, 137, 159, 163. *See
  also* Attachment theory
  on attachment behavioral
    systems, 9–10
  on biology, 131, 187–188
  comparison to Freud, 48, 50
  criticism of, 1–2, 114, 140
  on development, 68, 159
  extension of theories of, 13–14
  influences on, 15, 17, 84, 95, 116
  on mother-child relationship, 7,
    71–72, 74, 106
  and psychoanalysis, 17, 103, 106,
    162
  on relationships, 76, 126–127
  research by, 6, 157–158
  respect for empiricism, 3–4, 112
  secure base concept of, 79–80
  similarities with Erikson, 58–59
  similarities with Sullivan, 129
  and therapy, 147, 149
Brain, 37, 46

Bretherton, I., 4, 163–164
British Independent School, 82, 93–
  103
British Institute, 2
Britner, P. A., 45
Bromberg, P. M., 123
Burlingham, D., 3, 68
Byrne, R. M., 120

Caregivers/parents, 9–10, 14, 159,
    175. *See also* Mothers; Parent-
    child relationships
  abusive, 50, 174–175
  child's ambivalence toward, 72–
    73, 85
  child's efforts to maintain
    connection to, 150–151
  and child's internal working
    models, 12–13, 140
  child's perception of, 15, 108–
    109, 141–142
  in development of affect
    regulation, 171–173
  and development of
    mentalization, 166–167
  different relationships with, 69–
    70, 91–92
  disturbed, 43, 82, 88, 100–101,
    106, 153–154
  frightened/frightening behavior
    by, 15–16, 175–176
  hierarchy of, 10
  insensitivity of, 49, 91, 101, 109–
    110, 130, 158
  quality of parenting by, 26–27,
    59, 137–138
  response to child's behaviors, 7–8,
    46
  responsiveness of, 9, 12
  sensitivity of, 73, 88–89, 96–99,
    102, 160–161, 167–168, 188

Carlson, E. A., 43
Cassidy, J., 19, 21
Cassidy and Marvin system, 21
Catharsis, through recollections, 48
Cavell, M., 126
Child Attachment Interview (CAI),
    22–23
Childhood and Society (Erikson),
    161
Closeness, psychological, 8–9
Cognitive functioning, 102
    attachment theory on, 17, 92
    and coherence of attachment
        narratives, 142–143
    effects of harmonious mother-
        child relationship on, 100–
        101, 164
    effects of secure attachments on,
        28, 31
    of infants, 82, 159
    mechanisms underlying
        attachment behaviors,
        11–12
    mental model theory, 120–121
    in paranoid-schizoid *vs.*
        depressive position, 181–182
    problems in, 40, 49
Cognitive psychology, 15, 17, 146
Compromise formations, in ego
    psychology, 54
Conduct problems, and disorganized
    attachment, 40–41
Conflicts, 49, 63
    among internal working models,
        186
    in borderline personalities, 116
    in developmental model of
        psychopathology, 66
    in ego psychology, 54
    between individual and
        environment, 126

intrapsychic, 54
    in parent-child relationships, 153
    of parents, 155
Containment (holding
    environment), 103, 167
    function of, 88–89, 97–99, 102,
        165, 166
    need for, 100, 162, 171
Control, struggle for, 138–139. *See
    also* Attachment behaviors,
    controlling
Cortisol levels, 36–37, 46
Countertransference, 133, 152
Craik, K., 12, 120
Crews, F., 48
Crittenden, P. M., 159
Crittenden pre-school assessment of
    attachment, 21
Crowell, J. A., 25
Crying, as attachment behavior, 7–
    8, 187–188
Culture, effects on child's
    development, 59–61
Current Relationship Interview, 24

Darwin, C., 116
Death instinct, 82–83, 91
Defenses, 49, 66, 69, 98
    Balint's theories on, 95–96
    containment as, 88–89
    in Freud's structural model, 158–
        159
    infants', 155–156
    mechanisms, 146–147
Depression, 33, 35, 57
    of parents, 28, 37, 119, 172
Depressive position, 83, 84–87, 90,
    167
    compared to attachment security,
        91–92, 97, 144
    integration in, 181–182

Deprivation, effects of, 68–69, 88,
  184
  Freud and Bowlby studying, 48,
    157–158
  maternal, 6–7, 11
Development, 54, 77
  attachment theory and
    psychoanalysis compared on,
    50–51, 149, 159–160, 186
  continuities in, 68–69
  influences on, 9–10, 139, 160–161
  integration of actual vs. psychic
    reality as, 168–170
  of mentalization, 78–80, 165–170
  and model of psychopathology,
    65–66
  models of, 58, 66–67, 82–84
  and relationships, 63, 94–95, 164
  of self, 108–109, 112, 117–121,
    130, 161
  stages of, 48–50, 58, 73–74
Developmental determinism, 49–50
Disorganized/disoriented attachment,
    36–45, 69, 136–139
  causes of, 50, 73, 88
  and controlling attachment
    behaviors, 87–88
  Lyons-Ruth's work on, 136–139
Dissociation, 174
  and disorganized attachment, 16,
    32, 43
Dodge, K. A., 45
Dozier, M., 33, 152
Drive expression model, 58
Drives, 8, 51, 63, 70, 83. See also
    Aggression
  Bowlby accused of renouncing, 1–2
  in interpersonal school's theories,
    108–109, 131
  Kernberg's theories on, 111–112,
    114

libidinal, 93–94
primary vs. secondary, 3, 6

Eagle, M., 4, 33, 90, 95, 139–144
Ego, 63
  autonomous, 53–54
  defenses of, 69, 158–159
  development of, 2
  instincts of, 105, 107
  in paranoid-schizoid and
    depressive positions, 83
  in projective identification, 83–
    84
  resilience of, 33
  safety experience of, 79–80
  splitting of, 94, 181–182
  strength of, 90, 96, 116, 143
Ego ideal, 57
Ego psychology, 79, 107, 158
  compared to attachment theory,
    53–63
  mechanistic thinking in, 108, 110
Ehrenberg, D., 133
Emde, R. N., 78–79
Emotions. See Affect
Empiricism, Bowlby's respect for, 3–
    4, 112
Engel, G. L., 1
Environment, 90, 100, 126–127
Envy, 91
Epistemological perspective, in
    attachment theory, 17
Equilibrium, children's development
    of, 68
Erikson, E., 3, 57–63, 158, 161,
    180–181
Erotogenic zones, 57
Ethological perspective, 17
Evolution, 131, 146–147, 187–188.
    See also Survival value
Exploration, child's, 9, 100, 130, 141

Fairbairn, W. R. D., 93–94, 95, 102, 130, 162

Fallacy of Understanding, The (Levenson), 132–133

Families, risk factors in, 37. *See also* Caregivers/parents; Mothers

Fantasies, 15, 39, 83, 130
in Kleinian model, 82, 87, 92

Fathers. *See also* Caregivers/parents
of borderline personalities, 75
sensitivity of, 26

Fear, 136–138, 187

Fear system, 9

Felt security, as goal of attachment, 13–14, 139

Ferenczi, S., 49, 124, 158

Field Theory, used by Spitz, 55

Fixations, 66, 109

Fraiberg, S., 69, 138, 153–155

Franz, C. E., 63

Freud, A., 3, 158, 159
on attachment, 3, 67–68, 181
model of psychopathology, 65–66
theories of, 1, 69–70, 70

Freud, S., 83, 116, 131, 137, 167, 186
on anxiety, 48–49
comparison to Bowlby, 48, 116
on ego defenses, 158–159
influence of, 82–83, 127
on mental processes, 49–50, 120
moving topographical model, 48, 51
structural model of, 53–54, 65–80
studying early deprivation, 157–158
theories compared to attachment theory, 47, 50–52
theories of, 47–49, 65–80
on unconscious, 141, 146

Fromm, E., 124

Fromm-Reichmann, F., 124

Furer, M., 71, 175–176

Genetic predisposition, 82, 140

George, C., 22, 39

Gergely, G., 76, 170

"Ghost in the Nursery" (Fraiberg), 153

Gill, M., 17, 123–124, 141

Giovacchini, P., 107

Green, J., 22

Greenberg, J. R., 116, 123

Greenberg, M. T., 32, 46

Grice, H. P., 23

"Grief, mourning in infancy and early childhood" (Bowlby), 56

Griffin, D. W., 25

Guilt, 83, 85

Gunderson, J., 34–35

Guntrip, H., 94, 162

Hampstead Clinic, 67

Hampstead War Nurseries, 67

Hanley, C., 1, 62

Hartmann, H., 53–54

Hazen, N., 39

Hegel, G., 98

Heinicke, C., 6, 7

Heisenberg, 132–133

Helplessness, 138–139, 183

Hermann, I., 3

Hesse, E., 24, 36, 43, 50, 107, 175–176

Hofer, M., 16, 145

Hoffman, I. Z., 123

Holding environment. *See* Containment (holding environment)

Holmes, J., 4, 95, 119, 144–149, 152

Hostility, 33. *See also* Aggression

Hullian learning theory, 6

Human nature
  in interpersonal school, 131
  in object relations theories, 81–82
Hyperactivity, determinants of, 44–45

Id, 84, 105
Idealization, 108–111, 116
Identification, 90, 113, 154, 173
  functions of, 78, 106
  projective, 83–84, 87–89, 183–184
Identity, 61, 63
Images. *See* Representations
Independents. *See* British
  Independent School
Individuality, 125–126
Infant-caregiver relationship. *See*
  Parent–child relationships
Infant–mother relatedness, 4
Infants, 82, 111, 117
  cognitive functions of, 55, 159
  development of, 76, 94–95
  in Freud's developmental
    determinism, 49–50
  motivations of, 79–80
  observations of, 51, 86, 154
  physiology of, 36–37, 145, 187
  and relationships, 6–7, 94–95
  temperament of, 103, 116
Instinct theory, 103
Instincts, 53, 67, 114
  ego, 105–107
Interpretations, for borderline
  personalities, 178–179
Internal working models, 18, 20, 92,
  102, 109, 140, 186. *See also*
  Representations
  and attachment, 12, 69
  of borderline personalities, 75,
    188–189
  caregiver's, 154–155

compared to similar theories, 56–
    57, 59, 78, 113–114, 127–
    128, 164
  faulty, 39, 49, 113–114, 129,
    150–151
  ontogenesis of, *14*
  and repetition compulsion, 141–
    142
  of self, 12–13
  Stern's elaboration on, 118, 120–
    121
  therapy as attempt to modify,
    132, 134
Interpersonal school of
  psychoanalysis, 116, 123–134,
    143–144
Introjective pathology, 34–35

Jacobovitz, D., 39
Jacobson, E., 56–57, 163, 184
Johnson-Laird, P. N., 120
Joseph, B., 141

Karen, R., 90
Kernberg, O. F., 82, 111–116, 162,
    188–189
Klein, M., 103, 159, 160, 167
  and attachment theory, 1, 84–92,
    144
  model of, 82–84, 144, 181–182
Kohut, H., 82, 108–111, 161, 170
Kreppner, J., 44
Kris, E., 54

Lamb, M., 44
Levenson, E., 124–125, 128, 132–133
Lewin, K., 55
Libido, as drives, 93–94
Lichtenberg, J. D., 108–109
Lichtenstein, H., 71
Lieberman, A., 153–156

Lilleskov, R., 2
Liotti, G., 43
Locomotion, as attachment
    behavior, 8
Loss, 139
    and anxiety, 49, 158
    parental, 37–38, 137, 152
Love, desire for, 95
Luquet, P., 168
Lyons-Ruth, K., 32, 38, 71, 135–139

Mahler, M., 65, 71
    developmental model of, 66–67,
        117, 145
    observation of children, 159–160
    theories compared to attachment
        theory, 71–78
    work on borderline personality
        disorder, 74–75
Main, M., 163, 164, 175–176
    on adult attachment, 23, 61
    on disorganized attachment, 36,
        50, 107
    Slade's use of theories of, 150–
        151
Main and Cassidy attachment
    classification, 21
Main and Goldwyn classification
    system, 151
Marrone, M., 4
Marty, P., 168
Marvin, R. S., 45
Masson, J., 48
Masterson, J. F., 75
Maternal deprivation. *See*
    Deprivation; Separation
McDougall, J., 171
McLaughlin, J., 123
Memories. *See also* Internal working
    models; Representations
    and therapy, 150–151, 164

Mental functions. *See* Cognitive
    functioning
Mental model theory, 120–121
Mental organization, 55
Mental states, 84–86, 166, 173
    mirroring of, 169, 171–172
    reflection on, 27, 174–175
Mentalization, 165–170, 176–177
Metacognitive capacities, 166, 189
Metapsychology, Bowlby's criticism
    of, 3
Mirroring, 108–110, 161, 166
    and development of
        mentalization, 170–173
    in motivation, 110–111
Mitchell, S. A., 116, 123–124, 130,
        131, 132, 144
    contributions to interpersonal
        school, 125–126
    on sexuality, 128–129
Modell, A., 82, 105–107, 162, 183
Morality, 49
Moran, G., 173
Mothers, 7, 43, 49–50, 103, 153. *See
    also* Caregivers/parents;
        Parent–child relationships
    and attachment security, 25–26
    and child's affect, 170–173
    and child's separation and return,
        11, 74
    depressed, 28, 37, 119, 172
    frightened/frightening behavior
        by, 38–39, 107, 136–138
    good-enough *vs.* failings of, 96–
        97, 99, 103
    role in child's development, 55–
        56, 73–74
    sensitivity of, 25–26, 29, 39, 94–
        95
    separateness of, 66–67, 75–77,
        166

Motivation, 79–80, 110, 118, 131
  affect as system of, 111
  attachment-affiliation as, 108–
    109
  for forming relationships, 162–
    163
  idealizing and mirroring in, 110–
    111
  in self-object theories, 93–94
Mourning, 137
Murray, L., 172
Mutual cuing, 71

Narcissism, 89–90, 106, 183
  and detached-dismissing
    attachment patterns, 95–96
  Kohut on, 108–109, 110
Narratives
  attachment, 22–25, 147–148
  and attachment security, 142–
    143
  pathologies of, 148, 152
  use in therapy, 150–152
Nesse, R. M., 146
Neurosis, Kernberg's model of, 112–
  113
North America
  ego psychology in, 53–63
  object relations theory in, 105–
    116

Object, 108, 144
  attachment to "bad," 130, 142
  early perceptions of, 76, 102,
    141–142
  identification with, 83–84, 100–
    101
  representations of, 56–57, 111–
    114, 163–164
  separateness of, 86–87
  therapist as, 153

Object relations, 17, 71, 79, 89, 95
  and mother, 77, 160–161
  representations of, 74–75, 113–114
Object relations theories, 13, 102,
    105–106, 156, 162
  and attachment theory, 8, 139–
    144
  of British Independent School,
    93–94
  depressive and paranoid-schizoid
    positions in, 83–87, 91–92
  Kernberg's structural theories,
    111–116
  Mahler's developmental model of,
    66–67
  in North America, 105–116
  variety in, 81–82
Observation
  by Bowlby, 129–130
  of children, 66–67, 70, 159
  longitudinal, 121
  of parent–child relationships, 154
O'Connor, T. G., 44
Oedipus complex, 1, 109, 140–141
Ogden, T., 123
Omnipotence, 94–95, 108–111, 119
Oppenheim, D., 22
Oral phase, 62
Organ modes, 57
Other, 98, 127
Oversimplification
  criticism of attachment
    classifications as, 186–187
  criticism of Bowlby's theories as,
    56, 61
  criticism of Erikson's theories as, 61

Paranoid-schizoid position, 83–87, 144
  compared to attachment security,
    91–92, 181–182
Parens, H., 77

Parent–child relationships, 6, 51, 59, 71–72, 103, 110, 118, 138, 145
  consistency of, 97–98
  developmental effects of, 55–56, 78–79, 94–95, 164–165
  and disorganized attachment, 88, 138–139
  effect of attachment on interactions in, 28–31, 45, 88
  first three years of, 153–156
  give and take in, 58–59
  harmoniousness of, 100, 164
  motivation for forming, 162–163
  practicing subphase, 66, 77
  of rodents compared to humans, 16–17
  symbiotic subphase in, 75–76
Parents. *See* Caregivers/parents; Fathers; Mothers
Part object representations, 114
Past, *vs.* present, 128–129, 153–154
"Pathways for the Growth of Personality" (Bowlby), 2–3
Peer rejection, 40–41
Perception, distortions of, 49, 185–186
Perry, B., 187
Personality
  development of, 2–3, 68–69
  effects of attachment security on, 14, 30–31, 33
  parents', 27–28
Physiology, infants', 36–37, 145, 187
Piaget, J., 127
Pizer, S., 123
Pleasure, 94, 140
Pope, A. W., 41
Practicing subphase, 66, 71, 77
Present, *vs.* past, 128–129, 153–154
Pretending
  functions for child, 169–170, 176
  by parents, 175

Preverbal period, 67
Primary process, *vs.* representational unconscious, 141–142
Projection, 119
Projective identification, 83–84, 87–89, 119, 183–184
Protection, 9, 16
Proximity, to parent
  functions of, 89, 160, 162, 188
  as goal of attachment behaviors, 8–11
  and responses to reunion, 20–21
  use in adulthood, 53
Psychic structures, 112, 114
Psychoanalysis, 80, 90, 111. *See also* Therapy
  and attachment classifications, 182–184
  and Bowlby, 2–4, 61–62, 103, 106
  changes in, 18, 67, 81
  of children, 67
  contact with attachment theory, 10, 17–18, 44, 135–156, 158–163
  distance from attachment theory, 3–4, 17, 103, 185–188
  relationships in, 81, 126
  schools within, 76, 117, 124–128
Psychoanalysts, 11
  as object for children, 153
  as participant, 124–125, 130–132
  role of, 67, 129
  secure attachment of, 152
Psychology, 5, 13. *See also* Cognitive psychology; Ego psychology
Psychopathology, 77, 82
  emergence of, 44–46
  explanations of, 31–35, 62, 69–70, 106, 158
  models of, 65–66, 112–113
Psychosomatic illness, 33

Rage, and injured narcissism, 110
Rapaport, D., 17
Rapprochement subphase, 66, 73–74
Reality, 48, 130
    actual vs. psychic, 158–159, 168–
        170, 178–179
    perception of, 110, 185–186
    psychic, 174–178
    vs. representations, 163–164
Reductionist
    affect-trauma model accused of
        being, 48
    to biology, of attachment theory,
        132
    Bowlby accused of being, 2, 11
Reflection
    and attachment security, 166–167
    of borderline personality, 189
    effects of abuse on, 174, 176
    parent's on self and child, 27
Regression, 54, 66
Regulation, 16–17, 138. See also
        Affect regulation
Relatedness. See Attachment;
        Relationships
Relational diasthesis model. See
        Disorganized/disoriented
        attachment
Relational–intersubjective
        approach. See Interpersonal
        school
Relationships
    of adults, security of, 25
    attachment to early internal
        working models in, 102
    based on relationship with
        mother, 50, 78–79
    corresponding to attachment
        classifications, 182–184
    development of, motivation for,
        162–163

and development of
        mentalization, 170–173
    in development of self structure, 117
    different with different caregivers,
        91–92
    effects of secure mother -child
        relationship on, 29–31
    evolution of self through, 112
    as goal of basic strivings, 94
    importance vs. individual ego, 63
    infants' sensitivity to, in first year,
        76
    of infants with disorganized
        attachment, 39
    necessity as context for
        understanding, 132–133
    need for, 34–35
    peer, of infants with disorganized
        attachment, 40–42
    power of, 126–127
    in psychoanalysis, increasing
        focus on, 81
    psychopathology, interpersonal
        causes of, 158
    representations of, 163–164
        effects of disorganized
            attachment on, 45
    rigidity of, 177–179
    role of early attachments in
        current, 131
    as "schema of a-way-of-being-
        with," 118–121
    splitting of self and object, in
        paranoid-schizoid and
        depressive positions, 83
    in therapy of interpersonal
        school, 132–133
    types of, self-with-other, 118
    violence in, and disorganized
        attachment, 43–44
    Winnicott vs. Bowlby on, 103

Renik, O., 123
Repetition, 102
  compulsion, 141–142
  of trauma, 177
Representational systems, 13, 31
Representations, 12, 118–119. *See
    also* Internal working models
  of borderline personalities, 177–
    178, 188–189
  development of, 77, 160
  disruption of, 85, 114–115, 176
  in psychopathology, 112–114
  of relationships, 45, 163–164
  self, 109–111
  self and object, 102, 111–112,
    188–189
  self-other, 34–35, 78–80, 165–
    167, 172–173
  splitting of, 74–75
  systems of, 56–57, 67, 163, 170
Repression, as defense mechanism,
    146–147
Research, 112, 117
  on attachment, 19–46, 152–153
  observation *vs.* laboratory studies,
    180
  on parent–child relationships,
    154
  perspective of, 17–18
Reunion, and attachment, 7, 20–22,
    72–73
RIGs, Erikson's theories predating,
    59
Rinsley, D. B., 75
Riviere, J., 90
Robertson, J., 6
Rochlin, G., 1
Roife, H., 1
Roles, 164
Rosenfeld, H., 89–90, 183
Roy, P. R., 44–45

Safety. *See also* Felt security
  child's need for, 79–80, 97–98,
    181
  in disorganized attachment, 136–
    138
Sampson, H., 141
Sandler, J., 65, 67, 78–80, 111, 119,
    141, 164, 173, 181
Schafer, R., 62
"Schema of a-way-of-being-with,"
    118–121, 164
Schizophrenia, treatment for, 124
Schuengel, C., 38
Searles, H. F., 107
Secondary autonomy, 53
Secure base concept, 7, 71, 79–80,
    147, 181
Seduction hypothesis, Freud's, 48
Segal, H., 85–86
Self, 51, 54
  and attachment narrative, 147–
    148
  barriers to development of, 61,
    100–101
  of borderline personalities, 75,
    177–178, 189
  development of, 91, 93–99, 117–
    121, 161, 167–168
  false, 101, 103, 144
  Mahler's developmental model of,
    66–67
  and motivation, 93–94, 110
  representations of, 12–13, 45, 56–
    57, 75, 111–115, 163–164
  sense of, 106, 130, 144, 148
  threats to, 83, 100–101, 184
Self psychology, 108–111, 160
Self-awareness, parents', 27
Self-esteem, 50
Self-object theories, 93–94
Selfobjects, 108

Self-other boundaries, 57, 72, 77, 173
Self-other relationships, representations of, 34–35
Self-regulation, 56, 77, 89, 107. See also Affect regulation
Self-representation, 71
Separation, physical
  child's response to, 6–7, 11, 16–17, 20–22
  in Mahler's theories, 72–73
Separation Anxiety Test (SAT), 22
Separation-individuation, 4, 118
  achievement of, 86–87
  awareness of separateness, 166, 173
  and differentiation, 72, 94–95
  in Mahler's theories, 66–67, 71–74
  process of, 74–78, 96–97
Settlage, C. F., 73
Sexuality, 62, 106
  in attachment theory, 10, 128–129, 140
  as drive, 111–112
Shaver, P. R., 19
Shaw, D., 32, 116
Siblings, 29
Slade, A., 27, 149–153
Smiling, as attachment behavior, 7–8
Sociable behavioral system, 9–10
Social cognition, 40–41
Social competence, 29, 40–42
Socializing, behaviors signaling desire for, 7–8
Solomon, J., 39
Spillius, E. B., 86, 87
Spitz, R., 55–56, 117, 158, 165
Splitting, 87, 94, 146
  in paranoid-schizoid position, 84–85, 181–182
  of representations, 74–75

Sroufe, A., 13–14, 89, 95, 164
Stein, H., 25
Stern, D. N., 4, 59, 76, 98, 117–121, 141–142, 164
Stern, Daniel, 123
Stolorow, R., 125–126
Strange Situation test, 11, 23–24, 70
  and disorganized attachment, 36, 38
  effects of attachment security on, 20–21
Structural (tripartite) model, Freud's, 53–54, 70, 93–94, 158–159
  modifications of, 65–80, 80
Subjectivity, Mitchell's work on, 124–125
Sullivan, H. S., 124, 126–128, 129, 132–133
Superego, 83, 84
Survival value, of attachment, 8, 16–17, 116, 146
Symbiotic subphase, 66, 71, 74–76, 145
Symbolic representation, 21–22, 171–172. See also Cognitive functioning

Temperament
  and attachment security, 25–27, 32
  of infants, 25, 91, 103, 116, 140
Theory of mind, 100
Therapeutic relationships, 154
Therapists. See Psychoanalysts
Therapy, 66, 164
  with borderline personalities, 177–179
  of parent–child relationships, 153–156

process of, 35, 130–134, 143
use of attachment theory in, 147–153
use of narratives in, 148, 150–152
"Third," concept of, 87
Thompson, C., 124, 127–128
Thompson, R. A., 44
Topographical model, 48, 51, 53
Transference, 79, 125, 128, 141, 143, 154
Transitional relatedness, 106–107
Trauma, 49, 139, 152
  and disorganized attachment, 43–44, 136–138, 183–184
  effects of, 145, 158, 174–177
Trevarthen, C., 119

Unconscious, 1–2, 94
  in attachment theory, 17, 146–147
  representational theories of, 141–142

Van Ijzendoorn, M. H., 43
Vaughn, B. E., 25
Vocalizing, as attachment behavior, 7–8

Waddington, C. H., 2
Waters, E., 13–14
Watson, J. S., 76, 170
Weil, A. P., 71
Weiss, J., 141
Westheimer, I. J., 7
White, K. M., 63
Whittle, P., 5
Winnicott, D. W., 44–45, 93–94, 100–103, 141, 158, 162, 165
  on development of self, 94, 109
  influence of, 95, 119
  on mirroring, 161, 170
  on sensitive caregiving, 96–99, 167–168
Withdrawal, 74
Wolstein, B., 124